Chicken Soup for the Soul.

P9-DME-001

NEWMARK, A
CHICKEN SOUP FOR THE SOUL: LIF...

APR 2019

DISCARD

Life Lessons
from the Dog

PROPERTY OF
THOUSAND OAKS LIBRARY
1401 E. Janss Road
Thousand Oaks, California

Chicken Soup for the Soul: Life Lessons from the Dog
101 Tales of Family, Friendship & Fun
Amy Newmark

Published by Chicken Soup for the Soul, LLC www.chickensoup.com
Copyright ©2019 by Chicken Soup for the Soul, LLC. All Rights Reserved.

No part of this publication may be reproduced, stored in a retrieval system or transmitted in any form or by any means, electronic, mechanical, photocopying, recording or otherwise, without the written permission of the publisher.

CSS, Chicken Soup for the Soul, and its Logo and Marks are trademarks of Chicken Soup for the Soul, LLC.

The publisher gratefully acknowledges the many publishers and individuals who granted Chicken Soup for the Soul permission to reprint the cited material.

Front cover photo courtesy of iStockphoto.com/jmpaget (©jmpaget)
Back cover and Interior photo of dog with books courtesy of iStockphoto.com/Liliya Kulianionak (©Liliya Kulianionak)
Back cover photo of dog with cap courtesy of of iStockphoto.com/Ljupco (©Ljupco)

Photo of Amy Newmark courtesy of Susan Morrow at SwickPix

Cover and Interior by Daniel Zaccari

Distributed to the booktrade by Simon & Schuster. SAN: 200-2442

Publisher's Cataloging-In-Publication Data
(Prepared by The Donohue Group, Inc.)

Names: Newmark, Amy, compiler.
Title: Chicken soup for the soul : life lessons from the dog : 101 tales
    of family, friendship & fun / [compiled by] Amy Newmark.
Other Titles: Life lessons from the dog : 101 tales of family, friendship
    & fun
Description: [Cos Cob, Connecticut] : Chicken Soup for the Soul, LLC,
    [2019]
Identifiers: ISBN 9781611599886 | ISBN 9781611592887 (ebook)
Subjects: LCSH: Dogs--Literary collections. | Dogs--Anecdotes. | Human-
    animal relationships--Literary collections. | Human-animal
    relationships--Anecdotes. | Dog owners--Literary collections. | Dog
    owners--Anecdotes. | LCGFT: Anecdotes.
Classification: LCC SF426.2 .C454 2019 (print) | LCC SF426.2 (ebook) | DDC
    636.7/088/7/02--dc23

Library of Congress Control Number: 2019931155

PRINTED IN THE UNITED STATES OF AMERICA
on acid∞free paper

25 24 23 22 21 20 19   01 02 03 04 05 06 07 08 09 10 11

Life Lessons
from the Dog

101 Tales of Family, Friendship & Fun

Amy Newmark

Chicken Soup for the Soul, LLC
Cos Cob, CT

Changing the world one story at a time®
www.chickensoup.com

Table of Contents

❶

~All in the Family~

1. My Dog Mows Best, *David Warren*...2
2. Human or Dog? *Mya R. Schwartz*.................................... 4
3. Our Weather Forecaster, *Connie Beckman* 7
4. Canine FaceTime, *Sharla Hintz*... 10
5. Becky's Traumatic Journey, *Saralee Perel* 11
6. The Best Gift, *Rebecca Ruballos*... 13
7. The Definition of Faithful Is "Dog" *Elizabeth Delisi*...............17
8. First They Get Married, *Kelly Hennigan*............................20
9. Kitchen Sleepovers, *Natasha Lidberg*.................................23
10. Bananas Foster, *Julie Theel*..26
11. Taking a Chance, *Tara Flowers*...30

❷

~Who's in Charge Here?~

12. It's Not Insomnia — It's My Dog, *Ann Morrow* 36
13. Our Little Genius, *Diane Stark* 40
14. Walking Archer, *Winter Desiree Prosapio* 44
15. What Comes Naturally, *Sallie A. Rodman* 46
16. A Dog for a Nurse, *David Hull* 49
17. Christmas Blitz, *Irene Maran*..52
18. The Canine Tactician, *Lisa Mackinder* 54
19. All Ears, *Cheryl E. Uhrig*..57
20. The Bichon on the Bed, *Roz Warren* 60
21. Time for That Walk, *Jeana Tetzlaff*....................................63

❸

~Opening Hearts~

22. Then Came Stitch, *Diana L. Walters* 66
23. My Dog in Bhutan, *Evan Purcell* 70
24. Dogwood, *Lucy Barrett* 74
25. Joint Custody, *Rebecca Edmisten* 78
26. Choose Love, *Lori Fuller* 80
27. A Mastiff-Sized Trail to the Heart, *Lindsay Detwiler* 82
28. More than Worthy, *Brenda Beattie* 85
29. Operation Andy, *Diane Stark* 88
30. Don't Judge a Dog by Its Cover, *Marilynn Zipes Wallace* 91
31. A Lesson in Empathy, *Alicia Curley* 95
32. Thanks to Bentley, *Susan A. Karas* 99

❹

~Smart Dog~

33. My Rescue Dog Is So Smart, *Martha Roggli* 104
34. Bobbie, *Ellen Fannon* 107
35. Too Obedient? *Linda Meilink* 112
36. All the News That's Fit to Chew, *Lisa Taylor* 115
37. My Clever Dog Bubba's Tricks, *Ken Prehn* 117
38. The Reward, *Amanda Sue Creasey* 119
39. The Test, *Patricia Lund* 121
40. Model Behavior, *Zach Hively* 123
41. Captain of My Destiny, *Roz Warren* 127
42. Reflection, *Richard Matturro* 130

❺

~Canine Kindness~

43. The Gentle Backup, *Candace Sams* 135
44. Clean Paws, *Gwen Cooper* 139

45. Giving Until It Hurts, *A E Troyer* 142
46. Friends to the End, *Teresa Crow* 144
47. Retrieved, *Yvonne Kays* 148
48. Karma, *Cassidy Porter* 152
49. Soul Sniffer, *Jennifer Sienes* 155
50. Spreading Sunshine, *Jill Anne Berni* 159
51. Brodie, *Linda Feist* 162
52. Stormin' Norman, *Patricia Ayers* 166

❻

~My Very Good, Very Bad Dog

53. Cookie's Secret Life, *Kandace Chapple* 171
54. He Who Laughs Last Is the "Wiener" *Kathy Harris* 175
55. No Snacks for Judy, *Kay Presto* 177
56. I Should Have Remembered, *Polly Hare Tafrate* 179
57. Shell Game, *Lisa Timpf* 182
58. A Bad Puppy, *Vickie J. Litten* 184
59. The Hot Dog Thief, *Michele Bazan Reed* 187
60. Idle Paws, *Sheryl-Ann Odell* 189
61. Where's the Beef? *Louisa Godissart McQuillen* 193
62. Under Georgia Red Clay, *Rebecca Edmisten* 195
63. Two for the Road, *Marsha Porter* 198

❼

~Resilience and Forgiveness~

64. A Gentle Healer, *Nikki Rottenberg* 203
65. Mitzie Has Arrived, *Veronica Bowman* 205
66. Hazel's Resilience, *Abigail Smith* 208
67. Hope on Three Legs, *Leslie Garrett* 211
68. The Mayor, *Gwen Hart* 214
69. Finding the Way, *Suzanne M. Kurth* 217
70. Good Golly Miss Molly, *Tracy Falenwolfe* 221

71. I Remember Mama, *Cheryl Wright* 225

72. It's Never Too Late for Love, *Joyce Laird* 228

73. Ol' Spanky, *Roberta Messner* 231

8

~Canine Comedy~

74. The Unwavering Trust of a Dog, *Andrea Peebles* 236

75. Ruger, the Frog Prince, *Taylor Reau Morris* 239

76. Game of Chance, *Debbi Mavity* 241

77. Slow Learner, *Mary Vigliante Szydlowski* 244

78. The Mayor of Fox Den Road, *Sharon Struth* 248

79. The Three Musketeers, *Donna Collins Tinsley* 251

80. The Amazing Invisible Dog, *Lisa Timpf* 253

81. Eleanor's in the Room, *Bea L. Montecarlo* 256

82. In Full Flour, *Tammy Collins Gibson* 259

83. It's a Dog's Vacation, *David Martin* 261

9

~Always the Protector~

84. A Miracle Named George, *S.J. Wells* 265

85. Barely Awake, *Linda Kinnamon* 268

86. Buddy Barked, *Jude Walsh* 272

87. A Dog Knows, *Blossom Turner* 275

88. Springing into Action, *Michelle J. Nunnes* 278

89. The Accidental Hero, *Diane Stark* 281

90. The Dog Who Cried Wolf, *Lisa Timpf* 284

91. No Joking Around, *Valerie J. Frost* 286

92. His Chance to Save Me, *Ashley Bell* 289

93. Oso Concerned, *Nadia Ianakieva* 291

94. Lost and Found, *Jennifer Poff Cooper* 294

95. Harry, *Samantha LaBarbera* 298

96. The Golden Rule, *Jeaninne Escallier Kato* 301

97. Satchie's Gift, *Aileen Weintraub* 304

98. Hell's Bells, *Kelley Knott* 307

99. The Last Goodbye, *Jan Hopkins-Campbell* 310

100. I'll Take a Mulligan, *Jenny Filush-Glaze* 314

101. On Eagles' Wings, *Jenny Pavlovic* 317

Meet Our Contributors 321

Meet Amy Newmark 336

About American Humane 338

Thank You 340

About Chicken Soup for the Soul 341

All in the Family

My Dog Mows Best

You can usually tell that a man is good
if he has a dog who loves him.
~W. Bruce Cameron, A Dog's Journey

I had an audience as I put on my old, beat-up tennis shoes. Everyone in the house was familiar with my mowing shoes, and one member of the household was always thrilled when I put them on. She wagged her tail as I laced up the tattered strings. It was time to mow; Emmy, our Golden Retriever, was ready. Unlike me, the dog enjoyed every aspect of mowing.

I went to the shed to get our mower, and she followed along. She glanced up at me as if to say, "Let's do this." I took out our mower and tugged the pull string that started my trusty Toro. Emmy barked with joy as the engine revved. It was as if she were trying to compete with the mower to see who could be louder.

I began mowing rows of grass in our back yard, and the dog followed me as I cut each row. She marched in unison with the mower. It was as if she were a soldier; she followed along in perfect step.

As I made turns at the end of each row, I gently rubbed her head as if to say, "Thanks for helping me." Each time I did this, her tail wagged, and she looked up at me lovingly.

Once in a while, I came across a stick or a rock. I slowed down, picked it up and tossed it aside. Emmy chased after it every time and brought it back to me. She is a Retriever, so chasing after stuff is what she does best.

Every time she brought back a stick or rock, I gave it another hurl. After a while, Emmy settled down and sat in the shade as I continued to mow. She glanced up at an occasional bird or the wind blowing the trees, but mostly she kept her eyes on me.

Once in a while, she walked over to me and the mower, begging for another pat on the head. I would pat her again, and she would walk away satisfied that she was getting the proper attention. Finally, the back yard was finished, so I stopped the mower and went for a drink.

I pulled up a chair and sipped on my bottle of water. It gave me some relief after an hour in the summer sun. I made sure to fill Emmy's water bowl, and she lapped up some water as well. Then she came over and sat right next to me. She looked up at me again as if to say, "Are you ready to mow the front yard yet?" We rested a bit longer, and then she followed me to the front. I started the mower, and Emmy barked loudly again.

I mowed row after row, and Emmy followed in unison again. She was still able to keep in perfect step and still in need of a few pats on the head. She retrieved a few more sticks and rocks, just as she had in the back yard. I finished up as Emmy watched me from the front porch.

She followed me to the back door and watched as I took off my old tennis shoes. We went inside, and I washed up and grabbed more water. The summer heat had done me in for a while, so I headed for my favorite recliner in the family room. I dozed off for a little bit. When I woke, I looked down to see Emmy resting comfortably next to me. One of my mowing shoes was tucked under her furry chin. She was enjoying an afternoon nap, content as could be.

Emmy loves every aspect of mowing—the shoes, the rev of the engine, the pats on her furry head, chasing sticks and getting extra attention—but, most of all, she loves the company. I seldom enjoy mowing—it is tedious, and often hot and grueling—but thanks to our dog Emmy, I do love one thing about it: the joy we bring to each other!

—David Warren—

Human or Dog?

*When I look into the eyes of an animal I do not see an
animal. I see a living being. I see a friend. I feel a soul.*
~Anthony Douglas Williams

There's not enough time in this world. I rarely socialize with
my classmates or walk up to strangers. All work-related
dinner invitations are typically declined within an hour.
The only humans who know me well are family mem-
bers and potential future partners. My version of an exciting night
includes sitting at home, reading a good book while petting my dog,
and minding my own business.

Rei is sleeping comfortably on his oversized doggie pillow as I
write this. He will be two in November. It's hard to believe two years
have passed already. I remember him at eight weeks, so small and
fuzzy. The night I held him for the very first time, he fell asleep on
my shoulder. I wanted the moment to last forever, much like the way
a mother feels while holding her newborn baby.

I stare at him as he continues sleeping peacefully. In a few minutes,
I'll wake him for his afternoon walk. I keep him on a tight schedule.
After all, he's my baby and deserves the best. I crawl over to Rei and
gently rub his belly. He jumps on all fours and stretches his legs in
delight.

"Come on, Rei," I say. "Time to walk."

We walk across the golf course, enjoying the beautiful scenery.
Golfers drive by in golf carts and wave hello. Most of the time, the

waves are aimed at Rei. Sometimes, I wave back; other times, I don't. It sounds harsh, but typically strangers will engage in conversation with Rei while ignoring me. I find myself constantly reminding people that I'm the owner.

The golf course is part of a hotel that I often visit to retreat from my daily life. Rei always accompanies me because I hate walking alone. Occasionally, the manager reiterates the hotel's rules, which forbid walkers because golf balls could land on our heads and knock us unconscious. Needless to say, Rei's cute face comes in handy under these circumstances. I rely on his cuteness to get me out of trouble. Besides, I'm always careful, scanning my surroundings for danger zones, and trying to walk when no one is around.

I love the coffee shop inside the hotel. It serves my favorite drink: cafe mocha, a mix of coffee and dark chocolate. The hotel seems busy today, and the line is quite long. As we patiently wait our turn, I hear a sound behind me, and I turn my head to investigate.

A young man in his mid-thirties is rapidly tapping his foot against the ground. I keep my eyes on him for a few seconds before deciding that he's cute. I also can't help but notice that his shirt reads "AEPI," the Jewish fraternity on many American college campuses. My instinct is to let him know I'm Jewish and available. But my shy, quieter self begs me not to do anything stupid. Instead, I wonder silently if he's "the one," the Jewish prince I've been waiting for my whole life. I turn back around, facing the front, and dismiss the wedding fantasy floating in my head.

We are second in line when I hear an unfamiliar voice asking for permission to pet my dog. From the corner of my eye, I can see that it's him — the cute guy with the AEPI shirt. My heart skips a beat as I move up once again and now find myself first in line. Greg (as I later learned) assumes my silence to be a "yes." As the two engage in a new friendship, I find myself halfway between heaven and hell; somehow Rei's leash has wrapped itself around my legs forcing me into a standstill. I try to communicate with the cashier but I'm silenced by Rei's barks. His excitement is overwhelming, as he slobbers over Greg. It's unclear if the girl behind the counter can hear my voice. After my third attempt to speak, I finally place my order.

Still in shock that the mystery Jewish man initiated contact, I manage to untangle myself and we find a table in the corner of the coffee shop, away from the crowd. I sit across from Greg, unable to look away. He is very handsome.

Unsure of myself and what is considered to be a social norm, I begin the classic dating ritual of interrogation. I ask about his shirt. He reveals his Jewish identity and explains his association with AEPI during his undergraduate years. Forty-five minutes and twenty questions later, I learn quite a bit about my mystery man: Jewish, lawyer, and dog-obsessed. Wedding bells are ringing all around me. I imagine Rei in a bow tie.

"We should get together sometime," he says. I jot down my number and hand it over with a big smile on my face. Hopefully, he can't smell my desperation. And if he can, I pray he overlooks this and calls me anyway.

As Rei and I leave the coffee shop to head home, an uncomfortable thought crosses my mind: Is Greg into me or Rei?

At 8:00 the next morning, I wake up to the sound of my phone ringing. I jump out of bed and check to see who is calling. It's a text from Greg, asking me out to lunch and requesting I bring Rei.

The answer is clear.

Oh, well. As life has always shown me, it's never about the human, but always about the dog.

— Mya R. Schwartz —

Our Weather Forecaster

You can be in the storm, but don't
let the storm get in you.
~Joel Osteen

R ain is pouring down today, which brings back delightful memories of our German Shepherd, Bambi. Our family adopted her at the tender age of four months. The first time I met her, she reminded me of a delightful little fawn. She had the warmest brown eyes, which could melt even the hardest heart. She had long, pointed ears that seemed to be oversized compared to her little head. When I watched her playing in the yard, all I could see were ears, eyes, and legs.

Like all puppies, she was full of energy, inquisitiveness, and wonder. Our boys remarked excitedly that she looked just like the young deer, Bambi, in the movie they had watched recently. The name fit her personality perfectly.

Bambi also inherited all the fine physical characteristics of the German Shepherd breed. She was strong, yet gentle and shy. She was a handful at times. But we were a young family with two growing, energetic boys, so she fit right in with our lifestyle. Bambi loved the boys. She'd wrestle, romp and play with them until all three were completely exhausted.

When Bambi was almost two years old and considered a full-grown, mature dog, she became quite protective of us. She never failed to watch the boys. If a stranger entered our yard, she'd glare at the intruder with piercing, determined eyes and emit a low growl. The stranger sensed not to proceed any farther. Even though Bambi had this protective instinct, she never bit anyone. Nevertheless, she did manage to frighten away many welcome and unwelcome guests.

On one occasion, I had called a repairman to come to our home to fix our refrigerator. I was at work, and the boys were home with the babysitter. I informed the repairman by phone that we had a dog, but it would be safe to enter the house because the babysitter would be there to meet him. The repairman entered our yard and proceeded to the front door. Bambi was outside and she growled and glared at this intruder while she diligently guarded the door. The frightened man froze in his tracks. He didn't know whether to stand still, retreat or scream for help.

Finally, the babysitter and boys returned from their walk. They rescued the poor, frightened fellow from our guard dog. They reassured Bambi that it was okay to allow the man to enter our home. But even while the repairman was fixing our refrigerator, Bambi kept a constant, watchful eye on him. This man was very glad to finish repairing the appliance and get away from this beast.

However, there was a side to Bambi's personality that didn't match her bravery. She was so terrified of thunder and lightning that she'd immediately turn into a frightened, timid pup. On any summer day when the sun disappeared behind the clouds, Bambi would race to the door and demand to be let into the house. One time, Bambi was so relentless that she ripped a hole in our screen door and came galloping into the house. She seemed to have a built-in sense that told her it was going to rain. She was usually correct in her predictions because rain, thunder and lightning would soon follow.

But Bambi didn't feel safe enough just being inside the house, lying on her designated rug. The only place she felt safe was in our bathtub, curled up in a ball. Time and time again, with great difficulty, I tried to remove our terrified dog from the tub. Finally, I surrendered to the realization that it was impossible. The small, confined tub likely muffled some of the noise from the thunder, and I marveled at Bambi's ability to find a safe place to wait out the impending danger.

Like Bambi, I have fears and hang-ups about certain things and situations, and I do my best to deal with them as they arise. Sometimes, all I can manage is to retreat to a safe place within myself until the fear passes. Then I am able once again to face the day with joy and security. Bambi helped me realize that all of us have hang-ups and fears, but that doesn't define who we are as a whole.

As the years passed, Bambi became unable to jump in our bathtub, but this didn't prevent her from finding another safe refuge — our walk-in shower.

Bambi is no longer with us, but our wonderful memories of her remain to brighten rainy days. Today, there is a little less fear and more sunshine and laughter in my heart as I remember our furry weather forecaster curled up in the bathtub.

— Connie Beckman —

Canine FaceTime

*The greatest pleasure of a dog is that you may
make a fool of yourself with him and not only
will he not scold you, but he will make a
fool of himself too.*
~Samuel Butler

I like to FaceTime my daughter. She lives two hours away, but it seems like two billion light years away. However, sometimes our FaceTime gets hijacked. Her dog, Kona, likes to play with squeaky toys. When he makes them squeak, he mimics them with his puppyish yowly-whine. Then my dog, Arrow, responds by running from wherever he was napping and howling for his friend. Then Kona howls, so we show them to each other.

Pretty soon, our conversation has been taken over by moaning and bellowing that can only be understood by a canine. They are probably talking about naps in the sun, bones, and how well they have trained their humans. They have a lot to tell each other. They go back and forth in this verbal mystery as my daughter and I hold the phones up for them so they can see each other.

Clearly, we've lost control.

— Sharla Hintz —

Becky's Traumatic Journey

*Dogs are not our whole life, but they
make our lives whole.*
~Roger A. Caras

My husband Bob took our dog Becky for surgery to remove a lump the size of a baseball from her belly. Anxious thoughts overwhelmed me.

After surgery, when Bob left to pick her up, it was snowing heavily. My heart soared when they returned home safely.

Becky could barely walk because of the anesthesia, so Bob carried her. They couldn't get in the door because she was wearing a gigantic hard plastic cone around her neck to prevent her from licking her sutures.

I held the door wide open. She was miserable and crying. There was slushy snow inside her cone. It took over five minutes to get them in while Becky shook her head wildly to try to remove the cone. The sound of the cone hitting the door made her panic and cry even louder.

Once inside, she was so frightened that she kept her tail between her legs. She thought she had done something wrong. Her expression said, "I'm sorry for what I did that led to me having to wear this." She wouldn't take her special treat of a cube of cheese. We tried having her sit with us. She wouldn't sit. She wouldn't lie down. All she did was stand and cry.

"How long will she have to wear it?" I asked.

"Two weeks."

She wasn't allowed to jump on the bed where she sleeps. All night, we stayed with her on the floor as she trembled and whimpered. Whenever she moved, the cone banged loudly into furniture, constantly startling her and seemingly reminding her that she was a bad dog.

Once I nodded off, I heard the cone smashing against the wall. Becky was trying to drink from her water bowl. In a tender moment, I knelt on the floor and held her bowl to her mouth so she could drink. She kept trying to "kiss" me with her licks, but couldn't reach my face, which seemed to break her heart. I know it broke mine.

Our love for our dog is like a parent's love for a child. Two weeks is a long time to watch your dog cry.

Eventually, the day arrived when Bob took her to have her sutures removed. I desperately hoped they'd return without the cone.

Finally, they came home. Wearing no cone, Becky saw me, and then wiggled down the path where she greeted me with delight.

She had her cheese treat and her supper. Then she raced to Bob, who was on the bed. She jumped up and slathered him with kisses. I did the same thing.

All night, Becky kissed Bob and me. I pulled the quilt over us as we snuggled in the warmth together.

Our three-way hug, filled with gratitude and glee, will remain in my memory forever.

— Saralee Perel —

The Best Gift

Happiness is a warm puppy.
~Charles Schulz

It was my brother's idea. "Let's get Mom a Pug for her birthday. It might cheer her up." By the time our conversation ended, I had my assignment: find our mother a new companion.

Our father had passed away a few weeks earlier, and his sudden death had left us in shock. We were now faced with creating a new "normal," and none of us was sure how to do that.

Maybe a puppy wasn't such a bad idea. We had always had dogs around: Barney, the Belgian Shepherd/Labrador Retriever mix who people often mistook for a bear; Butch, the goofy Yellow Lab; Kizzy, the Black Lab mix who "pancaked" every time an unfamiliar man entered the room; and Luke, the Rottweiler who insisted that he was a lap dog. In fact, Mom had brought up the idea of adopting a Pug once, and Dad's reaction had been, "What do we need another dog for? We have Luke." But Dad and Luke were both gone now.

After an exhaustive search, I finally found an ad for Pug puppies in a local newspaper. A nearby family had a Pug who had just given birth to five AKC-certified male puppies! All had been to visit the veterinarian, had their first vaccines, and would be ready to leave their mom in a few weeks. I gave them a call.

The man who answered the phone listened patiently to my story and then made a suggestion. "You really should come along with your brother to meet the dogs. Chances are that you sound something like your mother, and you probably smell similar, too. A puppy will pick up on those things and will likely feel more comfortable when you introduce him to her later on." Okay, I could do that. The date was set.

When the day arrived, my daughter, her friend, and I piled into my brother's truck. We pulled up in front of some houses that sat along a narrow alley-like street. As we stepped onto the sidewalk, we were greeted by a chorus of barks. Two Pugs and an Akita had positioned themselves on the back of a sofa and were watching us through a large bay window. As we climbed onto the porch and rang the doorbell, more chaos ensued.

A tall, slender man with graying hair and a kind smile opened the door. As I reached to shake his hand, I could see the puppies behind him, running and cascading over each other to get to us. Each puppy wore a different color string around its neck.

We met the man's wife, who wore a similar friendly smile and welcomed us to her home. We met the puppies' parents and then set about the business of selecting a friend for our mother. We were informed that the "red" puppy had been spoken for, but the others were still available. There were four puppies and four visitors; the man handed each of us a dog. Three of the puppies looked up at us with large, curious eyes. The fourth one, who I was holding, began to wiggle excitedly and kiss my face. "Let's take this one! He's the one! Look how affectionate he is!" I said. As far as I was concerned, it was a done deal.

My brother wasn't convinced. "Let's take some time to get to know all of them." We spent the next hour or so sitting on the floor playing with a pile of puppies.

Eventually, we settled on a different puppy for our mom. The "purple" one was the runt of the litter and made up for his small stature with a large personality. He spent most of the time we were there either jumping on one of us or following his patient mother around asking for more to eat. We signed the requisite paperwork and agreed on the pick-up date. The woman asked what we would be calling the new dog so that she could use the name and help him get used to hearing it. That being done, we left to bide our time and get ready for "Doug's" arrival.

As we rode home, I listened to the excited chatter of the others, but my mind was elsewhere. When my brother finally dropped us off at home, I looked at my daughter and said, "I can't get my mind off the 'green' one."

"I know," she answered. "I think you should call and let them know that we want him." No sooner were the words out of her mouth than the telephone was in my hand. The next day, we went back to sign the paperwork, and "George" was ours.

Two weeks later, we picked up the puppies. We hid them around the corner in my mom's living room while she opened her birthday gifts. Just when she thought she was done, Doug walked across the room toward her. It took a moment for things to register, and then she began to cry. She knelt on the floor and scooped Doug into her arms. As she cradled and kissed him, she looked up through her tears and said, "There's another one!" George bounded around the corner. The dogs raced around joyfully, tagging each other and wrestling with the giftwrap. They had already begun to heal our hearts.

Pugs are often portrayed as the clowns of the canine world, and these two were no different. Doug loved to "help" with the household chores and would position himself on the open dishwasher door, ready for the prewash, or plate-licking, cycle. George sported a series of chic wardrobe pieces, including a floral Hawaiian shirt and a leather Harley hat. The brothers had regular "play dates," where they would often sit side-by-side and respond to human conversation with synchronized head tilts, like twin metronomes. The happiness they brought washed over our family and steadily tempered our grief.

Years have passed, and the dog that I didn't even know I wanted has become the one I can't live without. The gift I sought for someone else has become the best gift I ever gave myself. Through George, I've learned revealing lessons about myself, and I've learned larger lessons about life.

I've learned that grief can bring about positive changes. When my father passed away, I felt as if I would never be a complete person again. It took many nights of burying my face in puppy fur and sobbing for me to realize that I was complete, just different. I learned to see the joy in each day. If George stopped to smell flowers when we walked or sighed contentedly when he snuggled next to me, how could I ignore the ordinary miracles that came my way? And I've learned that God always knows our needs and fulfills them. He knew, even before I did, that I needed a dog, and he sent George to me.

— Rebecca Ruballos —

The Definition of Faithful Is "Dog"

There is no faith which has never yet been broken,
except that of a truly faithful dog.
~Konrad Lorenz

hen I was five years old, my mother decided she wanted a dog. My dad was neutral about the idea, but my sister and I were enthusiastic. We went to the local shelter where we discovered a Beagle who had been hit by a car. His back left leg was badly broken, and he was clearly in terrible pain, dragging it around behind him.

My mother wanted to take him. She launched into rescue mode and demanded to know what was being done for the dog. She was horrified to learn they had no intention of getting him any medical care. But the "dog warden" (as my mom called him) wouldn't let her have the dog. "I'm going to use it for hunting," he said. She pointed out his back leg was broken. "It'll get better," he replied.

Never one to give up easily, my mother found out who was in charge of the shelter and contacted him. She told him the situation, and he said, "If I arrange for you to have the dog, what would you do with him?"

Mom said, "I'd take him to the vet. If he can't be saved, I'll have him put out of his misery."

So he told us to return to the shelter, where the "warden" met us, quite disgruntled. "You got me in trouble with my boss," he said. "He told me I have to give you the dog." So he did. Thus, our search for a pet ended with us taking the dog to the local vet and asking him to put it to sleep.

The next day, Mom phoned the vet. "The dog and I had a conversation," the vet said. "The dog said he didn't want to be put to sleep, so I fixed his leg. He's in a cast for now, but he'll be fine." It took a long time to heal, and he had to be helped up and down the stairs to our second-floor apartment for weeks. The bad leg was always a little shorter than the others, but he got along fine. So, we had a dog.

Now our dog needed a name. My mother couldn't think of any name except that of a dog on a television show—a female Basset Hound named Cleo. Since our dog was male, my mom chose to spell it with a K: Kleo. He was her shadow, her faithful friend, and her companion. Kleo loved all of us, letting my younger sister and me put him in doll clothes, trim his fur, and sit on him without complaint, but my mom was his savior. When she left the house to run errands or get groceries, he howled at the top of his lungs until she returned. And when she came home, he was beside himself with joy.

Kleo went with us on vacation each summer, driving from our home in Washington State to our grandparents' homes in Massachusetts and New York. We never had to leash Kleo; we just opened the door and he hopped out, did what was needed and got back in the car.

One day, we stopped at midday for gas and a bathroom break at a station in the middle of nowhere. It had started to rain. Everyone tumbled out of the car and took off in several directions. A few minutes later, we were on the road again.

Hours passed when my mom asked suddenly, "Where's the dog?" Kleo was a quiet dog for the most part, so it took time to realize he wasn't in the car.

Everyone panicked. "Did anyone see him get back in the car at our last stop?" Mom asked. None of us had. We needed to call the gas station, but how? In the days before cell phones, the only way to make a call was at a phone booth or a home phone. Since we were in a rural area, there were no phone booths.

Finally, Mom insisted we stop at a house and ask to use the phone. An elderly couple answered her knock. "Oh, dear, come right in out of the rain," the woman said. Mom phoned the gas station, but by that time they had closed for the day, and there was no answer. So we turned around and headed back to that gas station as fast as we could.

It was dark by then and pouring rain. My mom didn't want to scare us, so she said, "Look along the side of the road. He might be trying to find us." But secretly I suspected she was looking for him lying along the roadside, dead.

We got all the way back to the gas station without finding Kleo. My sister and I were sobbing, sure we'd never see him again. We pulled into the gas station parking lot, and as our lights swept the station, I heard my mom gasp. Two eyes reflected back the headlights. There sat Kleo in front of the dark, locked station, soaking wet, with water dripping off his long ears, faithfully waiting for our return.

My mother jumped out and opened the back door. We had no blankets or towels, so she wrapped him in her sweater. We all laughed giddily, patted him and told him what a good dog he was. His face seemed to say, *What did you expect? I will always wait for you!*

It so happened there was a campground next to the gas station. The campground owner came over and said she had noticed Kleo earlier in the day. She was amazed at how he just sat there all day long waiting for his family to return. She had tried to lure him to her, figuring perhaps he'd been abandoned, but he wouldn't move from his chosen spot.

That night, Kleo was rewarded with as many hamburgers as he could eat. And from then on, Mom always asked "Where's the dog?" whenever we headed out on the road after a stop.

In the years since, we've had other dogs, and cats, and have loved them all for their own unique personalities. But there has never been and never will be another dog like Kleo... a loyal friend and the true definition of faithful.

— Elizabeth Delisi —

First They Get Married

Weddings to me are wondrous because they are so
filled with tomorrows.
~Mary Forsell

The boys overheard us talking about our German Shepherds Roxy and Cuda possibly having a litter of pups. They ran to us bursting with excitement. "Are the dogs getting married, Mom? They have to be married if they are going to have babies."

I looked at them in surprise and then eyed my husband Mike. Quickly recovering, I said, "Well. Why, yes, of course. They are getting married."

It was our good luck that Grandma came to visit at that moment. Sean and David threw themselves into her arms, bubbling with excitement about the dogs getting married and having puppies. Grandma did what all good grandmas would do in a similar situation. Without hesitation, she said, "I will make the veil."

The boys giggled and said, "Doggie biscuit cake, too?" They both got revved up by the thought of planning a wedding. "Can we invite people, too? Do we have music?" They fired questions so fast that we couldn't help but burst out laughing.

"Yes, we will take care of everything; don't you worry. But I think we'll just make it a small ceremony," I said. They nodded and ran off to play.

***

A couple days later, we were ready to go. Grandma arrived with the bride's veil. She placed it on Roxy's head and smiled ear-to-ear with pride. With a bobby pin here and there, the veil was set beautifully in place. Panting and wagging her tail, Roxy appeared somewhat apprehensive from under the veil.

The boys were so excited. Sean, age five, ran around the house in anticipation of the day's events. David, a year older, rushed to put on his black pinstriped vest. Even though they were young, each boy had an important role in the wedding, as witnesses.

Sean raced up to me and asked, "Does my suit look alright, Mommy?" I nodded and told him how handsome he looked. I gathered both boys and encouraged them to pick up the toys that were scattered around our dining room. I didn't get the usual tidying-up unresponsiveness. Instead, David grabbed the toy basket and hollered commands. "I got this truck, Sean! You get that brick." Sean was happy to pick up and help prepare our room for the grand event.

Mike hurried down the stairs with a conservatively appropriate beige tie. He secured the tie around the anxious groom's neck. I wore my sparkly pink eye shadow for the occasion. I had worked all morning making the unique dog-bone wedding cake and the flower arrangement that the boys helped me set up on the table.

We decided the time had come to get things moving with the wedding ceremony. Grandma started to hum the wedding march. Mike was ready to officiate the service. The boys asked, "What do we do now?" I directed them to stand beside their dogs. They proudly stood on either side of Roxy and Cuda. They placed their little hands upon each dog's back.

Mike's voice demanded respect as he recited the well-known vows. "Dearly beloved, we are gathered here today to witness the unification in marriage of this doggie couple." The boys shifted their feet in excitement. Grandma and I smiled at each other with the purest of joy. Our hearts filled with the gift of youth's simple and innocent delight.

Mike managed to coax out approving barks from the doggie bride and groom by dangling a bag of dog treats above them. From beginning to end, the ceremony went perfectly, as if it had a wedding planner at the helm. The dogs' destinies became sealed, and the boys happily hugged their broad shoulders. The early spring light seemed even brighter at that moment.

***

A few months later, I looked out my window and saw Sean and David sitting on the ground, their laps filled with three male and two female puppies. Roxy was a great mother, and Cuda was the most patient and loving dad. Both Sean and David helped to care for the puppies daily.

Years later, we all look back on that wedding as one of our best family memories.

— Kelly Hennigan —

Kitchen Sleepovers

*It is amazing how much love and laughter they bring
into our lives and even how much closer we become
with each other because of them.*
~John Grogan

"**W**hat about Domino?" someone suggested as our worn minivan rolled along.

"No," we murmured in unison.

Our new dog was a Labrador-Retriever mix — black all over with the exception of one white paw, a white underbelly, and a few white chin hairs. I took one more look into the loving eyes of this cute, little bundle and said, "What about Oreo?"

Everyone agreed it was the perfect name. "Hello, Oreo," I whispered in her ear. "Welcome to the family."

Once we arrived home, we were eager to show her off to all of our neighbors and friends. Everything about her was exciting — her little bark; the way she half-waddled, half-scampered down the gravel driveway; the way she got startled by bicycle horns; the way she turned up her nose at wet grass and refused to walk through it. We were smitten.

As her first day with us drew to a close, we were all exhausted from doting over her every move and celebrating her first-day milestones. However, a looming question begged to be asked. Where would Oreo sleep? My dad, in his wisdom, established that Oreo would not sleep with any of us because he did not want her getting accustomed to it.

"She will be our protector," he said. "And she can't do that if she is cozied in with one of you." We all swallowed hard, but agreed this was best. Heads hung low, we started shuffling our over-tired bodies to our rooms.

"However…" Dad continued. We all paused, hopeful about what he would say next. "However, puppies cry when they are alone, so maybe one of us should sleep with her — just for a few nights until she gets the hang of things."

These words rang out like an announcement of Christmas morning, and my dad now had the challenge of staring into the eyes of five pleading children, each hoping to be the special, chosen one for this incredible honor.

My dad shuffled for a moment, nodded toward my mother, cleared his throat and said, "Now, there are seven of us, and there are seven nights in a week. I think it only right if we each take a night. So, that's how we'll do it, fair and square." We all heartily agreed and then held our breath as we waited for who would get to be first. I tried to look good, but not too desperate.

Then my dad said something we did not expect. "I will take the first night," he said. Disappointed but not wanting to argue or make a fuss, we all kissed our parents goodnight and dragged ourselves to bed. We knew we wouldn't sleep a wink and counted the hours until we could get up and play with our furry friend again. My dad placed Oreo in her shiny, new dog bed and went to collect his things to settle in for the night.

In the early hours of the morning, I was awakened by a strange noise and went to investigate. My bedroom was the only one located on a different floor from that of my siblings. After looking around and deciding to dismiss the noise as a figment of my imagination, I decided to peek in on our new puppy. I crept quietly to the kitchen and peered into the tiny dog bed. To my surprise, it was empty. Confused, I glanced around, worried about where our little friend had run off to. I saw my dad sleeping soundly and moved closer to wake him. That's when I saw Oreo nestled safely in my dad's arms. I smiled and slipped out quietly.

I will never forget that image of my dad, a grown man, nestled in a tattered sleeping bag and lying on the floor just like he had done with each of us kids when we were sick. This time, he was cradling a tiny puppy in his strong arms to keep her from crying. I knew she must have felt like the most loved creature in the world.

From that day forward, she was known as "Dad's Dog." She followed him everywhere and cried when he was gone. Oreo's first week with us was so special, and we have never forgotten those kitchen sleepovers. Each night, my dad would announce the next person to spend the night with Oreo, and like a winner on *The Price Is Right*, that child would scream with joy and run triumphantly to collect a pillow and some bedding.

Despite being Dad's Dog, Oreo got to know us as an individual. She customized her approach to each of us. She could wrestle my brother and sit quietly with my sister. She knew to bark a warning if we were getting too rowdy, or to growl if a stranger approached. She taught us the value of quiet, still moments, and that love can be both simple and profound at the same time.

The years went on, and we five kids grew up and moved out. We still stopped by occasionally to grab a meal with Mom and Dad and share a quick moment with Oreo before returning to our busy lives. Then, one day, we got the call that we all knew would come. Dad notified us that Oreo was "not doing well." I felt a lump in my throat as tears streamed down my face. "I'll be right there," I said.

Oreo's last days were spent just like her first in our home, with each of us spending time with her lying on the kitchen floor. I watched as my dad slowly made his way onto the floor next to her to whisper in her ear and hold her close. Both of them were older and grayer than when they had their first night together. But Dad's still-strong arms caressed Oreo's silky fur. It was their final kitchen sleepover.

— Natasha Lidberg —

Bananas Foster

The bond with a true dog is as lasting as the ties
of this earth will ever be.
~Konrad Lorenz

When the nice lady asked my two young daughters if they would like to keep a doggy for a few weeks, you'd think she had just offered them a lifetime membership to Disneyland. They transformed into ecstatic little bobblehead dolls wildly nodding "YES, YES, YES" before she could even finish her sentence.

But Mommy bobblehead doll (me) was shaking her head in the other direction. We already had three dogs at home, but the lady was quick to elaborate. She explained that she was starting a new rescue that focused on saving the dogs that would otherwise be euthanized merely due to lack of space at the shelters. We would provide a temporary home for a dog while a permanent home was found. It would only be for a few weeks. We would save a dog's life. We would be... fosters.

Well, that was all I needed to hear. After all, any time I see a stray, I stop traffic to catch it and call the owner. I even "saved" our new neighbor's dog for a week... How was I supposed to know he lived there when I saw him out front? The poor guy was frantically looking for his dog. Oops!

So my bobblehead changed direction, and I found myself agreeing to help in any way we could.

A week later while shopping for art supplies at Michael's, we received the call. The lady had a dog for us. She had saved three that were to be euthanized that day, and they were in her car. Could she please bring the dog to the parking lot of Michael's? Absolutely, we said!

Minutes later, a rather harried-looking lady rushed toward us with a bundle of brown fur in her arms. Of the three rescues, this was the "healthy" one. One of the others had vomited all over the back seat of her car, and the other had coughed the entire way, no doubt kennel cough. Apologizing for the quick hand-off, she deposited the fur ball in my daughter's arms and the shelter paperwork in mine, and then ran off.

I read the details about our new foster dog: a female about two years of age. She was a white Poodle-Terrier mix weighing ten pounds. I told my daughters to start thinking of names for our new little foster girl.

Once we had the dog at home in my daughters' room, we realized that a few things didn't match the paperwork. First, she was very brown. It was hard to imagine she could ever be white, but then again it was impossible to see much through the two inches of matted fur. A trip to the groomer was our first priority.

The second thing we noticed was a bigger surprise. My younger daughter pointed at something on the undercarriage of the dog. She wanted to know why the dog had a "banana." While my older daughter broke out in embarrassed giggles, we realized that our female dog was in fact a male. I guess the shelter staff was either too busy for detail, or they needed a basic lesson in anatomy.

So our previous list of female names had to be discarded. My older daughter suggested the name Stevie, but my younger daughter fittingly liked the name Bananas. An argument ensued that quickly escalated into World War III, so we tabled the name choosing and opted to get Stevie Bananas straight to the groomer.

Four hours later, an exhausted groomer and a totally transformed white dog emerged. The groomer said she found fourteen ticks and a zillion fleas. Our hearts went out to this little dog in our care. He was going to need a lot of love, and we were ready to give it.

Back home, the girls settled a worn-out but clean Stevie Bananas onto their bed. He fell sound asleep with a Barbie pillow under his head, a sparkly pink blankie tucked around him, and my two daughters spooning him on either side. It was probably the first good night's sleep he had enjoyed in a long time, if ever.

Over the following days, Stevie Bananas' adorable personality blossomed. He perked up and became comfortable in his new surroundings. Our other three dogs welcomed him, and he loved the attention of his fellow fur-friends.

Then he coughed. And coughed again.

The veterinarian confirmed our fear: He had kennel cough, contracted from the shelter. It's very contagious, and it was too late for our other dogs. Before we knew it, we had a lovely chorus of incessant coughing from all four dogs, a complete barbershop quartet. Finding a home for our little foster would have to wait until we had a clean bill of health.

Round-the-clock care from my daughters and plenty of antibiotics restored our crew to health. We resumed our search for a happy home for Stevie Bananas by posting cute pictures on the rescue's website. We took him with us everywhere, hoping someone would spot him and want to adopt him.

Days turned into weeks. Summer came, and Stevie Bananas joined the family on our trip to Mammoth, riding the paddleboard with my daughters out onto the little lake in a cute doggy life-vest.

Then, one day, the phone rang. A permanent home in Portland had been found.

This was what we were hoping for, right? We were thrilled to have finally found a home for our foster, right? We had successfully completed what we had set out to accomplish, right? Save, foster, home, repeat... That was the plan, right?

The rescue organization had secured a spot on the dog shuttle to his new home in Portland the following morning. I was to have him there at 8:00 a.m., where he would be put in a crate for the nine-hour drive to his new family.

I didn't sleep at all that night. The girls went to bed sobbing. There was no doubt Stevie Bananas had become a part of our family. This was going to be the hardest thing I had ever done.

Stevie Bananas crawled up on my chest and kissed my nose, his little tail wagging. He knew something was up. As his big brown eyes looked deeply into my own, I was hit with the knowledge that was there all the time. Stevie Bananas wasn't being shipped off at 8:00 the next morning... He was already home.

We turned what could have been a miserable next day into a celebration. We threw a big welcome-home party for Stevie Bananas. All the dogs ate doggy ice cream, and we enjoyed plenty of—what else?—Bananas Foster!

—Julie Theel—

Taking a Chance

*I have found that when you are deeply troubled,
there are things you get from the silent devoted
companionship of a dog that you can get
from no other source.*
~Doris Day

I couldn't believe I was in the passenger seat with him sitting in my lap. How could I have allowed this to happen? He was shaking and frightened, not knowing where he was headed, but I remained resolutely unmoved by him.

"We shouldn't have gotten him," I cried to my brother. "He should not be the one coming home." It was completely unfair to place blame on this innocent, ten-pound Black Labrador puppy curled up under the red-checkered blanket — a blanket, I might add, that was a favorite of my mom's. I could not help the way I felt he was symbolic of what I had lost only weeks earlier.

My five-year-old son had been asking for a dog since he was three. The two of us had been living with my mom ever since my husband abandoned us shortly after Alex's birth. My mom stepped in as she had always done to love and support me. She was my cheerleader, my teacher, my one true thing. My father died when I was very young, so our bond was indescribably strong.

Probably from the minute Alex could talk, he would repeat, "Dog, me want." He was relentless with his demands much the same way I was in the Neiman Marcus shoe department. "Gucci, me want."

Sadly, neither of us would be getting what we wanted anytime in the foreseeable future.

Mom would let Alex have anything he wanted. There was no limit to her generosity and adoration of her beloved grandson. In fact, if he wanted the moon, she would have had it sent express to his bedroom. Unfortunately for him, though, a dog would be his Waterloo with her.

It wasn't that she was anti-animal. She had singlehandedly raised three sons, so she was quite accustomed to smelly, hairy things that ate her out of house and home. But she knew all the work that goes into raising a puppy, and she simply was not willing to give up her unchewed furniture and clean tile floors, even if it meant disappointing the love of her life.

She would say half-jokingly, "When I am dead, Alex can have his puppy, but not while I am living in this house."

I hadn't counted on that becoming a reality so soon. My mother passed away shortly before Alex turned six. The void she left was devastating, particularly to Alex. She had been his 24/7 companion since birth. With the realization that Alex would be starting school only a few weeks after her death, I knew the house would be devastatingly silent during the day.

Seeing how lonely Alex was, my brother Ted said to me, "He needs a dog. He needs to have something to love again." My mom's voice echoed in my head, and I refused. It was too soon. It had only been six weeks since we buried her. How could we even think of it?

The first morning I dropped off Alex at kindergarten, I was numb. I knew it would be overwhelming to return home alone. It was not only the home that I shared with my son and mother, but also the home where I was raised.

Later that morning, in that empty house, I received a text message. I clicked on it to find a tiny bundle of black fur with big brown eyes staring directly at me. It was obvious my brother was not letting go of this. His message read: "Look at his name and the day he was born."

Louie, born on August 8, 2014. My mother, Lucy, had died on August 8, 2014. It was a sign.

Reluctantly, I gave in. The dog was to be a surprise. So on the day of my son's birthday, we headed out to get "Louie" while Alex waited at home with not an inkling as to what was to come.

We needed a new name, though. Louie just did not sit right with me. The night before we were to pick him up, I finished watching the movie, *Taking Chance*. The young soldier whose story was being told had a Labrador in many of his in memoriam pictures during the closing credits. I suggested "Chance" — as in, "We are taking a chance on a puppy" and, more likely, "There's a chance I might go insane with this decision."

I hoped that I would melt instantly at the sight of this precious little guy, but I looked at him with resentment. All I saw was an interloper coming to take the place that belonged to Mom.

As expected, Alex was overjoyed. He was unable to stop hugging Chance from the moment we walked in the door. It was love at first sight, and I was truly thrilled for my son.

I was dutiful and did what was expected of a pet owner. I walked him, fed him, and bathed him. Not one of his physical needs was ever neglected. But I still saw him as an invader.

Every morning after school drop-off, I returned home to that house filled with forty years of memories. Despite my lack of affection, Chance would be waiting at the front door with his tail wagging, jumping around and wanting to play.

I would go into the basement to do laundry and Chance would follow right behind me. I would hop into the shower and Chance would sit outside the bathroom door and wait. His furry, little shadow followed me wherever I went. No matter what I did, he gave me unconditional love — whether I wanted it or not.

But I was still in so much pain without my mom. It had only been two months, and I could not take a step without seeing reminders of her. Notes on which she had scribbled recipes hung on the inside of cabinets. Her signature scent, Halston, wafted through the bedroom as soon as I opened her closet. I wanted her, not Chance. I knew it was unfair, but I couldn't help what I felt. Chance got more than enough affection from my son and my other siblings, so I wasn't too worried for him. I would just tolerate him.

In late November, about six weeks after welcoming the new addition to the house, I heard a knock at the door. I opened it in time to see the UPS truck pulling away. A small brown box had been left on the porch swing—the place where mom and I spent hours chatting about everything from what color dress I would wear for my junior prom to what type of mother I was going to be.

The label on the package said Bradford Exchange and was addressed to "Lucy Flowers." Ever since I was a little girl, my mom would start preordering things for the holidays as early as an entire year beforehand. She usually forgot about them until they showed up months later.

With Chance on my heels, I took the package into the dining room and debated whether or not to open it. Curiosity got the best of me, so I found my mom's old sewing scissors and cut open the brown wrapping.

The order form said she had placed a preorder in March of that year. I pulled off the shredded paper and bubble wrap and was taken aback. Inside was a snow globe from their *Saturday Evening Post* series. I picked it up and had to catch my breath upon seeing what was behind the falling snowflakes. On a street that looked similar to our own, a tiny black dog pulled at the red newspaper satchel held by a little blond boy.

Throughout the years when Alex had been nonstop in his demands for a dog, Mom did her best to provide him with stuffed animals, books about dogs, and movies about dogs. Clearly she had ordered the snow globe as this year's contribution to the anything-but-a-real-dog collection. I dropped to the floor with tears streaming down my face.

Chance ran to me instantly and licked my face. I yelled at him to leave me alone, but he refused to leave my side. He dug in his heels and kept watch over me for what seemed like hours.

That would be the turning point in our relationship.

Chance is now almost four years old, and we have even welcomed a little sister, Sophie, another black Labrador, into our home. To be honest, I always thought that people who treated their pets as family members were a bit eccentric. And while I still miss my mom every single day, I know that without the introduction of our four-legged friends into my life, I might never have found the strength to make it through those endless lonely days. I will forever be indebted to Chance for my new beginning.

—Tara Flowers—

Who's in Charge Here?

12

It's Not Insomnia— It's My Dog

If you live with dogs, you'll never
run out of things to write about.
~Sharon Delarose

Doctors recommend that adults get seven to nine hours of sleep each night. A good night's sleep improves heart health, lowers stress and increases creativity. Unfortunately, my dog can't read and has no idea what scientific data is. Nor does she care that sleeping is one of my all-time favorite activities.

After a long, busy day, there is nothing I look forward to more than some quiet time with a book and then a good night's sleep. But once bedtime rolls around, dealing with Maya, our mischievous Shih Tzu, is like parenting a toddler who refuses to sleep in her own bed.

Here's how the little monster enjoyed one recent night.

11:16 p.m. Just after I closed my book and shut off the light, Maya decided that the most comfortable bed in the house was ours. Without notice, she leapt up from the floor and landed on my abdomen. It startled me so badly that my arm jerked off the mattress and made direct contact with the headboard, hitting my funny bone. She then walked along my torso and made a U-turn at my chin. There, she snuggled under the blankets, burying her face in my armpit and settling her backside comfortably on my pillow. After thumping me three times on the forehead with her tail, she fell asleep. I learned something valuable that night: Freshly applied lip balm can instantly attract up to ninety-five dog hairs.

12:28 a.m. Maya woke me by galloping across the bed when she got up to patrol the house. I heard her toenails clicking on the tile floor in the kitchen, then through the dining room where she stopped to get a drink. As I listened to her slurps, I was reminded that I had forgotten to put the water dish up for the night. (I'd pay for that later.) She clicked back across the tile and down the hall into the bedroom. I knew she was standing next to the bed. I could feel her watching me. But she just stood there.

Rather than getting back onto the bed on her own, she sat on the floor and pointed her nose toward the mattress, asking for assistance. Her plea for help was not a bark or a whine, but more of a whisper. It started out like a soft *ffffftt ffffftt* and then morphed into a funny sneeze. Progressively, the whispers and sneezes got louder and more insistent, and were followed by strange, throaty dog verbiage that sounded a lot like Chewbacca from *Star Wars*.

Once she was on the bed, she walked up to my pillow and stared at me, her nose just an inch from mine. Her chin hair was still wet from the water dish; it dripped on my face and ran down my neck. Before I had a chance to turn away, she burped. Not a cute, doggy burp, but a full-on, carbonation-induced lumberjack belch — to which my husband woke just enough to ask, "What'd you say?" Little Miss Manners then spent the next three minutes rolling around on her back before falling asleep.

1:11 a.m. Someone was snoring! I nudged my husband and grumbled, "Turn over." With a grunt, he rolled to his side, but the snoring didn't roll over with him. I sat up and looked at the little dog lying on my bed. Maya was on her back. Her ears flopped out alongside her head. All four paws were in the air. *That's just great,* I thought. *Chewbacca has sleep apnea.* I turned her onto her side and pulled the blanket over my head.

2:18 a.m. I had a dream that transported me back to my childhood. Not only did I hear the bumps and thuds, but I *felt* them. No doubt about it, there was a monster under my bed! As the bumping and banging intensified beneath me, I realized that I was awake, and the little monster was Maya. She wasn't just under the bed; she was *inside* the bed. She'd managed to find a small hole in the fabric on the underside of the box springs, which she wiggled through. Happily, she explored the interior, tromping and running around like a child in a bounce house. I spent the next fifteen minutes with my head wedged under the bed, holding a flashlight and trying to coax Maya out of the same small tear she had entered through.

2:46 a.m. After a successful rescue mission, I was back in bed, trying to doze off. And I would have fallen asleep if Maya hadn't been digging beside me with badger-like fury. Evidently, the blankets weren't quite fluffy enough. Using her paws and teeth, she managed to drag all but the sheet off my body and into the center of the bed. I tugged at the bedding, trying to reclaim just enough of it to cover my legs and prevent frostbite. In one quick "whoosh," all the blankets were gone as my husband rolled over in them and muttered, "Stop hogging the covers." I pulled my bathrobe from the foot of the bed and curled up under it.

3:31 a.m. The sound of a snare drum jolted me awake. I buried my head in a pillow and tried to ignore it, but the rat-a-tat-tat continued. Maya was scratching furiously at the back door. As I stumbled down the hall, I stepped on something that sent a chill up my spine. Cold, sticky and wet, I knew immediately that my toes had encountered a well-chewed, soggy rawhide. I hopped to the door on one leg, trying to free myself from the leechlike object stuck to my bare foot.

When I slid open the door, Maya zipped past me. She ran across the deck, skidded to a stop and sat down. When I pointed toward the back yard, she stood up, spun twice and sat again with a look that said, "Let's play!" Her ears were perked, her tongue hung out, and the corners of her mouth turned up. She was smiling; I was not. Then, in a flash, she ran back across the deck, through the door and between my feet. After all that, she hadn't even remembered to pee! She disappeared down the hall where I could hear her in the bedroom, doing her best Wookie impression and asking to be picked up.

I peeked in and saw my husband reaching down to lift Maya onto the bed. As they both snuggled into the blankets, I pulled the door shut. "She's all yours," I mumbled, as I tiptoed back down the hall and into the living room. I sank onto the couch with an old afghan and enjoyed the best two hours of sleep I'd had all week.

—Ann Morrow—

13

Our Little Genius

No one appreciates the very special genius of your
conversation as much as the dog does.
~Christopher Morley

"**G**uess what Jordan did last night?" I said to my co-worker.

He smiled slightly. "What did the most amazing eight-month-old on the planet do last night?"

I launched into a ten-minute description of the adorable thing my son had done the night before. At the end, I expected my co-worker to be as delighted as I was with my son's precociousness.

Instead, he seemed almost irritated. "Diane, I have to tell you something, and you're not going to like it. But I mean it in the nicest way possible." He paused and blurted out, "No one in this office will ever think your baby is half as fascinating as you do, and the stories you tell aren't all that interesting to the rest of us."

My mouth dropped open.

He shrugged. "Sorry. I meant it nicely."

"So I've been annoying everyone here by talking about my baby too much?"

He nodded. "Yeah, but we were too polite to tell you. Well, until now, that is."

"I guess I appreciate your honesty," I said. "And I'll definitely try to cut back on the baby stories from now on."

And although I did try to talk less about my son after that painful and embarrassing conversation, I found it difficult to fathom that other people weren't completely enthralled by his existence on this planet. He was all I could think about, and the fact that others weren't even interested in his latest milestone was hard for me to imagine. He was, after all, just so fascinating.

As a dog mom, I often feel the same way. My Pomeranian-Poodle mix, Piper, is the sweetest, smartest, cutest dog on the planet, and the idea that a human being exists who wouldn't fall in love with her is unimaginable to me.

Take the furnace repair guy who came to our house last week. I answered the door, holding Piper in my arms. (She has a habit of darting out the open front door so we can play "tag" in the yard, whether I want to or not.) I expected the repairman's face to melt into the "Awwwww" face I make every time I see my precious pooch. But he merely walked in, put paper booties over his shoes so he wouldn't mess up my carpet, and got to work.

I was offended on Piper's behalf.

Even my own husband is guilty of not properly appreciating how utterly fascinating our sweet girl is. "Honey, guess what Piper did today?" I said one evening when he got home from work.

He pretended to think for a minute. "Um, slept? Chewed on a bone? Pooped outside hopefully?"

"Yes, she did all those things, but she also learned a new trick," I said. "Piper gave me a high-five on my foot."

He gave me a weird look. "Piper has been giving high-fives for months now."

"I know, but today I held up my foot and said, 'High-five,' and she touched her paw to my foot."

Another weird look. "I wouldn't really consider that a new trick."

I shrugged. "Well, guess what else she did. This is really impressive. It proves what I've been telling you all along about how smart she is."

Eric sighed. "Please tell me."

"I was upstairs folding laundry, and I heard Piper in the kitchen, pushing her water bowl with her paw. You know how she pushes it against the wall so we hear the sound and know that we need to fill it for her?"

He nodded impatiently.

"Well, she was pushing her dish, but I was busy so I ignored her. She came upstairs and stared at me, and then ran back to the kitchen to hit her dish again. I called out, 'Piper, I'm busy, honey. I'll fill it in a minute.'"

My husband nodded again. "Because she understands everything you say to her."

I stuck out my lip, pouting. "Piper understands twenty-seven human words," I stated emphatically. "That's a huge vocabulary for a Pomapoo."

Eric rolled his eyes. "The water dish?" he prompted.

"Yes, anyway, so when I didn't come downstairs to fill her dish, she rang her bell to tell me she needed to go outside. I was worried that if I didn't take her out, she'd have an accident, so I set aside the laundry and came downstairs right away. As soon as she saw me, she ran away from the door and back to her water dish. She pushed it with her paw and gave me a look that clearly said, 'I win.'"

"So she rang the potty bell as a ploy to get you to come downstairs and fill her water dish?"

I nodded triumphantly. "It was a genius move, don't you think?"

Eric smirked. "You're pleased that you were outsmarted by a Pomapoo?"

"An extremely intelligent Pomapoo," I corrected.

Eric rolled his eyes, but later that night, I caught him snuggling on the couch with Piper. "Who's a smart girl?" he cooed in her ear. "You are. You're the smartest, cutest puppy in the whole, wide world."

As I watched my husband with our puppy, I loved both of them a little bit more. I also realized that one of my favorite things about being married is the unique bond my husband and I share because we love the same little people the exact same amount. Eric is the only person on this planet who will ever be as fascinated with my offspring as I am. He loves my kids as much as I do, and I am blessed to be married to him. Plus, he will never tire of hearing stories that start with, "Guess what one of our little geniuses did today."

Even when that little genius is a Pomapoo named Piper.

—Diane Stark—

14

Walking Archer

Walk like a dog; it will lead you in the right direction.
~Author Unknown

I'd never been one for walking. I'm married to a guy who loves to run, and he would always ask me if I'd take a walk with him. My response was always "I have a car" — until I became the caretaker of an eleven-pound furry ball of relentless enthusiasm.

I say "caretaker" because one can't really *own* a creature that has this much enthusiasm. Our latest addition, Archer, is a Terrier who believes with all his being that every day is AWESOME. Every. Single. Day.

And the most AWESOME thing is going for a walk.

Every. Single. Day.

It started when we were having trouble with housebreaking. I have a theory that before he got to the shelter, and during his formative years, Archer lived in a back yard. This meant he grew up with the philosophy that the whole world was his to mark with a seemingly endless supply of yellow fluid.

Since none of our usual housebreaking methods were working, I thought I'd try walking Archer in the morning to give him an opportunity to get it all out of his system. The goal was to let him mark up the whole neighborhood to satisfy that urge to shout to every other dog in the universe that ARCHER WAS HERE.

It started slowly, just a walk down the block. The entire time Archer would prance with joy from mailbox to clump of weeds like I had just set loose a person on a carb-free diet in a room full of French fries. Periodically, a particular bush would require the big-dog treatment: the extra step of pawing at the ground in long, proud strokes to show just how large a dog had marked that particular spot.

Then, after a week, I started to get a little organized. My walk progressed farther down the block. My husband asked me how far I was walking, so I downloaded an app for my phone to track it.

It's been three months of walking, and Archer is fully housebroken. But if I try to skip the walk on any given morning, he looks at me like I've announced that all the bacon in the world has disappeared.

Last Sunday, we walked three miles — this from a woman with a perfectly functioning car.

I'll admit it is nice to walk, and it's fun to see Archer practically leap into his orange walking harness. I even like seeing the bar graph on the app showing how much farther I walk every month.

But every now and then, I look at this little dog and think, *Who is walking who?*

— Winter Desiree Prosapio —

15

What Comes Naturally

Instinct is a marvelous thing.
It can neither be explained nor ignored.
~Agatha Christie

My endodontist was apologetic. "I'm so sorry, Sallie. I don't think we can save the tooth."

"It's a front tooth. Can't you do anything?" I asked.

"The tooth took a bad hit when you fell last year. We can't save it. It's dying. You'll need an extraction, and then I would suggest an implant. We'll also send you home with a flipper — a false tooth that connects with wire to your other front tooth. It can be removed, but you'll probably want to wear it most of the time for cosmetic reasons until you've healed enough for your implant," he continued.

I left his office feeling distraught. The only flipper I knew about was an aquatic mammal that made funny chirping noises.

The day of the procedure came, and everything went well. But the flipper decided not to cooperate. It hurt to wear it and sent my sinuses into fits; also, I couldn't eat with it on. This made restaurant eating embarrassing, not to mention that I lisped when I talked.

Living alone, I talked to the one constant in my life: Mollie the Beagle. "I hate Flipper, Mollie! You'd think they would come up with a better idea. And the name, Flipper? Really!" I ranted at her each morning as I put it in. I knew she understood me because she looked at me with her big, brown eyes and whined. It was as if she looked right into my soul; Mollie understood my pain.

One gloomy winter afternoon, Mollie and I snuggled up on the couch with a book. It was the perfect day for a long nap. The next thing I knew, I was waking up an hour later.

I realized I had forgotten to put Flipper back in after eating lunch. I reached for its red case on the coffee table. It wasn't there. *Wow, that's funny*, I thought. *I always put it in its case when I'm not wearing it.*

Hunting around the house, confident that I had just laid it somewhere, I became more frantic as I searched. Where, oh where, was Flipper?

I was going to the opera with my daughter in two days. I had an invitation to lunch with my former boss. I couldn't walk around missing my front tooth! The more I looked, the more panicked I became.

Finally, pausing to take a breath as I rounded the corner into the bedroom, I noticed Mollie sitting on the bed. And there, next to her, was a little pile of silver wire and nothing else. Flipper had met its demise.

"Mollie!" I screamed. "Did you eat Flipper? Oh, Mollie, I can't believe you did that! What am I going to do?"

She just looked at me with a satisfied look as if to say, "I took care of that nasty Flipper dude you hated so much."

I rushed to the phone and called my dentist. His recording said he would be in first thing the next morning. The next day, I had the first appointment.

"You must have a dog," the dentist said with a sly smile as he took the mold for Flipper Number Two.

"How'd you know?" I asked.

"We get this a lot, especially with the hounds. You have one?"

"Yes, I've got a very devoted Beagle named Mollie," I confessed. "She's in the doghouse, Doc. No pun intended."

"Oh, that explains it. Don't be too hard on her. They love your scent on these appliances," he said, chuckling.

"Gross!" I replied.

"Not really. That is what gives them their natural ability to track and find items and missing persons. They have that nose for a reason."

So I left with a newfound respect for Mollie's nose. I went home and hugged Mollie. As I rubbed her nose, I told her I was sorry I had screamed at her, and that it was my fault for being careless.

Mollie's nose was a miracle of nature, but for the next two weeks, I put Flipper up high on a shelf when I wasn't wearing it—a very, very high shelf!

— Sallie A. Rodman —

A Dog for a Nurse

No animal I know of can consistently be more of a
friend and companion than a dog.
~Stanley Leinwall

I t happened right at the start of my summer vacation when I was in elementary school. "Well, you're overdue for measles anyway," my mother told me when I started showing symptoms. My cousins had recently suffered through measles, so my mother was anticipating the warning signs.

Honestly, I don't recall much about having the measles, although my mother has told me I had a very severe case. The only thing I clearly remember is our black-and-white mutt, Boots, who stayed near me the whole time I was sick. He kept me company, resting quietly with me during the day and snuggling warmly against me at night.

As I recovered from my illness, the doctor recommended plenty of fresh air and exercise. I must have been depressed after my sickness because all I wanted to do, even though I felt better, was lie on the couch and read classic literature: *Richie Rich*, *Casper the Friendly Ghost* and *Jughead and Archie*.

"You've got to go outside and get some exercise," my mother insisted one day. "The doctor said it will help you get better."

"I don't feel like it," I complained. I sat on the couch reading a comic book with the dog lying patiently next to me.

"You could go outside with Boots," suggested my mother.

Boots stood up, his tail wagging at the sound of his name. He jumped off the couch and headed for the door. My mother let him out. "Are you sure you won't join your dog?" she asked me.

I shook my head.

Later that evening, Boots did not return home at his usual time. After dinner, I called repeatedly for him, but he did not appear.

"It's not like that dog to miss a meal," said my mother. "You'd better go out and look for him."

For the first time in a long time, I headed out into the yard. I found Boots sitting in the back yard with his ball clamped in his mouth. He hurried to me when I spotted him, dropping his ball at my feet. I picked up the ball and threw it a few times for Boots. He chased it enthusiastically and brought it back to me. Then, after a while of play, the dog followed me back inside for his dinner.

The next evening, the same thing happened again. I called for Boots, but he did not come. For a second time, I went outside and found him sitting in the back yard with his ball. We played for a while in the twilight and then headed back inside.

This strange pattern continued day after day. Every evening, I'd have to go outside to get Boots. We'd play catch for a while, and then go back inside for Boots to have his dinner.

And without my really being aware of it, thanks to my frequent trips outside to find Boots over the next few weeks, I became stronger and healthier, finally recovering my good spirits completely.

Once I was back to my old self, Boots changed his routine and began coming to dinner as soon as he was called.

"That's weird," I said.

"Well, you weren't listening to the doctor's advice to get outside and exercise," replied my mother. "So, apparently, Boots decided he'd give you a helping hand and encourage you to get some activity. I bet you're the first kid who ever had a dog for a nurse!"

Looking back on the experience all those years ago, I can't help but wonder if it was just a coincidence or if Boots really knew what he was doing in helping with my recovery. Regardless, I'll always be grateful that I had a dog for a nurse.

—David Hull—

Christmas Blitz

Dogs are great. Bad dogs, if you can really call them
that, are perhaps the greatest of them all.
~John Grogan

When Blitz, a German Shepherd puppy, came home for his first Christmas, it was fun and chaos at the Reiss household. My daughter's tree was decorated with the loveliest ornaments and lights, handed down from generation to generation.

Packages were carefully wrapped and piled neatly under the tree. Blitz had chewy toys and gifts of his own to open, but when the rambunctious puppy spotted the bows and wrappings, he dove into them without warning, like any young pup would. He crashed into the colorful boxes headfirst, legs spread out, like a sled speeding down a slippery slope. He chewed the paper, the boxes, and all the satin ribbons. In five minutes, this beautiful holiday scene was turned upside down and trashed.

Yes, it was Blitz's first Christmas, and he loved every minute of it.

The second Christmas was much like the first, only this time the tree had fewer ornaments on it, and the gifts were stacked on the dining-room table for safekeeping. A little older now, Blitz must have liked the smell of the real tree because he took a whiz on it. It wasn't "O Holy Night" but "O Smelly Night." The tree was sprayed with a pine scent, but that wasn't enough, so it was picked up and carried out to the front porch. It was viewed from inside the large living-room picture window where we couldn't smell it.

The third year, after Blitz knocked over the tree, still in its stand and not yet decorated, we set it up on the front porch. It was not the cozy scene one would see in a Christmas card, but it was reality. The living room looked as sterile as a hospital, with no signs of Christmas anywhere. Blitz had stolen Christmas from my family.

This year, the decision to put up a Christmas tree was the main topic of conversation in my daughter's household. Blitz was now 130 pounds and had a mind of his own. Obedience school had proved unsuccessful, and "Blitz Rules" was the new family motto.

One afternoon, while my daughter Vicki was at work, her two adult boys decided to surprise her by putting up a four-foot tree to try and save Christmas. They wedged the tree tightly into a corner of the living room and placed a star on top. It held no dangling ornaments or lights to attract Blitz, just a blinking star.

When Blitz entered the room, he stared briefly at the tree and walked by. Maybe he thought it was dull and not worthy of attack. We looked at it as a Christmas miracle. Taking it one step at a time, packages were again assembled on the dining-room table, while cards and garlands hung from the fireplace.

Maybe Blitz finally got the message and realized that Santa would not bring him any treats if he was naughty again this year. Whatever the reason, we won't question it. Our family is just happy that Bobby and Brian saved Christmas and brought back our tree, even though it was not decorated. Well, there's always next year, depending on Blitz.

— Irene Maran —

18

The Canine Tactician

I've seen a look in dogs' eyes, a quickly vanishing look
of amazed contempt, and I am convinced that dogs
think humans are nuts.
~John Steinbeck

Marley's eyelids fluttered up and down as I held his mouth shut. His thick body eased to the hardwood floor in the living room of our old farmhouse. My husband and I watched him closely, guessing this to be another ruse. Marley's eyes eventually remained closed, though, and he gave a little snore. Our dog appeared to be snoozing, acting as if we'd given him a sleeping pill rather than his daily medicine. However, based on past experience, we weren't convinced.

"You think it's a trick?" my husband asked.

I shrugged. "He really looks tired."

After a few minutes, I let go of his mouth. Immediately, Marley jumped up, spit out the medicine and dashed out of the room. Hoodwinked. Again. We looked at each other and laughed.

Over the years, Marley routinely demonstrated his strategic thinking. Our first glimpse of this occurred the day he arrived at our house aboard an animal van from the state of Washington. Climbing from his animal-transport vehicle, the driver laughed and said, "You have a real Houdini on your hands. One minute, he's sleeping, and the next he's gone. You don't even hear him move!"

Indeed. Although topping out at 169 pounds, Marley maneuvered about our house like a mouse wearing padded slippers, appearing and disappearing at will—when he saw fit to do so. Other times, Marley flopped onto the floor with the grace of an elephant, shaking the house to the rafters. This usually occurred around dinnertime, along with Marley milling about, woefully dragging his feet across the oak floor while putting on his miserable "I'm starving" face.

Marley's tactical maneuvering took place on walks as well. He usually heeled like a professional. Passersby often commented on his nice manners. But then Marley discovered a potential loophole. What if he trailed behind us at a snail's pace? How long could he make his walk last?

Our walks got longer and slower—until we caught on to his shenanigans. But, as always, our dog had another scheme up his sleeve. Marley decided not to utilize bathroom breaks throughout the day in order to save up more ammunition for marking choice items during his walk. All that stopping and starting took forever.

Being a Komondor, Marley's knack for strategic thinking was interlaced with independence, courage and quick-wittedness. These Hungarian sheepdogs were bred to watch and defend small animal charges, and their owners often left them alone to watch over flocks—sometimes for weeks at a time. Today, many still work in this capacity. Others, like Marley, have become beloved family pets. But that doesn't mean they leave behind the innate qualities that make them excellent flock guardians.

These character traits provided Marley with a healthy dose of suspicions. Case in point: a distrust of telephones. He interpreted the device as a threat. In our house, a ringing phone equaled a barking dog. I worked at home, and this didn't work out well when speaking with clients. It took time to break our comrade of this habit. Until then, whenever the phone rang, I had to close my office doors before the "commander" stormed into the room. Extremely displeased by the interference in fulfilling his duty, Marley would stare at me from the other side of the glass.

Marley deemed another activity as suspicious, too—running in the house. In fact, even walking fast warranted misgiving. Those activities signaled danger. And running to catch a ringing phone? A double whammy.

All things considered, Marley's imitation of Rip Van Winkle that night shouldn't have surprised us. Marley never took off his thinking cap.

"Marley!" we called.

I sat with the pill in my hand. Finally, we heard the shuffling feet. Then, our big, white dog poked his head around the doorframe and offered a playful, perhaps slightly apologetic, grin.

— Lisa Mackinder —

19

All Ears

*If you think dogs can't count, try putting three
dog biscuits in your pocket and then give him
only two of them.*
~Phil Pastoret

A popular "dog whisperer" kindly donated her expertise to a fundraiser at our local shelter. Although I was a total skeptic, I happily made a donation and got a fifteen-minute reading for my dog.

Roxy was eight years old at the time. We had adopted her two years earlier from Golden Rescue. At first, she was timid and overweight, and spent a lot of time sleeping. Now, she loved her walks, oozed confidence, and was a head-turner with her beautiful reddish-gold fur, and svelte new figure. Roxy was also a people magnet and vital member of our family.

So in we went for our fifteen-minute session — Roxy the social butterfly, and me the skeptic. The dog whisperer welcomed us both. Kneeling down, she began by gently rubbing Roxy from head to toe. Then she got up and handed me a clipboard, paper and pen.

"What's this for?" I asked.

"To write down her thoughts," she said as she sat down in the chair across from us.

"Oh, thanks," I said politely, and promptly set it down beside me.

Roxy was now lying on the floor beside me, relaxed and content. The dog whisperer sat in silence, as if deep in thought. Then she blurted out, "Roxy loves you."

Of course, she does, I thought. *I'm her main caregiver. I walk, feed and take her to the cottage. Besides, every dog owner thinks their dog loves them just as much as we love them.*

"No, I mean she *really* loves you. You rescued her — not from a bad home but a busy one. Once the kids came, they just did not have time for her anymore," she said emphatically.

I grabbed the clipboard and started writing. How could she know this? That is exactly why Roxy had been surrendered. Her former family loved her but realized they could not give her the attention she needed.

"She feels beautiful. And she loves being able to swim and chase balls. Losing all that weight really helped."

This was getting freaky. Roxy had been very overweight, but swimming at the cottage helped her shed the extra pounds in no time. As the dog whisperer went on, I continued to write and write. Clearly, Roxy had a lot to say.

But the comment that really got me was about her dog food. Since we had to put her on a diet, our vet prescribed a specific brand of low-fat kibble.

"She's okay with the kibble you feed her," the whisperer went on, "but it's boring. She really likes when you spice it up a bit with cheese shreds or scrambled eggs."

By the time we left, I had more than three pages of Roxy's thoughts. Wow, who knew our little Miss Roxy was such a blabbermouth? Kind of made me wonder what else she might have said!

That evening, I shared the notes with my family. They found it all quite amusing and were just glad the money went to a good cause. I understood their skepticism, but I carefully tucked the notes in my desk.

The next morning, like always, I let Roxy out the back door while I changed her water and filled her bowl with kibble. When she came back, Roxy scooted down the hall to her food. However, instead of wolfing it down as usual, she just sniffed it. Then she turned and looked back down the hall at me as if to say, "Did you not hear a word I said?"

Without a second glance at her food, she walked right past me and into the living room. She plopped down on her bed and let out the biggest of all sighs. *You little rascal,* I thought. *You're not going to eat it.* So I sprinkled a little leftover rice from our dinner on her kibble. Roxy scooted back down the hall and ate her breakfast — licking the bowl clean. Unbelievable.

Years later, after our beloved Roxy passed away, we adopted another wonderful white Retriever named Fenway. Of course, I had to take her to the dog whisperer. And just like Roxy, Fenway had a lot to say.

This time, I was all ears.

— Cheryl E. Uhrig —

20

The Bichon on the Bed

If I loved a guy as much as I love my dog,
the guy would be in serious trouble.
Because I'm all over that dog, all the time.
~Maria Sharapova

Bichon Frise is a small, white and incredibly cute dog. We Bichon owners love our "fluffs," but this attachment can present challenges. One Bichon owner recently posted this lament on a Bichon-related Facebook group: "I'm breaking up with my boyfriend because he refuses to let my Bichon share the bed with us. I've had Maggie for ten years and have been with my boyfriend for just a year. I told him that she was here long before he was."

That's an interesting dilemma, I thought, anticipating that her post would spark a lively debate.

I was dead wrong. Within a day, she'd received 400 comments, but every one of them was supportive.

The clear consensus among the Bichon crowd? A boyfriend who wouldn't bed down with a Bichon deserved to be kicked to the curb. The posted comments expressed this sentiment in a variety of ways. Here's a small sampling:

A CHOICE BETWEEN A BOYFRIEND AND A BICHON? YOU CALL THAT A CHOICE?

I'd have done the same thing. Love my dog or there's the door.

Boyfriends come and go. Bichons are forever.

Bichons before boys, I always say.

Well, look who ended up in the doghouse… Adios, boyfriend!

A DUDE WHO DISLIKES DOGS? BE VERY SUSPICIOUS.

You can tell a lot about a man by the way he treats your dog.

If he doesn't treat Maggie well, he probably won't treat you well either.

MR. RIGHT WILL LOVE BOTH YOU AND YOUR DOG

I made the same call a decade ago. Best decision I ever made because I met and married a man who loves both me and my dogs.

When my husband proposed, I told him that my dogs had shared my bed long before he did and would continue to do so. If he hadn't been okay with that? I wouldn't have married him.

We share our bed with six Bichons, and my hubby loves it. Real men love Bichons!

Even folks who don't bed down with their Bichons applauded this decision:

Who needs a man who is jealous of a dog?

He wants to come into your home and tell you what to do? I don't think so.

My Bichon sleeps in a doggy bed. But having said that — I wouldn't let someone else tell me where my Zoey gets to sleep.

THE BICHON-ON-THE-BED TEST, IN FACT, IS AN EXCELLENT WAY TO SCREEN OUT MR. WRONG

A few final words of advice:

Get another Bichon to get over him.

Go to the dog park and find a man who loves dogs.

So, if you're thinking of dating a Bichon owner, great idea. But never underestimate our loyalty to the dog on the bed.

—Roz Warren—

21

Time for That Walk

Some of our greatest historical and artistic treasures
we place with curators in museums;
others we take for walks.
~Roger A. Caras

Dogs have enriched our marriage for thirty years. Our last dog, Chance, was definitely special and usually very laid-back. He was a mix of Labrador and Golden Retriever with a hint of Greyhound. His favorite things to do were walking, and chasing other animals, including cats, rabbits and deer.

Every day, Chance and I would take a one-mile walk. Sometimes, my husband would go with us, but usually it was just the dog and me. After having a total hip replacement in 2000, walking was the best form of therapy to keep my muscles strong. Chance was a good motivator since we didn't miss a day of exercise, plus he was a gentle guy while on the leash despite weighing a hundred pounds.

After cleaning up the kitchen one afternoon, I slipped on my tennis shoes and grabbed Chance's leash. I didn't have to say a word because he was already prancing to the door. My husband, Tony, was in the living room sitting in his favorite chair with the laptop across his legs.

"Are you going with us?" I asked.

"Sure. Just a minute," Tony replied.

I sat on the couch with the leash still in my hand, and the look on Chance's face was like, "Huh?" Immediately, he went over, stood in front of Tony and gave one loud woof.

"Okay, just give me a second," my husband told him.

Chance nosed the laptop hard enough that Tony had to grab it before it went flying to the floor. "Chance!"

After getting the computer settled back on his lap, Tony started typing again when the dog gave a sharp bark. For several moments, both man and dog fought over the laptop. Chance tried to nose it off my husband's lap while Tony tried to keep it from hitting the floor. It became a tug of war, and I was laughing too hard to distract the dog and help my spouse. Once I was able to contain myself, I stood up and got the dog's attention.

"Okay, time for our walk!" Tony managed to set down the laptop safely and get up from his chair.

Chance ran to the door but looked back at us with a huff, like we had kept him waiting too long. As soon as the door opened, Chance bolted out and waited on the patio for us to leash him up. There was no doubt about how he felt about waiting for his walk. We had to go. NOW! My husband and I laughed all the way down to the park and back.

After that display of doggy impatience, Tony always checked in with me before I came into the living room with my shoes on and the leash in hand. He would set aside his laptop and be out of his chair to avoid another nose attack when it was time for Chance's walk.

—Jeana Tetzlaff—

Opening Hearts

22

Then Came Stitch

When our heart is open,
everything we do becomes love.
~Mimi Novic

I grew up on a farm where we had dogs, cats, cows, goats, and pigs — animals that stayed outside where animals belonged. We milked the cows and goats, ate the pork, and used the cats to keep the mice under control. Our Collies were watchdogs who barked when the cows got loose, when a stranger came onto the property, or sometimes because they felt like it.

I didn't dislike animals, but I never understood why anyone would want one in the house. It seemed unnatural. They tracked in dirt from the outside, not even bothering to wipe their feet, let alone wiping other parts that got dirty.

When a co-worker mourned the death of her twelve-year-old Cocker Spaniel, I was sympathetic for a day or two, but after that I wanted to say, "It was just a dog, not a child. Get over it."

And when a friend told me she'd spent thousands of dollars nursing her cat back to health, I thought she was crazy. A cat, for Pete's sake! One could pick up a stray feline on any country road. Why would anyone in their right mind spend money on surgery and medicine for a cat? I concluded that animal lovers really weren't in their right minds.

Thankfully, my husband Rich wasn't interested in having a pet either. Even though he had a family dog when he was young, he didn't see any need to repeat the experience.

But, one day, my grown daughter Jennie asked, "Mom, can I move in with you and Rich for a little while?"

"Of course, honey," I replied without hesitation. I knew that her relationship with her husband was in crisis, and their bickering had become increasingly painful.

"I need to be away from Clark long enough to figure some things out," she said. "And I need to bring Stitch with me. Clark hates him." Stitch was a six-year-old Yorkshire Terrier.

I gulped. A dog in the house. That wasn't in my life plan. What would Rich think? However, I replied quickly, "Of course, you can bring Stitch — you can't leave him behind."

Jennie and Stitch moved into our spare room. When she wasn't working, Jennie spent most of her time behind closed doors, writing in her journal, praying, thinking, and sometimes crying. Stitch stayed by her side. When she left for her night shift, Stitch sat and watched the front door, waiting for her return.

"She'll be back, Stitch," I said.

In my effort to comfort him, I began taking him for long walks when she left. And I bought special treats for him. I watched Stitch bounce with excitement when I asked, "Do you want a treat?" Pretty soon, he didn't seem to mind her leaving.

I told a friend, "I can't say the word 'walk' around Stitch. I have to spell it if I'm not ready to go. He gets all excited, and I hate to disappoint him."

Patti replied, "Sounds like you're getting used to having a dog in the house."

"Well, maybe."

One afternoon, as I reported to Rich the bargains I'd found when shopping, I heard Stitch scratching at the door of Jennie's room, trying to get out. He didn't let up in spite of Jennie's firm command, "Stop that Stitch!"

I went to the door and said, "He can come out if you want him to." When I released him, Stitch circled me, joyfully wagging and wiggling. As I sat down in my recliner with a glass of tea, he leaped onto my lap where he stayed while I read.

After that, Stitch spent more and more time with me. If I went to the kitchen, he followed. When I went to the bathroom, he waited outside the door.

Stitch became a source of amusement for Rich and me. I reported his antics to anyone who would listen. "He finished eating, picked up his plastic bowl in his mouth, and dropped it at the foot of my bed. I guess he was asking for seconds."

"Stitch batted around a piece of dry dog food, throwing it up in the air and pouncing on it. I bought him a new ball, but he preferred to play with his food."

After a few months, Jennie announced, "It's time for me to get my own apartment." She'd sought counseling and had gotten involved in a variety of new activities to help her through a difficult time. She was ready to move on with her life.

As she began packing, I found myself suggesting, "You're gone so much with classes and work that poor little Stitch would be alone a lot. Maybe he should stay here with us for now." She thought that was a good idea.

Evidently, Stitch did, too. He no longer stared at the door waiting for Jennie. He was content to hang out wherever his "Granny" was.

When I prepared for bed on Jennie's first night in her new apartment, I missed her. I'd grown accustomed to her presence. I'd also grown accustomed to Stitch's presence. He curled up on the pallet of quilts I'd made for him at the foot of our bed. *I've got a dog,* I realized, and I smiled to see his furry little body close by.

Recently, a neighbor's Poodle was hit by a car. I helped her pick him up and race to the animal hospital. We cried together as we waited to see if Miles would be okay, and we rejoiced when the verdict came that his broken leg could be fixed.

Miles was a member of Candice's family just as Stitch was now a member of mine. I'd never understood that kind of bond.

I guess animal lovers aren't crazy after all — at least, dog lovers aren't. Dogs have personalities. They're practically human.

But cats — well, I'm not so sure about cat lovers. However, I'm willing to consider that I could be wrong about them, too.

— Diana L. Walters —

23

My Dog in Bhutan

*Fall in love with a dog, and in many ways you enter a
new orbit, a universe that features not just new colors
but new rituals, new rules, a new way of
experiencing attachment.*
~Caroline Knapp

No one owns dogs in Bhutan. In this tiny Buddhist country, most people believe that the animals around us are reincarnations of our lost loved ones, so animals are given free rein to do whatever they want. Dogs wander around the neighborhoods and often poke their heads inside open doors with expectations of food. They greet humans with either friendliness or apathy, but are mostly free to do their own thing.

I moved to Bhutan from another teaching job, in Tanzania, where my roommates and I took care of a mutt we'd found wandering the neighborhood. I was really sad to leave my dog behind, but I knew that my roommates would take care of him. I didn't know, however, that once I moved to Bhutan, I'd be surrounded by friendly dogs wherever I went.

A few dogs spent every day hanging out at my school. One of them—a mangy little guy with a head too big for his body—really took a liking to me. He started following me from school to home, and from home to school. I didn't own him—again, that's not part of Bhutanese culture—but I started thinking of him as my dog.

As I settled into life in Bhutan, I had trouble making friends. Sure, I was close with all the other teachers, but most of them were older and had families. Because of the language barrier (and my own shyness), it was hard to go out and meet new people. Therefore, I spent most of my time working. I really focused on my lessons, making them as perfect as possible. And every day, my little dog friend would wander into my classroom and sit quietly in the corner.

He was a cute guy, despite the mange. Small and eager looking, he was a mutt with an open face and a constantly dangling tongue. His fur was patchy in spots, but he seemed otherwise healthy.

Most of the other teachers would shoo him out of the classroom with a loud, "Hi-ya!" Just one word, and the little guy would bow his oversized head and scurry off.

I didn't shoo him away, though. Whenever he wandered into my room, I'd ignore him. He'd walk between the desks for a while before settling under the teacher's desk at the back of the room. It was his special place. He would get comfortable and then watch me for the rest of my lecture. He wouldn't sleep or chew on anything, just watch.

Over time, the dog became a regular part of my day. I'd see him on my walk to school, trying to keep pace with me. He'd attend at least one of my classes. At lunch, because he wasn't allowed inside the school canteen, he'd patiently wait outside the building until I was done. I'd give him a few scraps, and then he'd disappear somewhere.

I never gave him a name because I figured it wasn't my place. He was becoming my little mascot, my shadow, but he wasn't my property. Instead, I said, "Hey, dog," when he trotted into the room.

Weeks passed very quickly, and I was settling into the Bhutanese routine. Sometimes, I'd go out to bars with the other teachers, but I was always too self-conscious to go by myself. I enjoyed the lifestyle, but it always felt like something was missing, so I focused even more on my work. I started a drama program at school, entering our students in a national competition at the capital. I ran a writing club where my students worked on poems and short stories. And every night, I made sure my lesson plans for the next day were perfect.

The problem, though, was that Bhutan was a laid-back, stress-free place, and I was putting way too much stress on myself.

One night, I stayed late in the office, typing out spreadsheets. I was alone — the other teachers had left a long time ago — when my dog friend trotted in. Somehow, he knew that I needed someone to talk to. He started nudging my leg with his head, more like a cat than a dog.

"What's up?" I asked him.

In the months that I'd known this dog, I'd never heard him bark before. All he did was whine and yap at me. That night, though, he barked. Just once, but I knew he meant business.

I closed up my laptop and followed him out of the office. Together, we walked down the path back into town. When we got to the creek, the road split toward home. Normally, the dog and I would both go in that direction. This evening, though, he turned right, which meant he was walking straight into town.

He seemed so confident, too, like he was leading the way and wanted me to follow him. So I did.

Our town in Bhutan was very small, just two main roads filled with mostly restaurants, karaoke bars and snooker halls. Usually, I went to town for shopping, but because of my limited language skills, I didn't often go to those "hang-out" kinds of places.

My dog walked straight to the first snooker hall. From the street, I could tell that it was packed with Bhutanese people, all laughing, drinking and having a good time. I was a bit jealous, honestly.

I was about to keep walking when the dog wandered into the snooker bar, moving like he owned the place. I watched the open door and waited to hear the familiar "Hi-ya!" of the patrons shooing him away. But that didn't happen.

And that's when I realized that this dog had a lot to teach me. He wasn't shy or self-conscious. Despite his mangy appearance, he simply walked into situations. Sometimes, he was shooed away, but sometimes he'd make a friend. Like me.

I wanted to be more like him. So without second-guessing myself, I followed him into the snooker bar. And that was where I met my first group of friends. I've lived in Bhutan for about eighteen months now, and my friend group keeps growing. All I needed was a mangy little dog to nudge me in the right direction.

—Evan Purcell—

24

Dogwood

There is nothing truer in the world
than the love of a good dog.
~Author Unknown

The day my younger brother was born, our father purchased a tree. He shoved it in the back of his Subaru Forester and drove it across town to the hospital. My mother laughed at the sight of him dragging a nearly five-foot potted magnolia into her tiny hospital room, dirt spraying everywhere. My brother, who had previously been sleeping on her bosom, woke due to her deep belly chuckle. His bright, round eyes stared up at the soft pink flowers, and on the first day of his life, my parents swear his tiny mouth smiled.

The tree lived in our back yard, and from May to October, so did my brother. My parents liked to joke that he was the tree in many ways—blooming each spring and losing some of his spirit come autumn. When he turned three, he memorized the words to the book, The Giving Tree, by Shel Silverstein. He was too young to read on his own, but he would sit beneath his tree and recite the story in his soft, little-boy voice.

That tree and my brother spent more time together than most married couples do in a lifetime. Notch marks along the trunk of the tree inaccurately depicted the boy's height as he grew. He measured himself against it without second thought that the tree might also be growing.

When my brother turned five, my parents decided he needed a companion. Daily declarations such as, "When I grow up, I want to be a rock so I can be with my tree forever," had begun to worry them. One early June afternoon, my dad brought home a puppy. She had been the runt of the litter and had a diamond-shaped white spot on her chest, stark against the rest of her teeny, black body. When she walked, her large puppy paws always managed to carry her body a little crookedly. Her name was Agnes, and my brother adored her.

Perhaps what my parents hadn't anticipated was that Agnes would cement my brother's relationship with his tree. My brother, the tree, and Agnes—strange, I know. The tree served as a place of rejuvenation for my brother and Agnes. After an afternoon of Frisbee, the two would sit beneath the tree and read. He liked to make fairy houses under the tree, using rocks and flowers found in the garden. At night, my mother and I would sneak outside and leave small notes for my brother and dog treats for Agnes—all from the resident fairy.

Magnolia trees are known for their large, blooming flowers that will cover an entire back yard when the first cool breeze hits in autumn. My brother's tree was no exception. The first fall we had Agnes, she and my brother would sweep the flowers up into big piles and jump in them. They fastened flowers around their heads and pranced around the yard playing make-believe.

In the winter, they would make snow forts around the tree, ensuring that no critters would cross. It was quite amazing that Agnes developed the same adoration for the tree that my brother had. When he got old enough, he'd take Agnes for runs on a paved trail that ran behind our house. Instead of holding her on a leash, my brother would hold onto one end of a branch that had fallen from the tree, and Agnes would grasp the other end in her mouth. Together, the two of them would run for miles—my brother redirecting Agnes's ever-crooked gallop every few minutes. I think she would've followed him anywhere, but my brother swears that she only followed him because she knew the branch was from their tree.

The summer before my brother entered the seventh grade, Agnes's old age started to catch up to her. She stopped waiting on the front porch for my brother to get home from school, and the thump, thump, thump of her tail against our kitchen cabinets became less common. She no longer trotted all the way to the back corner of our property where the tree was when she had to use the bathroom.

"An autoimmune disease," the veterinarian said.

"A few more weeks, at best," my father repeated to us at the dinner table one night.

My brother slid off his chair and crawled over to where Agnes was quietly lying on the ground. He enveloped her in his arms and stroked the top of her soft head. Thump, thump, thump. In her last days, when she got too weak to walk on her own, my mom would carry her out to the tree and let her lie on a blanket in the cool breeze while everybody else was at work and school.

The day that my brother got off the bus and skipped into the house to find that Agnes was no longer there, his heart broke. He ran into the back yard, out to the tree, and sat with his head between his knees until far past suppertime. He ran his hand up the trunk and felt all the notches of his youth. Despite my brother's growing and changing and leaving, the tree had always been there.

We buried Agnes not long after that day. My brother wrapped his baby blanket around her cold body and held tightly to her paw as my dad placed her body in a hole we'd dug next to the tree. He held on as everyone piled dirt on top of her body until my mom gently pulled him back, and the rest of the hole was filled.

We each shared what we had loved about Agnes. My sister was grateful that Agnes always ate her unwanted vegetables. My mother said that Agnes had always been the most intelligent and soulful of dogs. My dad loved her willingness to ride around in the back of his pickup truck, and I spoke of the way she'd climb upstairs in the morning and wake me by sticking her wet nose in my face. My brother ended the ceremony with the perfect eulogy when he took out a familiar bright green children's book and began to read aloud his version of the almost lyrical tale.

"Once there was a tree… and she loved a little boy and a dog. And every day the two would come, and they would gather her leaves and make them into crowns and play king and queen of the forest....

"'I don't need very much now,' said the boy, 'just a quiet place to sit and visit my dog....'

"'Well,' said the tree, straightening herself up as much as she could, 'well, an old stump is a good place for a boy to visit and a dog to rest forever. Come, Boy, sit down.'"

And my brother did.

—Lucy Barrett—

25

Joint Custody

Before you get a dog, you can't quite imagine
what living with one might be like; afterward,
you can't imagine living any other way.
~Caroline Knapp

It's amazing what a dog can do for a marriage. Scott and I had always shared an interest in dogs. We took great care in selecting our first two Terriers, Lewis and Martha. They were truly our dogs, the kids before kids. And even after we had two human children, the dogs still held a very special place in our family.

But I'll never forget eight years ago on Halloween afternoon when Scott pulled into the driveway. The girls and I were inside, putting on costumes and make-up. I glanced toward the front window when I heard his car. He opened the car door and I saw a little dog. The girls and I went outside for a closer look. He had brought home one of the ugliest and least desirable dogs around. The mangy thing was blackish grey and short to the ground, with large ears and a freakishly long body. And while it was clear this dog was largely Terrier, I was still put off.

Scott made his plea. He was driving home and glanced into the weeds on the side of the road. Sitting there among brambles, twigs and debris was this little dog. He couldn't resist. Scott took the girls trick-or-treating that night while I stayed home with the newcomer. His demeanor was pleasant enough; he enjoyed a few treats and even seemed to be house-trained.

For two English teachers with a black dog found on Halloween, the perfect name for him was Poe, after the gothic writer Edgar Allan Poe. In the days that followed, we learned from the vet that Poe was about nine months old, and a trip to the groomer made a world of difference in his looks. Eventually, we learned that he was a full Cairn Terrier—not a show-quality Cairn—but a purebred dog nonetheless. As he became more and more endeared to each of us, I often wondered who sent him away or let him get away. It was their loss; Poe was a delightful addition to our family in every way! In the years that followed his arrival, Poe became one of the family, with a sweet, affectionate and fun personality.

Unfortunately, my marriage with Scott did not stand the test of time, and we got divorced. We did, however, part amicably—so amicably, in fact, that we not only share custody of our daughters, but we also share custody of Poe! He travels with the girls, and he has a leash and a goody bag at each parent's house. We've been doing this for a while, and Poe never misses a beat. He has his own little customs and routines with each parent and moves between us seamlessly.

But let's face it, there's nothing in this joint-custody thing for Poe; it's not like he's a human child who needs and deserves attention from both parents. Poe is a joint-custody dog because of the joy and pleasure he brings to Scott and me. He would be just as happy living with only one of us. I regret that Scott and I didn't work out as a married couple and that our family dynamic is very different than it was back on that Halloween. But for all the things that have changed, I am forever grateful that in our new relationship we can continue to share a much loved little dog, origin unknown.

—Rebecca Edmisten—

Choose Love

All, everything that I understand,
I only understand because I love.
~Leo Tolstoy

Because I volunteer with an animal rescue, friends and co-workers frequently give me donations for the animals. One evening, as I was delivering gifts to the shelter, I looked up to see a Pit Bull charging across the parking lot with her handler in tow. I quickly assessed the situation and bent down to greet the medium-sized blue Pit Bull. She lunged toward me as she stood on her hind legs and threw her front paws around my neck, showering me with kisses. I rubbed her head as her butt wiggled and her tail wagged furiously.

"Do you know her?" the handler asked me.

"No, I've never seen her before." I stood up and walked with the dog (I believe her name was Suede) and her handler into the kennel. In the lobby, where there was more light, I noticed that Suede had a lot of scars and had obviously given birth to many litters of puppies.

"Was she a fighting dog?"

"No," came the curt reply. "She was bait." My heart sank as Suede ran excitedly between her handler and me, asking for love from one and then rushing to the other for more.

Every Saturday for weeks, Suede went to the adoption shows in hopes of finding her forever home. Each week, she happily greeted anyone who walked by. People shopping in the pet store stopped to play with her, or just sat on the floor and petted her as her tail wagged non-stop. She was a favorite of kids and adults alike because of her willingness to love everyone she met. Her handlers shared her story with anyone who stopped. She amazed everyone with her tremendous heart and courage to love. Suede's scars kept some people from considering her, and others feared her breed. But one wonderful Saturday, Suede got adopted! After a thorough home inspection (they couldn't let her go with just anyone), her new home was approved.

She is now in a home where she is safe and spreads love to everyone she meets. She will never again be abused or have reason to be afraid of people.

I think about Suede sometimes. Before she was rescued, her only interactions with people resulted in abuse. Despite that, she happily greeted every stranger she came across and still expected nothing but love. She had every reason to be angry and afraid. Instead, Suede chose love.

My challenge to myself and to you: When the divisiveness and anger of the world get you down, remember Suede. Choose love.

—Lori Fuller—

27

A Mastiff-Sized Trail to the Heart

Dogs leave paw prints on our hearts.
~Author Unknown

We'd just moved into our first home, and I'd started a new job. A dog was the first thing on my husband's wish list and the last on mine. While he saw countless hours of playing fetch, lounging on the sofa, and being best friends, I could only see work I didn't have time for.

Still, my husband did something he never did — he ignored my threats of divorce and put his name on a waiting list for a brindle Mastiff puppy. Two weeks after we moved into our brand-new home, our first dog was ready to come home.

For two weeks, arguments like we'd never endured in our three years of marriage stewed between us. I cried. I yelled. I swore I wouldn't lift a finger for the mangy dog he was bringing home. I promised him I wouldn't like it, wouldn't care for it, and wouldn't love it.

He brought our twenty-four-pound, eight-week-old Mastiff puppy home on a Saturday. True to my promise, I didn't love the puppy. I barely managed a half-grin in photographs. I petted him apathetically, ignoring his puppy breath and whimpers. I rolled my eyes when he chewed my shoe and took delight in saying "I told you so" when he cried annoyingly the first night at our home.

Finally, about two days into the experience I was labeling a nightmare,

I decided to give our puppy a try. I resolved to give him a real chance. We'd named him Henry after the Cynthia Rylant series, *Henry and Mudge*. I told my husband if I was going to have a dog existing in my house, I was at least giving it a proper, literary name.

Two days after the dog I didn't want entered our home, I held him for the first time. His soft puppy fur and wagging tail eased my cold heart a little bit. With his wrinkled face looking up at me, I thought maybe, just maybe, I'd been wrong. Maybe I could make a little bit of room for him in my heart. I started seeing the games of fetch and the best-friend montage my husband had been promising all along.

And then it happened. A warm, wet feeling on my pants. Henry kept wagging his tail as I looked down in horror to see the growing wet spot on my favorite sweatpants.

He'd peed all over me.

Screaming, I vowed once more that the dog was never, ever going to be any friend of mine.

Over the next few months, things didn't get much better. There were destroyed shoes, popped cans of soda that sprayed on the ceiling, and chewed walls. There were barking and howling sessions and sharp, puppy-teeth lacerations. There were late nights of chasing a wily puppy around the yard in the snow, exhausted and enraged that he'd made "Come" into a game of chase. There were plenty of times I swore that I'd never, ever love Henry or even like him.

But that's the funny thing about dogs — they have a way of finding a trail to your heart, even when you're resistant. Their paws have a way of finding the path to you, of opening up your unconditional love. And once they do, there's no going back.

On a cold Sunday in November, I realized things had shifted. My husband was working, and it was just the two of us. I'd popped Henry into a Christmas sweater I'd purchased and walked him downtown for the annual holiday parade. Snow blowing, we plodded through inches of the cold stuff, my hood shielding my face and his sweater shielding his fur. His tail wagged as it always did, and when we got to our spot, he sat beside me, looking up at me with the emotive eyes I'd come to understand.

It was a small moment, really. Nothing significant happened. I stood there with his leash in my hand and looked down into the face I'd come to know over the past months. Something shifted. I realized for the first time that the dog sitting beside me wasn't the worst thing that could happen. Sitting beside me in his red and green sweater was my absolute best friend.

Somewhere between potty-training accidents, late nights, and chewed pant legs, he'd done it. He'd accomplished the impossible. His huge paw prints had walked right onto my heart, leaving impressions silently behind. I hadn't noticed it at the time, between my stubbornness and pride. Standing there, though, on the side of the road in our hometown, I realized I wasn't lonely. The love I felt for this dog was not only strong and powerful, but beautiful, because it was something I'd never expected.

Five years later, I can't imagine my life without Henry. He's been there for me through all of the tough times. From lost friendships to difficult decisions, his huge paw is right there on my shoulder, comforting me when the tears flow. He's there on the good days, the boring days, the at-home days, and for every day in between. He's there to eat cupcakes with me on a rainy day, to stretch languidly in the sunshine in the summer months, and to dance in the living room on a boring Monday.

He reminds me to live life to the fullest, and that real life is lived in the simple moments and small memories.

I don't say this lightly because it's not easy to admit, but my husband was 100-percent right in his decision that day. By bringing Henry into our lives, he showed me that sometimes the things we dread most in life turn out to be the most beautiful.

Most of all, he showed me that the love of a dog is something we have to experience firsthand to understand — and once we do, life is never, ever the same.

— Lindsay Detwiler —

28

More than Worthy

To err is human — to forgive, canine.
~Author Unknown

When I was a kid growing up on a farm in Indiana, I had every type of pet one could possibly think of. There was no animal I didn't love. But there was one animal I stayed away from, the poor Collie that lived across the street from my best friend.

His family kept him on a five-foot chain all the time. He had a doghouse to get out of the weather but they never played with him or took him off the chain. I felt so sorry for him. If anyone got near him, he would go crazy, snarling and jerking at the end of his chain. I was also afraid of him, but I saw such sadness in his eyes. The neighbors called the police so many times to complain that they finally gave them an order to get rid of the dog or else.

The people who owned the dog believed that nobody in their right mind would take him, so they decided to shoot him. I begged my dad to save the dog's life; I tried to convince him that he would make a great farm dog. I pulled out every card in the deck to sway my dad to take the dog before they killed it. For whatever reason, he finally agreed.

I'll never forget the day we took him home to the farm. We had to tie him up and wrap his head in a burlap bag so he wouldn't bite us. He fought us every step of the way. When we finally got him out to our farm, we had no idea what would happen next. We untied him and stood back, and he took off running straight for the woods. I didn't blame him; I would've done the same thing after being chained up for so long. We didn't see him for a very long time. I figured he was living in the woods.

Then one day as I was doing chores I saw something out of the corner of my eye. I realized that it was the Collie. He wasn't growling or snarling, just watching me. At first, I was very scared, but I saw a very different animal from the one we had set free. I went up to the house, got some food, and put it out by the barn where I'd seen him. The next morning, the food was gone, so I kept putting food there every day.

After a couple of weeks, I decided to try something new. I brought the food down to the barn and waited. A little later, the dog showed up. I held the food in my hand and reached out to him. At first, he didn't move, but then I guess hunger got the better of him. He started toward me, and I was scared because I had no idea if he'd bite me. Little by little, he crept up to me, but he looked as scared as I did. He finally reached me, snatched the food out of my hand, and ran away. It was only for a minute, but at least I'd made contact with him. I started doing that every day, at the same time, and he showed up like clockwork.

Over a period of a few weeks, we began to bond. He started staying longer, even letting me pet him. It took a long time, but eventually he began to trust me.

That dog became the best friend I ever had as a child. I named him Bobby. He was my supporter when I was in trouble, my protector when I was in danger, and my comforter when I was sad. I'll never forget crying on the porch, and Bobby patting me on the shoulder with his long nose. It was as if he were trying to say, "It's okay."

That formerly abused dog had so much love to give. I had a small white kitten that would crawl up on his back, dig around to make a nest, and then fall asleep with him. Gone was the angry wild beast. In its place was the sweetest dog ever.

Bobbie taught me very early in life never to give up on someone. Bad behavior and a nasty disposition could have been caused by a lifetime of pain and hurt. Bobby was a marked dog, destined to be executed, deemed unworthy of redemption. Others saw no hope for him, but he turned out to be the most amazing dog ever.

—Brenda Beattie—

29

Operation Andy

A dog will teach you unconditional love. If you can
have that in your life, things won't be too bad.
~Robert Wagner

"I wish I didn't have to leave for camp next week," I told Mom.

"But you love camp," she said. "It's usually the best week of your whole summer."

I shrugged. I had always looked forward to camp. But this year, things were different. "We just got the new puppy, and I don't want to leave him so soon," I said.

Mom nodded. "I understand. Andy is an adorable little thing, and he'll still be adorable when you get back from camp. It's only a week."

I sighed. A week sounded like forever. Although I never would have admitted it, I wanted to be Andy's favorite person in our family. But I was at a disadvantage. In six days, I would be leaving for camp. And I just knew that while I was gone, my siblings were going to sneak in and steal my spot as #1 in the new puppy's heart.

I had to make a plan.

That night, I lay in my bed, willing myself not to fall asleep until after my parents went to bed. The new puppy was in his bed in the kitchen, and Mom had put up baby gates to keep him from venturing onto the carpet unsupervised.

My parents turned off the lights and went to bed. And that's when the whining started. Andy was in a dark kitchen by himself on his first night in a new house.

Operation Andy was going exactly according to plan.

I grabbed my pillow and comforter and headed to the kitchen. I spread out the blanket and lay down. "Come here, Andy," I whispered to the little Sheltie. He was so cute, like a little Lassie. He stopped whining and snuggled his tiny body next to me.

I stroked his fur and tried not to notice how hard the kitchen floor was. Soon, Andy was breathing deeply, but I lay awake, too uncomfortable to sleep. I wanted to return to my own bed, but my desire to bond with the puppy was stronger. I lay awake most of the night, and at dawn I trudged back to my bedroom so my parents wouldn't know I'd spent the night on the kitchen floor.

The next day, I was exhausted and sore, but when Andy licked my nose and I smelled his sweet puppy breath, I decided it was worth it.

I spent as much time with Andy as I could that day. That night, I enacted my plan again.

As soon as my parents went to bed, I dragged my pillow and blanket into the kitchen and snuggled up with Andy. His little body was warm and soft, but the floor seemed even harder than the night before.

I tossed and turned all night, and at dawn I snuck back into my room again.

I slept on the kitchen floor the next three nights. I never got more than a few hours of sleep, but I was convinced my plan was working. The previous afternoon, Andy had been sitting in my sister's lap, but when I sat down on the couch, he got up and came to sit with me instead. Although my sleepless nights were not all that pleasant, they were definitely paying off.

Several times, my mom gave me an odd look and asked if I was feeling all right. I hid my exhaustion as well as I could, but I think she knew something was going on.

That night, I gathered my bedclothes and went into the kitchen to execute Operation Andy for the last time. I was leaving for camp the next day.

Andy had just snuggled in when the kitchen light came on. "What are you doing?" Mom asked.

"Sleeping with Andy," I said. "So he won't be scared."

She put her hands on her hips. "How long have you been sleeping on the kitchen floor?"

"Since the night we got Andy."

She shook her head and started picking up my blanket. "Nope. You're not doing this again. You need your sleep before you head to camp. You are sleeping in your bed tonight."

"Mom, I can't," I said. "I am leaving tomorrow, and I won't see Andy for a whole week."

"The dog will be here when you get home from camp."

"But by then, he'll have forgotten all about me," I said quietly. "He'll like everyone else better."

"Oh, honey, Andy has room in his little heart for all of us."

Tears filled my eyes. "But I wanted to be his favorite. That's why I've been sleeping in the kitchen all this time."

"Diane, you're exhausted. You're sleeping in your own bed tonight. But after Andy gets housebroken, maybe he'd like to sleep in your room sometimes."

"Really? I would love that."

Mom led me to my room and tucked me into bed. I was nearly asleep when I heard Andy start whining. "Mom, he's scared," I said. "He's not used to sleeping by himself."

And then I felt Andy's body settle into the blankets beside me. I looked up and saw Mom smiling at me. She shrugged and whispered, "I've got to wash your blankets anyway. You've had them on the floor all week."

The next morning, I left for camp. And just as Mom promised, Andy loved me just as much when I came home a week later.

Turns out, I'd worried for nothing. The truth is that dogs have great big hearts, and everyone who loves them becomes their favorite person.

— Diane Stark —

30

Don't Judge a Dog by Its Cover

The least amount of judging we can do,
the better off we are.
~Michael J. Fox

When we lost our beautiful Golden Retriever, Cookie, after eleven years, we were devastated. We'd had her since she was eight weeks old. My husband Alan felt that the best way to heal the pain was to get another dog as soon as possible. I wasn't so sure.

"I think that this time we should adopt a rescue dog," Alan said. "Cookie had a good home with us from day one. Not all dogs are that lucky." His rather emotional approach was hard to resist.

We contacted our friend Tim who worked for a local animal sanctuary. He came over with photos of the rescue dogs currently in residence. We scrutinized them with care, but none appealed to us enough. There were other animal shelters in the area, but we trusted Tim to find the "right" dog for us, so we were prepared to wait.

A week later, he phoned. "I've brought home one of the dogs whose photo I showed you," he said. Tim and his wife lived on a farm, and sometimes they would give animals at the shelter a little "vacation" by taking them home for a few days. "Her name is Sadie, and she is just delightful. If we didn't already have three dogs, we'd think seriously of keeping her ourselves. I'd very much like you two to see her."

When we arrived at the farm, Tim took us into a paddock where Sadie was lying on the grass. She got up immediately and padded over to him, tail wagging.

"What breed is she?" Alan asked, looking at this very bony creature with a rather sparse, fawn-colored coat.

"She's what the British call a Lurcher, which usually is a Greyhound crossed with another breed. In Sadie's case, she's a Greyhound crossed with a Saluki. We think she's about a year old, but we don't know her history."

"What's a Saluki?" I asked.

"Salukis were originally Arab hunting dogs. Like Greyhounds, they are deep-chested and run like the wind. Sadie's plumed tail and feathery legs and ears are Saluki characteristics, as is her coloring." Despite his salesmanship, we both viewed her as singularly unattractive after our richly coated and very huggable Retriever.

Sadie stood quietly next to Tim, who methodically stroked her ears. She seemed gentle, as was our beloved Cookie. I reached down to stroke the length of her long back. She looked up at me with intense eyes that were startling in their directness. Then she moved over to me, sat down on my foot and leaned her body against my leg. I was surprised at her boldness, but also flattered by the intimacy.

"I can understand your reluctance," Tim said, "but why don't you keep her over the weekend on a trial basis. If you don't connect with her, I'll take her back to the shelter."

I rather liked the body contact that I'd just experienced, but Alan was less won over. Nonetheless, he agreed to have her with us for the weekend.

We dog lovers attribute many "human" characteristics to our pets, in some instances quite ridiculously so. But that weekend we were introduced to Sadie's incredible intuitive abilities. She seemed to understand that I had already fallen for her but that Alan was the stumbling block.

That evening, Alan and I took our usual places on the sofa to watch TV. Because we'd always allowed Cookie on the sofa, which was protected with a big throw, we didn't resist when Sadie came over and climbed up, planting herself between us. Then she leaned over and laid her long neck on Alan's shoulder so that her head rested on his chest. It was uncanny but, to my eyes, there was no doubt that Sadie was applying all of her feminine charms to win him over.

By the time Sunday evening came around, we knew we couldn't part with her. And over successive weeks, she continued to enchant us.

Taking her out for walks was a real joy. We'd get to the middle of the park and then let her go — and she'd charge off like a shot. And when she bounded back to us, we'd swear she was smiling, as if to say, "Oh, how I love to run!" Whenever I walked her on my own, she would never go very far from me. She'd dash off but always circle back to make sure I was okay, as if protecting me instinctively.

When we settled down in the living room after a busy day, Sadie would join us. She would stare intently at one or the other of us. It felt as if she was looking into our very souls. The contrast of her dark eyes in that fawn coat was striking. And around those expressive eyes, it looked as if someone had applied eyeliner. Then she'd begin the nightly ritual of "talking" to us. We had no idea what she was trying to say, but we reveled in her attempt to communicate.

Almost imperceptibly, this scrawny, almost hairless dog blossomed into a beauty. Why? Because we'd fallen in love with her.

I have to admit that she wasn't perfect, but the only "naughty" thing she ever did was to periodically dig holes in the lawn. We just couldn't break her of that habit.

We had Sadie for eight wonderful years. When poor Alan was given the sad task of burying her in our garden, we both started to laugh at the irony of the situation. There he was digging a hole in our precious lawn — the very lawn that we tried to stop her from destroying.

To Alan and me, Sadie was living proof that beauty is in the eye of the beholder. She was our ugly duckling that turned into a swan. Although she never changed physically, unlike the duckling in the famous fairy tale, our perception of her certainly did.

Thank you, dear Sadie, for teaching us that one should never judge a dog by "its cover."

— Marilynn Zipes Wallace —

31

A Lesson in Empathy

Empathy is seeing with the eyes of another,
listening with the ears of another,
and feeling with the heart of another.
~Alfred Adler

This past winter, I started having panic attacks. My heart hammered in my chest. My body flushed with heat. I struggled to catch my breath as my mind raced. The fear I experienced during my attacks seemed life threatening, and I urgently wanted to flee. I felt alone; no one could experience the intensity of what I was going through.

My panic attacks were diagnosed as symptoms of burnout, depression, and anxiety. I worked with professionals to get better, and by the time spring turned to summer, my health had improved. But as the storms inside me started to calm, the storms of summer were only beginning.

Until a year before, thunderstorms hadn't bothered Moose, our seven-year-old mixed-breed dog. Then something changed. Moose seemed to experience storms for the first time. The roaring thunder. The flashing light. These things now existed in her world, and they were scary.

One Friday evening, we had our first storm of the summer. I slept unaware of the storm moving through, but I woke the next morning to a sleep-deprived husband. A clanking sound coming from Moose's room jolted him out of bed in the early morning hours. Moose was trying to shove her head through her doggie gate to escape the storm. My husband deterred Moose from her escape attempts that night by covering the gate with a blanket, but I worried she would hurt herself during the next storm.

Unaware of the forecasted storms the following Monday night, I didn't understand why Moose was barking and yipping until I heard thunder rumble moments later. I settled into bed, assuring myself she would settle down, too.

Clank.

Clank!

CLANK!

I ran to Moose's room and found her slamming her twenty-five-pound body against her gate. She was panting, whining and barking. She paced back and forth. She leaped at the gate, trying to escape. Moose was having a panic attack.

My chest tightened. I tried to cover the gate with a blanket to block Moose's attempts to squeeze her head through the bars. She leaped at the blanket. We battled on. I tried to get the blanket over the gate, and Moose did everything she could to get out of her room.

My heart pounded while my frantic brain searched for a solution. The blanket wasn't going to work. With my husband away on a work trip, I was alone to figure out how Moose and I were going to survive the night.

Moose has never slept in our room. I wasn't willing to cave on this, but I needed a way to get some sleep. With limited patience in the early hours of the morning, I compromised and put her in the en suite bathroom. I turned on the bathroom fan and hoped it would drown out the sounds of thunder. With her doggie gate placed at the entryway, Moose had her own "cave" to hide in, and I didn't have a dog in my bed.

The storm seemed to quiet down, and so did Moose. Glancing at my clock, I prayed I would fall asleep.

Bark! Bark! Pant. Pant.

CLANG!

The gate crashed to the floor, and I heard Moose rushing toward me. I scooped her up and plopped her back in the bathroom.

"ENOUGH! CUT IT OUT!" I yelled. I set the gate down with a loud *CLANG*. Moose winced. She stepped back and cowered, ears back, tail tucked, her brown eyes glassy.

I didn't mean to upset you, she seemed to say.

I huffed back to bed, angry and upset. Angry that I wasn't getting any sleep. Upset because I had yelled at Moose and made her cower. The thunder continued, and I listened to her cry and pant while berating myself for what I had done.

When the storms finally moved on, Moose quieted down, and I drifted in and out of sleep.

Moose was fine the next day, but I felt different. I was bothered by my lack of empathy and understanding for Moose's behavior. I expected Moose to see thunderstorms the way I did — nothing scary, a natural phenomenon. I was too caught up in my own needs (sleep) that I couldn't see her fear was real.

During my own panic attacks, I had wanted others to be there for me, even if they couldn't relate to what I was going through. How could I ask others to be there for me when I neglected to be there for Moose? She didn't ask for her fear, and I didn't ask for mine. She asked for help and support during the storm, and I reacted not out of concern for her, but for my own needs. That is not how I wanted to treat anyone I loved.

Earlier in the year, I had learned about things I could do to make my panic attacks less scary and more manageable. Meditation, for instance, helped me in the thick of my distress, and as I progressed in understanding how to manage my anxiety, the panic attacks relaxed their grip.

I didn't think I could teach Moose how to meditate, and I couldn't snap my fingers to make the storms or her fear go away. But I figured that I could do something much easier than all of those things — I could show empathy for Moose. I could be more flexible in our house rules and provide her a comforting place to feel scared. Most importantly, I could support her by being there, without judgment, when she experienced fear.

When the next storm came, we were ready. Moose received a new calming treat. We moved her bed into a corner of our bedroom and, for the first time, invited her to stay with us. Uneasy at first, Moose barked and whined, racing back and forth from the bedroom to the hallway. Alert and on edge, she seemed to be waiting for us to escort her back to her room. We continued our bedtime routine, and when we were ready to turn out the lights, we called Moose over. She didn't hesitate to join us, and after we showed her to her bed, she settled in.

That night, we didn't stop the storm. We didn't take away Moose's fear. But we did help her by weathering the storm and her fear together.

—Alicia Curley—

32

Thanks to Bentley

*Today I choose to live with gratitude for the love that
fills my heart, the peace that rests within my spirit,
and the voice of hope that says all things are possible.*
~Author Unknown

The morning was still as I hugged my robe around me and made my way downstairs to the kitchen. It had been another fitful night, with dreams I couldn't remember. The reason was clear: I still hadn't adjusted to living alone. My husband had passed some time ago, but I was still steeped in sadness. The house felt big and empty, yet I hardly left the confines of its protective walls.

To combat the loneliness, I'd brought home a little teacup Maltese. The plan had been for him to keep me company and offer comfort. He would sit on my lap as I watched TV or read a book and snuggle beside me when I climbed into bed at night. But Bentley wouldn't cuddle for long. After a few minutes, he'd wriggle to get away. "Maltese are supposed to be lap dogs. They like to be close," I'd remind him with a frown.

As the months wore on with no change, it became clear he didn't seem to care a whit about my plan. I was looking for some love, and Bentley wasn't very accommodating. It was disappointing the way he'd scamper off to his little house and the solitude of his own bed.

Training didn't go any better. Bentley continued to run away when I said "stay" and jump up when I said "down." I did my best to work with him, but it was difficult to be consistent when I was feeling so low. The one thing he didn't resist was the wee-wee pad. I was relieved he took to it right away. Not having to go outside helped me avoid running into the neighbors — with their sympathetic glances and offers to come in for a cup of tea. It wasn't that I didn't appreciate their concern; I just wasn't up to socializing.

Bentley didn't seem to mind being housebound. He was content to lie down and stare at me as I pecked away on my laptop. But I often wondered if he was bored and if I was a bad mommy. To assuage my feelings, I'd grab his yellow squeaky duck or one of the other toys from the basket and wave it under his nose. Tossing it way down the hallway, I'd shout, "Fetch!" trying to put some excitement into my voice. He'd lift his head, but rarely budged.

Anytime I'd stroke his soft ears and ask, "What's the matter, boy?" he'd give me a low, cranky growl. "Rrrrrr…" It wasn't the least bit menacing, just his way of saying, "Leave me alone." Still, it was obvious that I needed to put more effort into our bonding experience.

"Come here, Bentley," I cooed one day when the sun shone bright and the skies were especially blue. We'd been inside for so long; I decided it wasn't fair to Bentley. No matter how content I was to hide out in the house, he needed some fresh air and exercise.

"Go for a walk?"

One look at the cherry red leash, and he tore off in the opposite direction. Even with his tiny legs, he could run faster than me.

"You don't want to play; you don't want to walk!" I cried out. My arms raised in frustration as I rounded the corner, trying to catch him. "What dog doesn't like to walk?"

When I finally had him leashed up and moved toward the front door, he planted his behind firmly on the floor. I picked him up and put him on his feet. "Heel!" I commanded, tugging on the leash. Bentley dug in, and his bottom went down again.

I wasn't about to argue with a dog no bigger than a pocketbook. Instead, I carried him to the street as he whined and wiggled. Once he was on the ground, he fought every step of the walk. He kept looking over his shoulder toward the house, and we only got as far as the end of the block when he completely revolted. He stopped with such force that his back legs lifted clear off the ground. He almost somersaulted.

"Okay," I relented. "I guess that's enough for now."

When we turned toward the house, he began running like a racehorse. The little guy was more anxious to get home than I was!

As soon as we stepped over the threshold, he hurried straight to his bed, let out a long sigh and promptly fell asleep. My shoulders slumped. No matter how I tried, I couldn't understand what was wrong with him.

The phone rang, interrupting my thoughts.

"No, thank you, Pam," I said, declining an invitation to lunch, the same answer I'd given my other two friends when they'd called to invite me out. It was kind of them to think of me, but I just wasn't in the mood to do anything. I returned to my comfy chair with a book in hand, content to be by myself.

Then it hit me. Be by myself... just like Bentley.

I sat up straight and set aside my book. Bentley didn't like leaving the house, just like me. And Bentley didn't feel like doing anything, just like me. And like me, Bentley didn't like to listen, just like I didn't listen to my friends who told me I needed to get out — that I'd start to feel better if I'd stop isolating and push myself a little more. I'd practically growled at them to leave me alone, the way Bentley growled at me.

It was a sobering revelation. I'd become almost a recluse. And what had I done to my poor puppy?

"Bentley Beauregard, wake up! We have work to do. We're starting over fresh, right now."

I picked up the phone and dialed Pam back. "Is that invitation still open?" I could see it all in my mind's eye. Pam would serve one of her fabulous meals out on the patio while her sweet dog, Indiana, pranced around the yard, waving his happy tail.

"Sure, come on over," she said.

"Would you mind if I brought Bentley?"

"Of course not. He and Indy can play while we have lunch."

On the drive over, I looked at Bentley, curled so sweetly in his seat, and I smiled for the first time in a long time. The little guy had helped me to see a big truth: It was time to open my hurting heart and allow the love in from family, friends and neighbors who never stopped reaching out to encourage me. Thanks to Bentley, I was on the road to a long-overdue healing, and I was taking him with me.

—Susan A. Karas—

Smart Dog

33

My Rescue Dog Is So Smart

Dogs got personality. Personality goes a long way.
~Quentin Tarantino

My dog is so smart, and he is only six years old. Well, yeah, technically, he's forty-two if you want to be all scientific and nitpicky about it. Anyway, my dog knows how to tell time, and he knows what day of the week it is! That's pretty amazing for an animal at any age, if you ask me.

First of all, he has known what time it is since he was housed in the animal shelter. I found him — or rather the school custodian found him — in the gutter outside the country school where I taught. Walking into my room, holding a puppy out at arm's length for the kids to see, he asked them if they had ever seen him before or knew where he lived. I held out my arms to the janitor, took that dirty white puppy to my chest, and hugged his furry body. I could hear his little heart pounding, and when he put his tiny paws on my shoulders, I melted. I knew we belonged together.

When I finally put down the puppy, I noticed that he couldn't stand on one of his back legs. As soon as school was over, I rushed him to the country vet who told me he had a broken leg and had probably been hit by a vehicle. I still had a month of teaching left and knew I couldn't leave an injured puppy at home alone all day. With tears running down my face, I allowed the vet to call the local shelter, which agreed to take him as soon as his leg was put in a cast.

Driving home, crying hysterically, I realized I couldn't give up that puppy so easily. The next day, I called the clinic and told them I had changed my mind. Without thinking about how I would manage it, I told them I wanted to keep the puppy and would pay his medical expenses. But it was too late. The shelter had already picked him up! I tried calling the shelter, but got only a recorded message. I was devastated. I swore to myself to do everything possible to recover him.

Every day on the way home from school, I stopped at the shelter to visit him. And every day I told him I'd see him tomorrow. When I pulled into the shelter's parking lot, I could hear his bark. And when I got to his cage, he was already at the front of his kennel whining, his paw on the fence in greeting. Looking up at the clock on the wall of the enclosure, the volunteers would comment on how that dog always knew when I was coming. "He must be able to tell time," they'd laugh.

My students wrote stories about him, imagining how he came to find his way to our school. I dropped the stories off at the shelter and asked the staff to give them to the person in charge. I also reminded them that I really wanted to adopt that puppy. I told them my class had already voted to name the pup Sonny, in honor of the custodian who had rescued him.

Our destiny was fulfilled when Sonny's cast was removed the very day school got out. I got the call from the shelter in my classroom, and the students cheered while I cried tears of relief and joy. After school, I pulled up to the shelter for the last time, and headed home with Sonny.

Now, six years later, Sonny still amazes me with his time-telling acumen. Late for a walk? He's at my side, whining. Breakfast most mornings is between 6:00 and 6:30 — no later or there's a loud barking reminder. He awakens from his afternoon snooze and ambles into the living room at exactly 2:00, when he knows treats are forthcoming before his human companion settles in for an hour of her latest Netflix series.

Okay, I can hear you skeptics. All dogs can learn such a precise routine fairly easily, especially when it pertains to all the things they love. But Sonny also knows the days of the week. Show me a dog who knows those!

He's aware when it's Saturday, the night my sister-in-law comes over for a *Scrabble* game, hors d'oeuvres, and dinner. He waits patiently by the door at 4:45 for her arrival by five. He knows that he has to get up early and wake me for my Jazzercise class on Monday, Tuesday, Thursday, and Friday mornings, whereas he allows himself a longer snooze on Saturdays and Sundays. But the most amazing display of this phenomenon is on Wednesdays.

A few years ago, we changed waste-management companies. One Wednesday morning, Sonny was enjoying his usual morning constitution — smelling and marking — when his body froze suddenly, his ears rising straight up.

"What is it, boy?" I asked. I looked around and listened, but I couldn't see or hear a thing.

He began whimpering and shaking, and foam started forming on his lips. Severely agitated, he tugged me forward frantically. I heard a distant *ping, ping, ping*, and then the loud rumbling and lights of the garbage truck. That's when he completely lost it. He bolted up the street, ripping the leash from my hands as I fell face forward on the asphalt.

I stumbled to my feet and ran up the street calling him. Finally, I found him hunkered down under some bushes far down the road. I was dumbfounded by his reaction until I remembered the vet's words that his leg had most likely been broken by a vehicle. Could it be that a garbage truck had hit him? Did he still associate the pinging with imminent danger?

All I know is that come Wednesday, he refuses to go outside at the regular time. When I forget what day it is and whistle for him, he comes as far as the mud room, and then he looks at me with an imploring look that says, "Hey, you know it's Wednesday. Monster day," until I finally remember and feed him his breakfast inside.

Pretty amazing, right? My dog is so smart! Now, if he'd only learn how to sit, come, and stay!

— Martha Roggli —

34

Bobbie

Appreciation is a wonderful thing: It makes what is
excellent in others belong to us as well.
~Voltaire

Bobbie came with a little blue cape identifying him as a guide-dog puppy in training. He wore it whenever we went out in public. The first place I took him was a veterinary continuing-education conference, where he mostly napped under the table — that is, until I caught him chewing on the tablecloth! Next, we went to a video store, where he stubbornly sat down and refused to go in. I ended up having to carry him through the store.

Soon, Bobbie went everywhere with me. He went to work with me every day, where he sat in the reception area and pooped on the carpet. He went to Cub Scout meetings, where he was the best-behaved boy in the group. He even went to church every Sunday, and one evening when my son was supposed to be watching him, Bobbie walked down the aisle for Jesus during the invitation! He also believed in foot washing and happily licked any bare toes during the service.

Working dogs have always amazed me with the incredible number of duties they are able to perform, whether it be detecting bombs in war zones or guiding a blind person safely across a busy street. As a veterinarian, I have been privileged to be involved in the healthcare of several of these remarkable animals, including military working dogs, dogs from Canine Companions for Independence, Wounded Warrior

Dog Project, guide dogs, and other types of service dogs. The sheer intelligence of these animals is mind-boggling, yet they are still dogs in every respect.

Although I have interacted with many working dogs in a professional capacity, when I decided to volunteer as a puppy raiser for Southeastern Guide Dogs in Palmetto, Florida, working dogs became very personal to me. Puppy raisers are tasked with teaching basic commands, socializing the puppies, and exposing them to as many different environments as possible. When the puppies are somewhere between one-and-a-half and two years old they are returned to Southeastern for advanced training. I submitted my application, and after an interview with the area coordinator, I received my puppy — Bobbie, an adorable, nine-week-old black Labrador. Since my stepson's name is Bobby, this evoked some amusement in our family.

Twice a month, our area puppy raisers got together for training. After training sessions, we often took the dogs as a group to various places and exposed them to different surroundings. Bobbie was taken on bus rides, into stores, restaurants, a county fair, sports events, schools, concerts, museums, railroad tracks, and the beach. When it was my turn to plan an outing, we took the dogs to a horse stable and then to a restaurant for lunch — ours, not theirs — where there had apparently been a mix-up in my communication with the management because we were all handed menus in Braille!

One of my favorite outings was to a home out in the country, where the dogs were turned loose and allowed to play. It was sheer joy watching them just "be puppies," so thoroughly enjoying themselves. They ran for a while, grew weary, and then made their way back to sit by their puppy raisers until they got their second wind. At the end of the day, all the puppies were "dog tired."

As time went on, it became evident that Bobbie's eyes were not quite right. His lower eyelids turned in (a condition called entropion), which caused irritation to his eyes and a constant discharge. Ordinarily, this would have disqualified him from being a guide dog, as a dog with eye problems of his own obviously cannot be the eyes of a visually impaired person. However, because of my association with a veterinary ophthalmologist, Dr. Don Carter, who volunteered to do corrective surgery for free, Southeastern gave permission for surgery. I will always be grateful for Dr. Carter's help and his part in helping Bobbie on his road to becoming a guide dog.

It also became apparent that Bobbie had quite a stubborn streak and a mind of his own. Because I was a first-time puppy raiser, people with more experience expressed concern about Bobbie being difficult to control. After being dragged numerous times at the other end of Bobbie's leash from his strong, insistent pulling, I found a Gentle Leader to be a miracle. The Gentle Leader has a strap that goes over the dog's muzzle and tightens as he pulls, hence teaching him to walk under his handler's control. "Dog swaps," in which puppy raisers exchanged dogs for a couple of weeks, also helped Bobbie become more manageable under more experienced puppy raisers.

In spite of his stubbornness, however, Bobbie was a sweet-natured dog. One of my technicians remembers lying on the floor with him, sobbing, after a traumatic event in her life. He just lay with her, giving her his unconditional love.

Bobbie was also incredibly intelligent. During my lunch hour, I often walked Bobbie around the inside of the veterinary clinic, teaching him "right" and "left." He caught on to directions in no time. In fact, later, during training at Southeastern, the trainers had to spell r-i-g-h-t and l-e-f-t in front of him so he didn't turn whenever those words were spoken.

About a month before Bobbie returned to Southeastern, I noticed an abrupt change in his stubborn, goofy, Labrador puppy phase. He morphed into a mature, adult working dog. Now came the tough part. I had spent hours with Bobbie, literally taking him everywhere with me. I had done all the hard work and had an excellent dog to show for it. But it was time for him to leave.

I never realized how difficult it would be to let him go. Of course, I knew this was the goal all along — to get Bobbie to the point where he could be trained as someone's eyes. I clung to that greater purpose as I tearfully watched him pile into the back of a van with several other dogs from our group headed back to Southeastern. Still, he took a little piece of my broken heart with him.

Not all dogs make it as guide dogs. Some are "career changed" into other forms of service animals. Some are released for pets. So I was thrilled when I learned that Bobbie had made it! Visually impaired students spend several weeks at Southeastern training with their new dogs. Bobbie was matched with a young, single mother.

At the end of the training period, puppy raisers are invited to come for the graduation to meet the student who was paired with their dog and say a final goodbye. My family and I drove to Southeastern, several hours from our home. All the puppy raisers attended an orientation and were then allowed to watch their dogs work. We stood in a grassy area, quite a distance away so as not to be a distraction, while the students and their guide dogs walked past us on the sidewalk. As Bobbie approached directly in front of us, he apparently caught our scent. Suddenly, he turned his head in our direction for a split second, and I saw a look of surprise on his face. Then he turned back and continued with his duty of leading his new owner. My heart overflowed with pride! I knew he wanted to run to us, but he chose, instead, to do what he was trained for.

Later, we were able to meet Bobbie's new owner and visit with Bobbie. We were asked not to speak to the dog until the owner gave permission. Bobbie sat stoically by her side until she released him to greet us. Then he was all over us, his tail wagging in ecstasy, and unable to hold his "licker." We visited for as long as possible, and then had lunch with Bobbie, his owner, and her family. Sometimes, owners keep in contact with their puppy raiser, and they may even visit each other. Bobbie's owner chose not to, and we had to respect her wishes.

I have often wondered about Bobbie and his owner over the years. Did he wonder why we "abandoned" him? Was he a blessing to his owner, giving her the independence and confidence to live as normal a life as possible? Were there any behavioral or medical problems necessitating retraining or removal from service? Is he still alive? If so, Bobbie would be fourteen years old now. Surely, if he is alive, he is no longer working. If not, does he live with his owner as a pet?

Raising Bobbie was one of the most rewarding experiences I ever had, even if he did steal a little piece of my heart that I will never get back. I will always miss him. But the loss is tempered by the joy of knowing he fulfilled his purpose with grace and dignity.

—Ellen Fannon—

35

Too Obedient?

Food is not just eating energy. It's an experience.
~Guy Fieri

Hambone was a rescue dog. By that I mean he tried to "rescue" himself from our house every time we went away. He had been adopted several times, and by the time he reached us, he had decided he did not like being home alone. He tore out screens and learned to open windows that were cracked just an inch. When that failed, he tore the woodwork around the door completely off, sometimes even eating the plaster around it.

He was always proud of himself when we got home and found him lying in the front yard.

When we called the Humane Society, we learned that we were the fourth family to rescue him. To send him back meant certain death.

"Get him a companion," said the rescue lady, assuring us that the best way to fix the problem would be to double down on it. And we were crazy enough to try it.

"He has anxiety," she told us gently. "He feels abandoned when you go away."

I went back to the rescue center to take a look at the dogs. The minute I stepped through the door, they all went wild—some barking, some whining, some clawing at the cages. I hated that moment. I wanted to open all the doors and let them run free.

But one medium-sized hound dog sat quietly at attention. I went over to look at her. I praised her a little and then started to move on.

As I turned away, she barked just once, and very politely at that, as if she was saying, "Hey, take another look at me."

I had found my companion for Hambone.

Sadie was very subservient to her new friend, except when it came to eating. She gulped her food and then went to beg from Hambone, who was, more often than not, willing to share. She gained thirty pounds. I began setting his dish apart from hers.

Hambone had dermatitis, and when acupuncture didn't work, we began serving both of them raw meat and vegetables.

We had been married about a year but had never had been able to schedule time for our honeymoon—a trip to Europe. About six months after we adopted Hambone, we were finally ready to go. We would stay in New York for a few days to catch a Broadway show, and then fly to England and France for two weeks. We made arrangements for our dogs at an expensive retreat, and I packed dozens of plastic containers containing their meals for the duration.

We had a great time in New York and were packing to leave for London when the phone rang. It was the doggie retreat.

"Are you sure this is the food your dogs usually eat?" the worried attendant asked. "Because... well, I don't know how to tell you this, but your dogs won't eat."

"They won't eat?" That was really odd to me. Sadie loved her food.

"Did you feed them together?" I asked.

"Yep." I nodded my head.

"Do you have a special command you give them to eat?" he asked. "Some dogs are trained just to eat on command."

I was perplexed. After the call, my husband and I went to dinner, thinking that we would soon be changing our flight and heading back to California. Europe would have to stay on our bucket list for a few more years. We couldn't take a chance that our dogs would starve.

When we got back to the hotel, we called the boarding facility. They had tried to feed them again, but with no luck.

"They seem to be starving," he said. "They look at each other, but then they don't eat. Are you sure you don't have a special word you use?"

"I don't have a special word, but…" Suddenly, it occurred to me. I did have a special ritual. I disliked their jumping on me as I got their food ready, so when they followed me in the kitchen at feeding time, I said, "Stay." That meant for them to sit while I prepared their food.

Then, because Sadie would always head for the largest dish, I would put her food in front of her and say, "Sadie, eat." Then I would present Hambone with his dish and say, "Hambone, eat."

I had done this twice a day for six months without even thinking about it.

They went out to the kennel where the two dogs boarded together, presented them with their food, and then repeated the magic words.

"They must have been starving because they tore into their food."

By the time we arrived home from Europe, the dogs had grown to love their new vacation home and enjoyed going to "summer camp" for many years. They grew to love each other. Hambone outlived Sadie by just a few months.

—Linda Meilink—

36

All the News That's Fit to Chew

Everyone thinks they have the best dog.
And none of them are wrong.
~W.R. Purche

I was determined that my chocolate Lab pup would learn to fetch the newspaper. The rest of the family laughed at the idea, but four-month-old Annie was eager to give it a try.

In the early days, she could barely pick up the neatly bagged newspaper that arrived on our lawn daily. She struggled with its weight, dragging it upstairs by the bag, often tripping over it as she walked, but she was always anxious to please and proud of her contribution to the daily routine of the family.

When fully grown, she could bring in the paper with ease, even on advertisement-packed weekends and holidays. She charged down the stairs each morning, enthusiastically performing her important job before breakfast. It didn't matter if the paper was in a bush or partially under the car. She'd hunt it down and bring it in — a true Retriever through and through.

On October 28, 2012, Annie brought in the *The New York Times* just like any other day. But for us, it wasn't just any other day. We were anxiously watching the weather and making preparations for Hurricane Sandy, the biggest storm to hit the New Jersey coast in over a generation, and one of the costliest storms in United States history.

We needed more immediate news than the printed paper could deliver. The unread newspaper sat, still bagged, on the kitchen table.

The next day, there would be no newspaper. We were forced to evacuate as the ocean flooded the entire coast, wiping out gas, power, water, and sewer lines. It would be two months before we were allowed back to our town. In the interim, our family found temporary shelter at a friend's house in a senior development about forty-five minutes from our home. We adapted, and so did Annie. She settled down to life in a smaller home, without a fenced yard.

On our daily walks, Annie scanned the neighborhood looking for newspapers, not realizing that in this community they were delivered to specially designed plastic mailboxes in front of each house. Once a week, however, a free newsletter of local activities was tossed in the yard of each home in the development. Finally, something to do! Excitedly, Annie delivered the weekly news. For now, this would have to suffice.

Two months later, enough services were restored that we could move back home. Unfortunately for Annie, newspaper delivery service was not one of them. For the first two days, she raced to the front door each morning to do her job, perplexed when she could find nothing in the yard. That's when my husband noticed that the October 28th newspaper was now tucked away on a kitchen bookshelf. He had an idea. Secretly, we tossed that same newspaper out the second-floor window every morning and watched as our happy girl went back to work doing her favorite job.

For two months, Annie brought in the same newspaper every day—never suspecting that something was amiss. It had to be re-bagged many times (she's a toothy Retriever), but it held up fairly well.

When newspaper delivery resumed, only the local paper was available, but Annie was perfectly happy to deliver the *Asbury Park Press*. After all, she's a Jersey girl at heart.

—Lisa Taylor—

37

My Clever Dog Bubba's Tricks

*Dogs travel hundreds of miles during their lifetime
responding to such commands as "come" and "fetch."*
~Stephen Baker

I adopted Bubba as a puppy and decided to train him by using hand signals. It took months, but working painstakingly for many long hours daily produced excellent results.

If I extended my palm downward, Bubba would lie down. Holding one pinky up and wiggling it signified "Bubba, dance." To my delight, Bubba would rise up on two legs and dance. My hand cupped to my ear prompted him to bark. Placing my index finger to my lips meant "stop." The pup grew, as did the number of tricks he'd mastered.

Soon, my pal Bubba accompanied me on errands and road trips, as well as to parks, picnics, and my veterans groups' outdoor reunions.

One spring afternoon, we went to a backyard cookout. Vern, our host, greeted me. "Nice pooch. What's his name?"

"Bubba," I replied.

"I'm great at training dogs," Vern boasted. "I'll bet I can teach him to do some neat tricks if I try."

So I sat back on a lawn chair, folded my arms, and observed.

"Bubba, sit," the host commanded while attempting to place him into a seated position. Zero response emerged from my dog.

"I'll give you a nice treat," the would-be trainer continued. "Come on, sit." Bubba remained standing.

This series of failed attempts ensued for twenty minutes. Then a rather frustrated Vern intensified efforts, turned away from me, and stood above the bewildered pup. This created a perfect opportunity for me to step in unnoticed.

"Okay, Bubba, since you're already on all fours anyway," Vern continued, "stand up on two hind legs for me." With that, he lifted the dog's front paws, but Bubba dropped them right back down again. Now, I silently commenced effective action. With my eyes meeting Bubba's, I slipped my right palm upward — the signal I'd taught Bubba for "stand on hind legs."

"Yippee, I succeeded!" a naively jubilant Vern shouted. "Now dance for me, Bubba." I wiggled my upraised pinky to signal my pet to commence dancing.

A crowd of onlookers gathered and quickly understood what was happening. The louder the observers laughed, the more it convinced Vern of his expertise in dog training.

Finally, I mercifully clued my host in on the ruse. He seemed to take it like a good sport, but then I wondered whether he'd ever invite me to one of his backyard picnics again.

Months later, Bubba and I visited Mexico. In a park while signaling to my dog using my left hand, I'd call out the Spanish word for "left." He'd whirl around toward his left. I switched to the Spanish word for "right." Bubba obeyed the sign I had formed right-handed. "Amazing!" the spectators said. "He taught his dog to understand Spanish."

"He also understands Chinese," I claimed rather inaccurately. I repeated those same hand signals while faking what I thought sounded like Chinese.

This time, I didn't explain my sneaky tactics to the enthralled observers. *It's a party,* I figured. *Let them have their fun. Later, they'll go home and tell their families about the amazing "multilingual dog's antics" they saw demonstrated in the park today.*

—Ken Prehn—

38

The Reward

Ever wonder where you'd end up if you took your dog
for a walk and never once pulled back on the leash?
~Robert Brault

A few years ago, while staying with my parents at their house near the Potomac River in the Northern Neck of Virginia, I embarked on my regular morning walk with my dogs, Jack and Sadie. As I do for every walk we take, I already had a route planned in my head. On this particular morning, my plan was to walk a route my family and I refer to as Barn Road Loop. Though my dogs and I had been in the Northern Neck two days and had already enjoyed four walks on the nature trails and throughout the neighborhood, we had yet to traverse Barn Road Loop. Today, I had decided, was the day.

We completed the first half of the predetermined loop, but when we got to the road that would take us to Barn Road, Jack rebelled. He often does, having quite a mind of his own. When I tried to coax him into turning left, he locked eyes with me, planted his feet in a posture reminiscent of a stubborn mule pulling against his lead, and held his ground. Sadie stood by placidly, watching to see who would win this battle of wills.

Although I was reluctant to alter the route to which I had already mentally committed, I gave in. Jack won. He often does. We weren't in a hurry, after all, and we could still walk Barn Road after this little detour.

No sooner did I stop pulling his leash in the direction in which I had intended to go, relinquishing our walk to his will, than my triumphantly tail-wagging dog led Sadie and me down his own chosen path.

When we got to where he was headed, I was so glad I had let him take the lead.

He had taken us to The Point — a peninsula of land where Cod Creek flows into the Potomac River, which eventually opens up into the Chesapeake Bay. We were rewarded for our detour with the absolute picture of peace. The morning was cloudy, but the clouds were starting to break, and their reflection shone like an impressionist painting in the water at our feet. There was no one else around, not even a car in the parking lot of the nearby clubhouse.

It was just me, my dogs, the seabirds, and the rippled reflection of the sky in the river. Gratitude and serenity washed over me like the lapping waves over the sand, and I realized that sometimes letting go — letting someone else take the lead — is the wisest decision one can make. I could have forged ahead with my own agenda, but in relinquishing my will to that of my stubborn dog, all three of us were rewarded. It is a moment I still look back on when I need some serenity and a reminder that I don't always have to hold the reins.

— Amanda Sue Creasey —

39

The Test

Whoever said you can't buy happiness
forgot little puppies.
~Gene Hill

omet, our Lab/Shepherd mix, had come into our lives unexpectedly. When we first saw him, he was eight months old. He sat obediently, did not bark, and was tied to a tree. The family that asked us to take him lived in a rural area, already had several dogs, and did not want this beautiful black puppy who had been dropped into their hands. The husband was going to "do away" with him.

Needless to say, Comet was soon in the back seat of our car, riding to his new forever home. We built a fence around the yard, and he loved to play with the kids outside and the two cats inside. He was very smart, but we did not know just how smart until he faced a challenge one day.

Comet loved to carry around an empty plastic ice-cream bucket by its plastic handle. He also loved to have a ball thrown to him, and he would run away with it in his mouth so that we would chase him for it. My two kids decided to put him to the test to find out which activity he liked better. As one child threw Comet's bucket to him, the other threw the ball.

Comet took a moment to assess the situation. Then he ran to the ball, picked it up in his mouth, dropped it into the bucket, and took off with both prizes!

That awesome dog made us chuckle many times over the years, but he always had our greatest respect.

—Patricia Lund—

Model Behavior

*A dog can express more with his tail in seconds that
his owner can express with his tongue in hours.*
~Author Unknown

It was just a normal Saturday morning. Wally and I were making a routine visit to the dog park. We planned to take a normal walk, under the normal sun, along the normal river.

The entirely normal morning snagged like a jacket on barbed wire when we saw the not-so-normal sign tied to the dog-park gate:

AUDITIONS TODAY
10:00
MAIN ENTRANCE

I rued the posted notice. In about an hour, the dog park was going to be transformed into a zoo. The auditions were for the local dog-treat company that had become a national hit. Their packaging always featured dogs with their humans in the wilderness around our small Colorado city. Everyone and their mother's pooch were bound to show up for their shot at bite-sized glory.

Personally, I've always been turned off by advertising. The thought of appearing on bags of training treats held zero appeal to me. Granted, Wally would make an outstanding model. He has a noble bearing for an indeterminate mutt. Chiseled jaw. Intelligent ears. Rich fur, the colors of dark chocolate s'mores. All graham cracker and marshmallow and exuberance.

He would sell a lot of doggie delectables. No doubt about it. Too bad he was my dog; the world might forever be denied his dashing profile. We didn't linger by the sign. Instead, we set off on our miniature adventure before the fame-seekers crashed upon the park.

I have visited a few dog parks in more urban areas, and they help me realize just how fortunate we are (dogs and humans alike) to have this particular dog park in our little town. There's no concrete anywhere in this acreage. And we're talking acres, alright. Practically boundless high desert terrain.

We trekked along the Animas River on one side of the dog park, and then back along the feet of the steep mountain face on the other side. With all this expanse, dogs are essentially free to be themselves. They can tuck tails and tempt each other to chase them. They can get crazy-eyed and run in beautiful, pointless circles. They can sniff and posture. With no corners and no crannies, they have room to play — and room to avoid each other. I've never seen a serious scuffle at this park because every dog has an escape route in every direction.

Yet the people fascinated me this morning — as they do many mornings — when they refused to let their dogs be dogs. A chocolate Lab started trotting up the trail toward Wally, and its human yelled for it. "C'mere," she said. "Leave that dog alone."

Leave him alone? Why bother coming to the dog park just to leave other dogs alone?

Another couple let their dog start the sniffing circle with Wally. Then, about three seconds in, one of them said, "That's enough. Stop it. Come on."

Stop it? This smelling ritual is the canine introduction protocol. Tails wagging, curiosity abounding, no one was threatening or imposing on anyone else. Still, when the dogs don't listen right away, the humans get irritable and start talking in capital letters.

"Come ON. CUT it out. RIGHT NOW. Get OVER here."

The dogs in every case were only good girls and good boys. They weren't doing anything that wouldn't be permitted by well-bred dogs backstage at Westminster. Wally certainly wasn't instigating anything;

he's not aggressive or a humper, and he listens to me when he needs to.

But I noticed something in every one of these instances. While the dogs were fine, the people seemed embarrassed.

I sensed that not a single one of these humans actually minded that their dogs were sniffing or greeting or striving in vain to play. Yet I also sensed that they thought I might mind. (I didn't.) Therefore, to avoid awkwardness or humiliation, they tried to show they were in total control of their dogs. (They weren't.)

They wanted their dogs to perform every step of the way. Even here, the one place in the county where dogs could be dogs without leashes, they still had their humans' befuddled sense of propriety tied around their necks.

Just in the nick of time, we made it back to the top of the park and made our way to the exit. We were skirting a small swarm of people and dogs clogging the entrance when a man with a clipboard intercepted us.

"He's a very handsome dog," the man said. "What's his name?"

I told him, and he asked, "Are you interested in auditioning him to be the next dog-treat celebrity?"

"Well," I wavered, "we do have someplace to be. But you're right. He is very handsome."

"I can get you third in line," the man said. He pulled a number 3 off his clipboard to prove it.

For all I knew, Wally would love having his face adorn bags of dog treats across the nation. He took majestic photographs. What kind of human would I be to deny my pal this chance at glory?

"Sign us up," I said.

Wally and I joined the throng of soon-to-be-disappointed auditioners. When the woman with the camera called for number 3, Wally and I strutted to the center of the circle. I asked Wally to sit. He sat.

What a guy.

"I'm just going to ask you some questions while filming you interacting with Wally," the woman said. "How long have you and Wally known each other?"

"Oh, about —" I started, when Wally darted off without warning to join a scuffling pack of dogs well past the ring of aspiring celebrities.

"Wally, c'mere," I hollered. "Come HERE."

Wally ignored me. I gave him my most sincerely charming smile and finished answering the woman's question.

"And how old is, ah, Wally?" she asked.

"He's five," I said. "And he's a great dog." I looked past her and saw my great dog attempting to mount another dog.

Wally had never acted like this — never once since I adopted him. Why did he have to act up when we were on camera? I wanted to stomp over to him so badly, take his collar and make him finish the audition with me.

Just like every other human in the park, I was embarrassed by my dog being a dog.

I took a deep breath and smiled, this time genuinely warmly. "I suspect we're done here," I said to the camerawoman. I handed her my number 3 and walked over to where Wally had advanced to playing a standard game of "chase me chase me oh god please chase me."

"Come on, bud," I said. Wally bounded over to me, just like normal. I petted his face and kissed his graham-cracker head.

"Tell you what, fella," I said. "How about neither of us ever has to perform for the other. You be you, and I'll be me, and we'll always love each other just the way we are. Deal?"

We had a deal. And even though we did not get a callback, we stuck to that deal — neither of us ever expecting the other to perform or act like anyone but his truest self.

— Zach Hively —

41

Captain of My Destiny

I have found that if you love life,
life will love you back.
~Arthur Rubenstein

I recently treated myself to a full body massage. As my massage therapist began gently massaging my scalp, which felt absolutely wonderful, I suddenly realized something. This is what it feels like to be Captain!

Captain, the Yorkie-Poo I share with my sister, loves getting his head scratched. Now I know why: this felt incredible! So utterly relaxing. So ridiculously pleasant.

I could have happily gotten my own head scratched for hours, which is exactly how Captain feels about it. Captain, at just five fluffy pounds, is a lap dog who will receive a scalp massage to his tiny noggin endlessly. If your hand stops scratching his little head for more than a few seconds, he'll poke at you gently with a paw until you resume.

Clearly, Captain knows how to live! In that moment, I decided that my resolution for 2019 would be to be more like my dog. So what exactly does this mean? I will seek out more massages and head rubs, that's for sure, but it also means to relax!

I spend a lot of my time getting things done, whether it's errands, housework or social obligations. Meanwhile, Captain is happily dozing the day away in a patch of sunlight. It's not as if I'm about to stretch out on the floor in the sunshine myself, but I could spend less time being productive and more time napping on the sofa or relaxing with a good book.

• And WALK! Captain never turns down the opportunity for a ramble through the neighborhood. Dogs know that going out the door is always an exciting adventure. The world is full of cool things to see and hear and smell. Of course, the smells that the two of us enjoy are very different. But we both love being out and about. The take home for me? When you're not relaxing — move!

• And ENJOY YOUR CHOW! Captain is always thrilled with dinner. He has never once felt guilty about eating anything. Of course, if given an opportunity, he'll eat himself sick. So I don't want to go overboard with this one. But to thoroughly enjoy every bite of my own dinner? I can do that.

• And PLAY! If Captain can't interest one of us in a game of "Yorkie-poo in the middle" or "Which hand is holding the treat?" he'll bat a piece of kibble across the room and then chase it down, just for the fun of it. I've accomplished a lot in my life. I am valued at my workplace. My writing is published everywhere, and my career as a writing coach has flourished. But how much time do I spend just unproductively goofing off? Not enough!

• And TREATS ARE GREAT! When you offer Captain a treat, he never turns it down with, "I don't deserve this." He grabs it, enjoys it thoroughly, then looks for more. Treats make life fun. However you define them, from freshly baked cookies to binge-watching *Doctor Who*, grab as many as you can.

• And APPRECIATE YOUR LOVED ONES! When I come in the door, Captain is always there to greet me, tail wagging. The clear message? "I'm thrilled that you're here." I can't wag, but I can appreciate my loved ones and always make sure they know how much they mean to me.

• And LIVE IN THE MOMENT! Captain, at twelve, is starting to head toward the end of his life span, just as I, at sixty-four, am starting to head toward mine. The difference between us? He has no awareness of his own mortality and so never gives it a thought. Unlike Captain, I know I won't last forever, but like my dog, I can choose to fully enjoy the moment rather than fret about the future.

• And LIFE IS TO ENJOY! Captain's purpose is simple — to enjoy life and be a good dog. This year I plan to get in touch with my inner Yorkie-Poo. I will enjoy life and be a good person.

— Roz Warren —

42

Reflection

To hold, as 'twere, the mirror up to nature.
~Hamlet

His face alert, his ears pricked up, he sat at the foot of the bed gazing at his own image in the full-length mirror. I watched, fascinated. "It's you," I said to him, knowing that he could not understand me.

He's an eight-month-old purebred German Shepherd, fifty pounds already. He looks nearly like an adult on the outside, but he is still very much a puppy on the inside. We got him when he was seven weeks old. Mary carried him on her lap while I drove us home.

Like any new parents, we pored over how-to books on the subject of raising a dog. There were new approaches I'd never heard of: crate training, for instance (it works), and clicker training (the jury's still out for us).

On the subject of housebreaking, the dog books caution against getting a puppy in the winter. It's already bad enough to be roused from bed for a midnight excursion to the back yard. Why compound the inconvenience by adding ice and snow? Since he entered our household in December, we had thrown that particular caution to the wind and paid the price.

Also, like new parents, we learned the melancholy truth that youngsters crave attention but only tolerate love. Much as we ached to hug him sometimes, the puppy clearly preferred chasing a ball or chewing a glove.

Everything happens quickly in a dog's life because its lifespan is a mere seventh of ours. Dogs grow quickly. They attach to people quickly. They learn habits, good and bad, quickly. And then they break our hearts by quickly getting old and dying. But within their brief lives, sometimes we get to glimpse a mystery.

Mary was working late that night, and I was doing the laundry. While I folded towels and laid them in a neat stack upon the bed, the dog amused himself by sniffing out whatever memories lay between the old pine floorboards. I made a sudden motion, and his head snapped up. He had seen the movement in the mirror and now was watching my reflection there.

I had always wondered how well dogs could see in a mirror. Their color vision is more restricted than ours, of course, but that limitation needn't prevent them from distinguishing things. The more interesting question, though, was how they understood what they saw.

When we had first brought him home and took him up to the bedroom, he had looked at himself in this same mirror. At that time, the reflection must have looked like one of the six brothers and sisters he'd left behind at the breeder's. He pawed at the glass and tried to get behind it. After a while, though, he ignored the mirror. But now he was looking at my image there with recognition, I thought. I put down the towel I had been folding and tried an experiment.

We had been teaching him a few basic commands: "sit," "down," and "stay." Recently, I had started accompanying these voice commands with hand gestures. Since he was sitting with his back to me, all he could see was my reflection in the mirror. Without speaking, I pointed toward the floor, the hand signal for "down." He watched me in the mirror, hesitated, and then slowly pushed his paws forward and settled upon his chest. I praised him lavishly, and only then did he turn around to look at me.

I let a few minutes go by until he was standing again and distracted by something else, and then I repeated the experiment. I made a motion to attract his attention to the mirror. Silently, I gave him the "sit" command, rotating my palm upward. Obediently, he sat. I followed it with the gesture for "down." He dropped to the floor. Again, I praised him, and he looked over his shoulder at me.

It appeared obvious that he could see my image in the mirror, but how did he interpret that image? Did he know it was merely a reflection, or did he think that somehow there was a second me in there? I walked over to him. Sitting by my side now, he looked up at me, and then at my reflection in the mirror. Finally, almost as an afterthought, he looked at himself. Suddenly, the earth stopped under my feet.

There were only the two of us in the room. If he recognized one of the images in the mirror as me, who did he think this other creature was — the shorter, hairier one that he was now looking at? I've read that dogs have no concept of self. According to animal psychologists, it is the very notion of self that separates primates from the rest of the animal kingdom. But if he didn't identify with the entity sitting next to me, who did he think it was?

I watched his eyes for some clue to what he was thinking. "It's you," I said.

He continued to stare at the dog in the mirror. Presently, he got up and went to it, casually brushed his nose against the glassy surface, and then came back to nuzzle me.

I faced him toward the mirror again. "Can't you see that it's you?" There was a note of pleading in my voice. "Aren't you curious about what you look like? You're such a handsome fellow. Don't you want to see?" But he was no longer paying attention.

Though I can never be certain, he may very well have concluded that it was his own reflection in the glass. His nonchalance seemed to bear that out, for if he thought there was truly another dog in the room, his reaction would not have been so calm. But his disinterest still bothered me for some reason. That's when I grasped the real pathos of the incident.

Tempted neither to admire himself nor to fret about his looks, he had a supreme indifference to his own image, a quality we ascribe only to saints — and dogs. From the mixed blessing of self-knowledge comes the unique loneliness of human beings on this planet.

He looked up at me now with mild anxiety, as if fearing he had done something wrong. I knelt down and petted him.

"It's all right," I said softly. "The fault is mine, I assure you. All mine."

— Richard Matturro —

Canine Kindness

43

The Gentle Backup

We give dogs the time we can spare, the space we can
spare and the love we can spare. In return, dogs give us
their all. It is the best deal we have ever made.
~M. Acklam

When I was twenty-one, being a police officer meant more to me than anything in the world. At the Texas police department where I was hired, I was one of the very first women on patrol. That meant something to me. I was filled with a sense of pride and accomplishment. I wanted to be the best cop the station ever had.

However, obstacles were thrown in my way. A few men didn't want women working there, and they had no trouble letting me know it.

The one thing that made life bearable was a little, dark-eyed ball of fluff that I found at the back of a neighbor's garage. I named her Heidi.

Heidi was part St. Bernard, part German Shepherd. Nobody wanted her because they knew she would be huge. At first, I figured that I couldn't afford such a large pet. But the way she acted when she was a few days old let me know that I had no choice.

With her eyes still closed, Heidi growled at everything — except me. She'd scoot into the depths of the garage and snarl at everybody else, as if she were under attack.

I couldn't help but admire that fuzzy baby taking on the world like she owned it. Thus, I made a vow to economize so that she and I could be together.

During those first years, Heidi grew to an enormous size. I gave up some of my food so she could have the best dog chow and medical care.

She returned every favor in full.

She helped me hold it together when things at the police department got rough. She wasn't just my responsibility — she was my friend.

During the first year of her life, she quit growling altogether. As ferocious as she pretended to be when she was a pup, she became gentle as an adult.

Everyone was her friend, and she offered her front left paw to let them know it, a behavior I had never taught her. She did it once, and my shocked response must have triggered her into repeating the gesture with anyone who came near. The gentler she became, the more I needed that tenderness.

Some of the men with whom I worked became unbearably crude and degrading. I got through it because I knew I would come home to the sweetest angel that ever walked on four paws.

One day, a detective from the police department showed up at my front door. In a time before cell phones existed, I assumed the detective was there for some serious reason. It occurred to me that I did have a landline, and that my supervisor could have called if there was some emergency requiring all officers to respond to the station.

This wasn't one of those situations.

When I opened the door to speak to the detective, he demanded to see my duty weapon. This scared me. Badly. I had never heard of someone from the detective ranks calling on officers to inspect their weapons — certainly not without warning or when the officer was off duty.

Because the weapon I was issued belonged to the department, I retrieved it and handed it to him. I was smart enough, however, not to let him inside my apartment. We stood at my front door with him inspecting my revolver — right there for anyone in the neighborhood to see.

Eventually, the detective handed back the weapon, but he told me he could make calls on me for any inspection any time. I asked him why he couldn't have waited for me to be on duty. The guy just smiled and reiterated that if he wanted to show up at my door he could do so. Obviously, this was nothing more than harassment.

I was on the verge of grabbing that detective by his throat when a sound stopped me.

I'd lost track of Heidi. I thought she was still asleep on my bed at the back of my apartment. When I heard that shuffling sound from nearby, the detective heard it, too. We both looked toward the driveway in front of my apartment.

Heidi was standing behind the detective like an avenging angel.

My apartment was on the ground floor. I didn't know it until later, but Heidi had decided that she didn't like the way I was behaving, or maybe she didn't like the way the man at the door was acting. Sensing something was wrong, she found a first-floor open window, pushed out the screen, and worked her way outside and around the building.

Heidi didn't growl. She didn't bite or show any aggression. She simply grabbed the detective by the pants leg and pulled him away from the door. As big as she was, the detective wasn't going to push his luck. He simply went with her.

Once they were about fifty feet away, Heidi let go of the detective. Then she sat and faced him. She was between him and me.

The message couldn't have been clearer: Leave my human alone.

It occurred to me that, if he had a weapon on him, he could shoot her and say that she'd attacked. I bolted from the door, grabbed her collar, and led her back into the apartment. I closed and locked the door behind us.

That detective never showed up again.

At the police department, I told everyone what had happened. A few weeks later, that detective was fired, along with the Chief of Police. I hadn't made a formal complaint, but apparently someone else had.

From that point on, things got better at work, but Heidi never let me go to the door alone. For the next ten years, I had a constant companion whenever the doorbell rang.

On that day so many years ago, Heidi taught a human cop how not to retaliate. Had I struck out at that detective as I wanted to, I would have lost the job I loved. I would probably have been arrested for assault. It has occurred to me that an enraged response was exactly what that detective was trying to elicit. He wanted to get me riled so that I'd lose control and he'd have a reason to take my badge.

Maybe that was the reason Heidi became so gentle. Maybe she understood that because I was always so angry over my work situation, one of us had to be the adult. She took up that role.

I've come to learn that friends come in all shapes and sizes. Mine happened to have four paws and a massive heart.

—Candace Sams—

44

Clean Paws

*Being a hero to someone, even if it is a dog, is a feeling
like no other. Though it can be frustrating, it can be
the most rewarding thing to give someone a second
chance at a happy life.*
~Elizabeth Parker, Finally Home:
Lessons on Life from a Free-Spirited Dog

It had been three months since we lost our beloved Terrier and
Bluetick Coonhound. My husband wasn't sure he was emotionally ready to get a new dog, but we had both grown up with
dogs, and he eventually conceded that the house felt too empty.

We began looking at local rescues and stumbled across a one-and-
a-half-year-old Bloodhound named Hunter who was being fostered by
another family near our home. We began the application process, and
within the week had a day and time set up to meet Hunter.

Hunter had been through roughly five homes in his short lifetime,
and he had been severely malnourished in his most recent home,
causing him to lose forty pounds. His incredible foster parents had
taken him back in and begun the process of putting some weight back
on the poor dog.

When we met Hunter, he was a happy, playful boy with boundless energy — not what one thinks of as a typical Bloodhound that
likes to laze around on a wooden porch. He was friendly and had the
most adorable floppy tongue that hung from his mouth, which always
seemed to be pulled back into a smile. My heart melted. I knew he

was a perfect fit for our little family and my husband agreed.

Hunter's amazing foster parents brought him over to our house the next evening to help transition him. We would take him for the weekend, and as long as all went well, he would become the newest member of the Cooper family. We were ecstatic.

While Hunter was the sweetest, liveliest pup, he had been through so many homes that he seemed to be unsure of the permanence of this one as well. It was a process of learning his behaviors and demeanor for us, as well as for him. We had many adventures with chewed-up shoes, mail, gloves, and tape measures. But we persevered and worked patiently with him every day, providing him with a plethora of plush, squeaky toys, ropes, and balls, as well as plenty of food and water. He learned what belonged to him and caught on to commands and our schedule. He learned he would never go without food in our home, and eventually we got him back up to a normal, healthy weight. Every day, we grew together. And while Hunter always had an energy level that could wear out a three-year-old hyped up on sugar, he was a loving, dutiful boy.

One evening, the three of us were lying in bed, snuggled together and watching television. Hunter was enjoying a nice ear rub and grumbling happily. My husband commented, "Hunter really seems to be settling in. You know, I think he feels more at home and knows this is where he belongs."

"I think you're right. He seems to know that he is here to stay. Isn't that right, Hunter?" I replied, joining in on the ear rubs.

We continued cuddling and watching television that evening, and Hunter began cleaning his paws as he always did before bedtime. Then, something new happened. Once Hunter had completed cleaning his paws, he reached over to me and began licking my hands. He had such a gentle mouth and he cleaned them thoroughly, even gently, nibbling on my fingers to get them to a proper cleanliness. Once he completed my hands, he moved on to my husband and began cleaning his the same way he had cleaned mine.

"What are you doing, sweet boy? Do I have some good leftovers from dinner on my hand still?" my husband chuckled. Once Hunter was finished with our hands, he did the same thing with our feet. We held back smiles as his soft, loving tongue tickled the bottoms of our feet generously. Once he was done, he came back with his floppy tongue and a smile on his face, and we snuggled again.

"I think he just cleaned our paws like he does his paws every night," I told my husband.

"I think you're right," he said incredulously, smiling and rubbing Hunter's lovable hound ears once more.

This new tradition continued every night. Hunter would clean his paws and then he would come and clean our "paws." It marked a turning point — he had fully settled in and knew we would be his humans forever. He realized we would always take care of him, and this seemed to be his way of showing us that he would always take care of us, too. He has been a good reminder that while it may take time to build trust, it becomes unbreakable once that foundation has been laid.

— Gwen Cooper —

45

Giving Until It Hurts

A kind gesture can reach a wound
that only compassion can heal.
~Steve Maraboli

I heard the back door open and looked up as my sister Joy entered the kitchen holding a raggedy doll in one hand. "Anita, what am I supposed to do with this?" she asked.

She had come in from spending a few minutes with Mose, my six-month-old Border Collie pup. During their time together, she had tried to explain to him why she was so sad that day.

Joy's cat had been sick, and at eleven years old there was nothing that could be done for her except to put her down.

Even though Mose hated cats, he was a sensitive dog and felt bad for Joy, so he gave her his most prized possession: a doll named Doll. In the past, anytime Mose was sick or scared, I would find him with his head curled around Doll, seeming to draw comfort from her. Now he was hoping that Doll would bring comfort to Joy.

As Joy and I looked at each other and wondered what we were supposed to do with Doll, we burst into fits of laughter until we could no longer laugh. Then we cried until we burst into laughter again. The humor of the situation provided a much-needed emotional release for what had been a draining day.

But our situation still hadn't changed. What were we to do with Doll? I decided to spend time with Mose to see if I could figure out what he might have been thinking. It didn't take me long to see the sad look on his face and to realize just how big of a sacrifice he had made to give Joy his Doll. I couldn't do anything to cheer him up. Finally, I went back inside and conferred with Joy as to what we should do.

We knew that the only way to cheer up Mose was to give Doll back to him, but we didn't know how he would respond. At first, he just looked at her and walked away. Clearly, he wanted Joy to keep her. Once again, the humor of the situation got to us. As soon as Mose saw us laughing and acting "normal" again, he grabbed Doll and put her into his crate of toys.

Later that evening, I laughed and cried as I reflected over some of the day's events. But time after time, I kept coming back to Mose's sacrifice. He hated cats, yet was touched emotionally himself when he saw how sad Joy and I were over the death of one. He was willing to give up the thing he treasured most in order to bring comfort to Joy. As the enormity of his sacrifice sunk in, I felt ashamed of my own selfish ways. So often when I see a need, rather than giving until it hurts, I give from my surplus. Yet Mose gave until his heart ached. And when Doll was returned, he wouldn't take her back until he knew that Joy had been comforted.

Seven years later, I still get emotional thinking about that day and the lesson I learned from Mose about giving until it hurts.

— A E Troyer —

46

Friends to the End

True devotion is motivated by love alone
and devoid of selfish entanglements.
~Rick Hocker

His given name was Tracks, but we just called him Pup. He was a red merle bundle of fuzzy fluff with the most amazing icy blue eyes. He was given to us by a friend when he was eight weeks old, and it didn't take long for him to steal our hearts.

Pup was an Australian Shepherd, a herding breed. Because of their extreme intelligence and uncanny instinct, they can be trained to herd sheep, cattle, goats, or even ducks. They excel in just about everything — herding, agility, dock diving, etc.

I live on about thirty acres of beautiful West Virginia rolling hills. Keeping this land cleared would not be possible without the help of my dedicated goats. They are excellent at munching away the multiflora rosebushes and honeysuckle, which makes them a necessity on my small farm. I have a Heinz 57 mixture of goats — a few Boers, a few Alpines, and a few minis. Needless to say, spring often brings numerous babies to the farm.

As I said, herding dogs are extremely intelligent, and Pup was no exception. I never trained Pup to herd, but I decided to put him to the test when he was about two years old. He was absolutely amazing to watch. Using his body, moving from side to side and crouching down low, he had those goats in a circle in no time — all on instinct.

It didn't take long before he could herd them all back to the barn. He had a working relationship with the goats. They weren't his pals, and he didn't hang around with them or play with them. They were his job — which is why what happened later was so amazing.

It was a dark and stormy night, and that's not a cliché in this case. Rain was pouring down, and the sky was streaked with lightning — a real gullywasher. It was cold and just plain miserable. I came home after an evening out and was surprised that Pup was nowhere to be found. He had a horrible fear of thunder and lightning. If it looked remotely like it was going to thunderstorm, he would be under the table in the living room, shaking. He wasn't there, though, and I knew something wasn't right.

After calling for him in the house and looking in all his hidey holes, I heard barking in the distance. I opened a window slightly and could hear Pup barking — not a happy bark, but an anxious bark — and it was coming from the goat barn. Flashlights in hand, the whole family sopped our way through the mud to find out what was going on with Pup.

We found him behind the barn, barking, crying and whining. Something was very off. This was highly unusual. Pup had a fear of storms, and here he was standing outside in the middle of one. As I made my way closer, I saw what he was doing, and my heart melted. He was standing over a dark little critter. I couldn't tell what it was until I got right up to it and moved Pup out of the way. What I found was a newborn goat — tiny, cold, wet and covered in mud. Pup had been out there in the storm trying to protect the baby with his own body. I grabbed the drenched little babe, wrapped him in old towels, and rushed him back to the house to get him warmed up.

Momma goats seldom leave their babies, so I was very concerned that she wasn't there. Did she die after giving birth? Was she somewhere suffering? With the baby inside my coat, I trudged back out into the downpour to look for Momma. I found her the first place I looked — standing in the barn with the rest of the goats, warm and dry. I tried putting the baby back with her, but she wouldn't have anything to do with it. Sometimes, that happens. This was a first-time momma, and it looked like the baby might have been a little premature. She might have felt that the baby wouldn't make it and left it there alone to die. That's the way of nature sometimes, but Pup had other plans. He was attached to this baby for some reason.

Since Momma wouldn't let the baby nurse, I had to intervene. While my son held Momma, I helped the baby nurse. There's no substitute for the colostrum a baby gets from its momma right after it's born. I could raise the baby on store-bought goat milk, but I needed to get that first colostrum in it. Pup was there the whole time, daring Momma to be uncooperative. It was like his new purpose in life was to save that baby goat. I could have understood it better if Pup was a female dog with maternal instinct, but he was a male.

I brought the little goat inside the house once again, put him in a basket and named him Little Britches. After I washed off the mud and muck, I found he was solid white and cute as a button. As with any newborn, he had to be bottle-fed quite often, especially since he was such a tiny thing. The whole family took turns feeding him while Pup sat there observing it all.

It didn't take long before Little Britches was up and running. Since he didn't have Momma, he became very attached to Pup. Everywhere Pup went, Little Britches was right behind him, kicking, bucking and running like all little goats do. Pup had a doggy door in the basement, and he taught Little Britches how to use it. When Pup climbed the basement steps, we could hear the sound of little hooves trotting right behind him. When Pup rested underneath the oak tree in the back yard, Little Britches would climb onto his back and jump off, acting like he had just jumped from the highest ledge in the world. The two were always together.

I let this continue until Little Britches was able to fend for himself with the other goats in the pen. He was becoming more like a dog every day, and I knew it was time to reintroduce him to the other goats. There was an adjustment period, but Little Britches finally settled into his new home in the barn. He never lost his dog-like personality and would often try to sit on my lap even though he was close to seventy pounds. He and Pup continued playing together, though on opposite sides of the fence. They remained friends until the very end. I've never had another dog and goat with the same relationship as Pup and Little Britches. That was one special dog.

— Teresa Crow —

47

Retrieved

Did you know that there are over 300 words
for love in canine?
~Gabriel Zevin

On a beautiful August day, I stopped at the overlook to let my dog Yainex out of his crate. He sniffed the air, ready for adventure.

Snow-capped Diamond Peak stood like a sentinel above Odell Lake, one of the largest natural lakes in Oregon. Tucked into a glacier-carved basin high in the Cascade Mountains, the lake is six miles long and over a mile wide. Sunlight glinted on the dark blue water as several boats bobbed on the surface.

Getting back into the car, I followed signs to Trapper Creek Campground on the southwestern shore of the lake and began to search for my parents. They had driven from Texas with their camp trailer to meet my dad's sister and her husband from San Diego at this favorite spot, and we were joining them for the weekend.

Cruising slowly through the campground, I caught sight of their trailer and the California motorhome. As I pulled into the campsite, I spotted them playing cards at the picnic table in the shade of a huge fir tree.

Leaping out, I gave hugs all around until I heard a muffled "Woof!"

"Okay, I'm coming!" I called. Opening the back door of the car, I released my young golden Lab/Retriever from his dog crate, snapping the leash on his collar.

"This is Yainex. He's just learning to obey, and he loves people. I'm afraid he's not much of a guard dog — he'd probably lick a burglar to death before he'd growl or bite," I said with a laugh as he eagerly pressed forward to receive pats from everyone.

"And this is Nancy, our granddaughter," my Aunt Ruth said proudly as a tanned, dark-eyed teenager with a shy smile emerged from the motorhome and walked toward us.

"Yainex and I need to stretch our legs, and I want to check out the fishing spots." I looked at Nancy. "Care to join us on a hike down to the lake?"

She nodded. "Sounds great."

We chatted as we left the campsite, and I released Yainex from his leash to explore once we were in the woods. The trail meandered through huckleberry patches and under dark fir trees along a rippling Trapper Creek. Yainex bounded back and forth, but stayed close, checking back to be sure we were following.

Finally, we emerged from the forest at the lake. Sediment had created a shallow gravel bar extending out over thirty feet from the mouth of Trapper Creek. Fishing lines cast from the bank couldn't reach the deeper water where the rainbow trout and kokanee salmon congregate in the heat of the summer.

"Do you like to fish, Nancy? Tomorrow morning we can float out past the gravel bar on the raft I brought and catch some trout."

"Sounds like fun!" Nancy replied.

Suddenly, Yainex barked. He splashed into the water toward a mallard duck swimming close to the shore.

The startled duck squawked and flew about twenty feet out into the lake, settling back down on the water.

"Yainex, come."

Totally focused on the duck, he swam after it.

My voice became more urgent. "Yainex, come here now!"

The duck quacked again and flapped its wings, traveling another thirty feet out toward the middle of the lake.

Yainex continued his pursuit of the elusive creature.

Odell Lake is deep, with the average depth of the frigid waters over a hundred feet. Terrified by the thought of hypothermia and possible drowning if he swam out too far, I called sternly, "Yainex, come! Come back here now!"

The mallard made another short hop. Yainex followed determinedly.

When the duck finally flew off across the lake Yainex turned and began to swim back toward shore.

"Good boy. Come here," I offered encouragement as he paddled through the water.

Visibly exhausted by the time he touched bottom, Yainex staggered through the shallow water of the gravel bar and onto the shore. As I reached him, he shook violently, spraying me with ice-cold water.

I hugged him, but had to scold. "You need to mind," I told him as I snapped on his leash.

"I'm glad he's okay," Nancy said, relief in her voice.

With a tired young dog in tow, we hiked back to the campsite, and then drove over to the lodge to purchase fishing licenses.

After a delicious beef-stew dinner, we roasted marshmallows over the campfire for s'mores while we told family stories and then headed off to bed. An exhausted doggy slept quietly and peacefully through the night in his crate outside the camper door.

Early the next morning, I pulled out my fishing equipment and the inflatable raft I'd packed in the trunk. Because of the unpredictable winds, I'd brought a hundred-foot-long rope to tie the raft to a tree on the shore.

I feared Yainex's claws would puncture the raft, so I left him in camp with my parents when Nancy and I carried the raft and fishing gear down to the lake. After inflating the raft, we put on life jackets, loaded our tackle, and pushed off from the shore with our paddles. Finally floating peacefully at the end of the rope, we baited our hooks and waited.

A slapping sound shattered the air like a gunshot. Startled, we turned to see a large beaver peering up at us. Then he dove, swimming back toward the mouth of the creek.

"Wow, I never saw a beaver before," Nancy exclaimed.

"Now we know why they call this Trapper Creek," I said with a smile, grateful Yainex wasn't here to chase this fellow.

Soon, we had pulled in several rainbow trout. While waiting for another bite, the sound of barking drew my attention.

I turned to see Yainex looking at us from the shore, pacing up and down. My parents emerged from the forest, calling his name. Yainex ignored them and waded into the water.

"Yainex, go back." I pointed at the shore.

He stood in the water, barking frantically. Then he stopped barking and began to swim toward us.

"Yainex, go back now!" I ordered, still pointing.

He thrashed through the icy water. As he drew near the raft, he opened his mouth and grasped the rope firmly in his teeth. Turning around, he swam back toward shore, towing us with him. Whether we liked it or not, our retriever was retrieving us!

I started reeling. "Nancy, pull in your line."

When Yainex reached the shallow water, he braced his feet and continued to tug hard on the rope. Backing up onto the shore, he pulled and pulled until the raft beached on the bank.

My laughter brought tears to my eyes, and Nancy chortled. My parents were grinning from ear to ear.

Yainex bounded to us as we disembarked, proudly wagging his tail and leaping up to give doggy kisses.

What a rescuer! Somehow recognizing danger, he wanted us to be safe on shore.

I bent down to give him a hug. "And I said you weren't a guard dog. I have to take that back. You certainly pulled us to safety today."

He taught me two big lessons that day: Always take care of those you love, and whatever you do in life… do it with enthusiasm!

— Yvonne Kays —

48

Karma

Acquiring a dog may be the only time a person
gets to choose a relative.
~Author Unknown

On a hot spring day in 2004, my father Paul and our family dog Champ made our weekly drive down to the River Valley Trail. My father had been taking me there since early childhood. I'd catch and release tadpoles, snakes, frogs and whatever other critters would let me hold them a minute. "The Creek" was also our favourite spot to let Champ run.

Being unusually hot for a spring day, neither Newfoundland-born Dad nor Cariboo-born me was fond of the heat. We cut short our outing and started driving back up the winding, dirt road. Rolling down the windows, something caught my ear, and I felt my dad press the brakes. I knew he must have heard what I had heard, although at the time I had no idea what it was other than some type of animal crying out in distress.

My dad backed over the bridge we had just crossed and parked so we could get out and pinpoint the sound. Whatever this poor animal was, it needed our help desperately.

We came to the shoreline just under the bridge, and the yelping became louder and more urgent. It came from across the creek. Knowing there was no point in convincing me otherwise, my dad found me a makeshift walking stick, and I began the trek through the water. Carefully placing one foot at a time, pausing in between steps as the current became stronger on my legs, I could only hope I would not slip. The water was deep, up to my chest, and I remember thinking, *So much for my cute white pants*, as I reached the other side.

Then I spotted her: a little grey fluff ball hiding in the shrubs, crying and fearful.

"It's a puppy!" I yelled across to my anxious dad, the relief palpable in his eyes. (I later learned he thought it might have been a bear cub.) She backed away from me, so I sat slowly on the ground, knowing if I took one more step toward her, she might fall into the raging waters below.

I sat still and talked to her gently, coaxing her, until she finally chose to trust me and melted into my arms. I held her tight against my chest, our nervous heartbeats echoing one another's. It was an instant and deep connection, but I had no idea it would last well into the next decade. With the walking stick in the other hand and a newfound determination, I stepped into the water and somehow got us both across safely to the other side, reuniting with a very relieved dad and a very curious Champ.

The puppy was hot to the touch, and we realized she was not actually grey but black. The grey was baked-on mud from the hot sun beating down on her, also meaning this tiny pup had been in that raging water.

How she ended up there, we'll never know, and the thought of her possibly having had littermates will always haunt me. But she was strong — and lucky. By some miracle, she made it to shore. And by some miracle, she cried as the right car was driving by, at the right time, with the windows down, with the right people inside. Karma. We'd call her Karma.

She slept hard on my chest for hours, only waking to eat and drink a little. Whatever journey she'd been on in her estimated four small weeks of life, I imagined it must have been a rough one. But she was safe now and in her new home.

Champ had been a spoiled, only child for the first eight years of his doggy life, so his snout was more than a bit out of joint when he realized Karma wasn't leaving. Eventually, though, he came around.

One day, as we sat on the deck admiring how Karma had begun to come out of her shell, we noticed that Champ was walking around her and then behind her. At first, we were confused as to his intentions, but then the answer clicked. He was herding her from the deck edges, blocking her from falling off. It reminded me of walking with my dad to get ice cream when I was a child. He'd casually move me to the side of his body that was farthest from the road and cars. It was an inner parenting instinct, so naturally present in both humans and animals, to protect their young. In Champ's case, he could no longer hide or deny the truth: He loved Karma. And the rest was history.

Champ and Karma spent years together as teacher and student, sharing love, adoration, adventure, and respect. Champ's bond with Karma was extraordinary, and he even came to love two additional rescues, Amy and Buddha (but that's another story).

Years went by, lives changed, and Champ was long gone. Finally, I was ready to bring another animal home that could use some TLC, so my spouse and I adopted Odin, a Pit Bull mix who had been badly injured and neglected.

We were a little nervous to bring Odin home as Karma never took easily to new dogs. But, to our amazement, the elderly Karma was thrilled. She took to Odin immediately, shocking us all! She calmed him, nurtured him, played with him, and loved him. It was like watching a re-run of a different lifetime, of her and Champ many years before.

Karma and Odin snuggle every night, and Odin loves to give Karma "nibble massages" where he gently chews her face and neck. Sometimes Karma reaches out a creaky, old paw to tap at him when he stops, asking him to continue.

Odin stares at Karma much like she once stared at Champ, and I can't help but worry about Odin's heartbreak when he loses Karma. It's hard to believe it's just shy of fifteen years since we found her. No doubt, Odin will one day pass on the love that came down to him via Champ and then Karma.

— Cassidy Porter —

49

Soul Sniffer

Compassion is so often the solution.
~Author Unknown

Einstein shifted to attention, watching the group of seventh graders as they jostled their way to my classroom. Within five minutes, the little Bichon would be asleep under my desk, unable to handle the stimulation of another group of kids who vied for his attention. It wasn't often that Einstein accompanied me to school. The noise level was a little much for him, but I thought the socialization was important for him. Plus, the kids loved it.

"Hey, Ms. Sienes. You brought Einstein today!" A couple of the girls dropped to their knees to give him a scratch and a hug, and they didn't care that twenty other kids jammed up behind them.

Einstein moaned in ecstasy as Michaela rubbed just the right spot under his chin.

"He's so cute." Her high, squeaky voice rose an octave.

"Well, he certainly likes you, kiddo."

The kids passed Einstein, one by one, and most greeted him with a quick pat on his soft head. His tail wagged in response, but he stayed glued to my side. Once everyone passed, I started to pull the door closed. Then I spotted Sam. Eyes downcast, he walked with heavy steps.

"Are you okay, Sam?" I asked when he drew closer. "It's not like you to be late." He was my most enthusiastic student and one of the brightest I had that year.

He shrugged, and then his face crumpled.

"What's wrong?" I did a quick scan for evidence of an injury, but saw nothing.

"Someone stole all my video games. I had them in my P.E. locker." Einstein stepped up to Sam and whined, as if tuned in to his mood.

"Video games? Why did you bring them to school?"

"I was gonna sell some of them. My mom's gonna be really mad. She told me to leave them at home, and now they're gone." He sniffled as tears pooled in his eyes.

"I guess that's a hard lesson in obedience." I knew my response was less than compassionate, but there always seemed to be some kind of drama with Sam.

"What am I gonna do?"

"Did you report it to the office?"

"Yeah."

"Well, there isn't anything else to do then. Let's go into the classroom and focus on the day's assignment."

I called the class to order as Einstein moved to his favorite position under my desk. This was the last of three groups of students, and he was as ready to go home as they were.

"Okay, let's go over today's quote and history mystery." That ought to get Sam's attention. His was always the first hand in the air when we had a history trivia question. But when I looked to him, his head was buried on folded arms on his desk.

"What's Sam's problem?" Quentin asked. "Somebody die or something?"

I reprimanded Quentin with a look, but found it difficult to drum up sympathy for Sam myself. Maybe a little distraction would work. "Hey, Sam. You want to give the history mystery a shot?"

Head still down, he shook it in an emphatic NO.

Best to ignore the situation. "Anyone else?" Three hands shot in the air, and Sam was all but forgotten as we got into the classroom routine.

Ten minutes later, I moved to my desk to retrieve the day's assignment and realized that Einstein was no longer there. I quickly looked at the door to be sure it was closed. The last time he came to school with me, he snuck out, and I didn't even notice until the school secretary called to say he was with her in the office. But no, the door was shut.

"Has anyone seen Einstein?"

Michaela pointed toward Sam.

I crouched down to peer under Sam's desk. Einstein's head was nestled in Sam's lap. Sam's head was still down, but he had one hand tangled in Einstein's ear. My heart melted a little at the sight of my gentle dog. He had reached out to people who needed him from the time he was a small pup. On our first ever walk in town, he tugged on his leash to get to a distraught baby in a stroller. It was in his nature to soothe and comfort.

The truth was my dog was more compassionate than me. Some days, it was a chore to deal with middle-school misery: homework that never got done; students who were more interested in who wore what than in a decent education; entitled attitudes. My heart had hardened a little each year I taught.

With my focus back on the day's agenda, I passed out the assignments and explained the objective. In the midst of being taskmaster and teacher, I'd all but forgotten about Sam's misery until I heard laughter from his side of the room.

The obvious glee drew a smile from me. "What's going on there?"

"Look at Einstein," Quentin said, finger pointed toward Sam.

Sam was upright again, a huge grin on his flushed face. Einstein had both paws on Sam's chair as he pushed his wet black nose into Sam's hand — a demand to be petted. This was not Einstein's usual M.O. He loved attention, but he never sought it out with someone he didn't know. The more Sam giggled, the more Einstein played with him.

"What's Einstein trying to do?" asked Michaela.

I laughed. "I think he wants to make Sam happy again. It looks like he's succeeded, too."

A few minutes later, his objective complete, Einstein made his way back to his place under my desk and went to sleep.

An hour later, as the class was being dismissed, Sam knelt next to

Einstein and gave him a belly rub. "You're a good boy, aren't you?" he crooned to the dog before he headed out the door with a group of boys. Smile in place, it seemed he'd all but forgotten the stolen video games.

After the classroom was empty, I dropped into my chair as Einstein eased out from under the desk. He propped his chin on my lap with a sigh.

"You certainly are a good boy," I whispered to him before I dropped a kiss on his downy soft head. "I need to be more like you, buddy." I combed his silky soft ears with my fingers as a lump of shame rose in my throat.

He had well-tuned radar for the broken and sorrowful, and it was his nature to bring a little love and compassion to each soul he encountered. It was a lesson I needed to be reminded of more often. That day, my sweet dog was the teacher.

— Jennifer Sienes —

50

Spreading Sunshine

Dogs don't rationalize. They don't hold anything against
a person. They don't see the outside of a human
but the inside of a human.
~Cesar Millan

I finally received the call. My therapy-dog mentor was on the line, ready to give me our first assignment. "Jill, I'm hoping that you'll consider taking a difficult assignment. It's for a long-term-care home in a tough, low-income neighborhood. These people really need to have a therapy dog in their facility, and I'm having a difficult time filling this position. Will you do it?"

I looked down at my dog, Sunshine. She looked up at me, her tail wagging. I didn't hesitate. "Yes," I said. "We'll do it."

Three years before that fateful phone call, Sunshine was found outside the city pound one cold morning. Her eyes were swollen shut from infection. When a dog rescue was notified that a beautiful Golden Retriever was on death row, they came to pick her up and take her to a veterinarian for surgery. One of the rescue volunteers told me, "Sunshine never stopped wagging her tail. She knew we were there to help her."

I had called the rescue looking for a dog, and that's when I heard about Sunshine. When we went to the rescue to see her, she ran to my husband and sat down beside him. He looked up at me and smiled. "I guess she's coming home with us!" After all she had been through — being abandoned and suffering — Sunshine was eager to forgive and move forward.

When Sunshine and I started our therapy-dog sessions, I soon discovered that walking with her through the halls of the long-term care facility was like being in the presence of a movie star. The residents adored her, and she reciprocated. Once, when we were leaving, a caregiver came up to me with a lady in a wheelchair and asked if we could visit. The lady saw Sunshine, and her eyes lit up. With her hands shaking, she cupped Sunshine's head and began to whisper to her. The caregiver was stunned. "Amazing," she said. "Ethel hasn't spoken to anyone in years." Yet, we could distinctly hear her telling Sunshine how lovely she was.

Beautiful miracles like that happened all the time. One instance occurred with a new arrival at the home, a gentleman who was once a farmer. When he saw Sunshine, tears started to roll down his cheeks. "You don't know what this means to me," he said. "I never thought I would see a dog again." He then began to reminisce about the dogs he had in the past. As we were leaving, his wife mouthed a tearful "thank you."

The residents wanted to give back, too. The majority of them had very little — they lived in a home with the barest of amenities. But these people would save sandwiches or cookies from their plates and offer them to Sunshine. One resident in particular tried to give me a quarter to "help pay for Sunshine's food." It touched me deeply. Perhaps these folks didn't have a lot, but they wanted to give what they could because they were so appreciative that we visited them.

We were also assigned to the Alzheimer/dementia floor in the long-term care facility, and this is where I witnessed Sunshine's forgiveness once again. A gentleman was patting her and humming to her. Suddenly, he struck her hard across her face. I was absolutely horrified and pulled Sunshine away, but she had other ideas. Calmly, she walked back over to the man and placed her head on his lap. He continued to stroke her head and hum. That was the power of Sunshine. She quickly forgave whatever horror befell her, whether it was being abandoned at the pound, blind and alone, or being hit by a stranger.

We volunteered for six years until Sunshine started to have

difficulties with arthritis. I often think of the power of her love for humankind. She had been neglected and abandoned in her past, yet continued to give unconditional love and affection to everyone she met. Sunshine's lesson of forgiveness and her willingness to connect had a lasting impact on so many lives, especially mine.

—Jill Anne Berni—

51

Brodie

When I needed a hand, I found your paw.
~Author Unknown

My daughter's voice quivered over the phone as she traveled back from a volleyball tournament. "I don't know if colleges will want me now, Mom. I can't believe this happened!"

At the age of sixteen, well on her way to an athletic scholarship, Bree had torn her ACL. The fallout was devastating. While friends were going to prom, and her club team was getting ready for nationals, she sat with ice on her knee and faced weeks of physical therapy before surgery.

It was going to be a long haul, but my daughter was a fighter; she'd rise above this injury. Still, I thought she needed a friend. That's when Brodie came into our lives.

A jet-black Labrador/Spaniel mix, Brodie was a year old when I rescued her from the pound. In appearance, she was all Lab, but the Spaniel genes had kept her stature puppy-like. People always commented, "What a cute puppy," despite her age.

Brodie eased my daughter's pain and disappointment and became a vital part of our family.

The physical therapy, surgery, and strengthening of Bree's knee took a year, but it paid off. She was back on the volleyball court with her high-school team and playing club ball once again. She received a full scholarship to a Division 1 school.

With Bree away at college, my husband working erratic hours, and my job requiring travel, we faced another dilemma. Who would care for Brodie?

At a family gathering, my cousin confided how lonely his dad had been since my aunt had passed away. "What do you think about Brodie keeping your dad company?" I suggested. So off she went to a new home. She and my uncle became fast friends, and Brodie was just a few towns away, which allowed me to visit whenever I felt the need.

A year later, my uncle sold his house to move to a nursing home. Luckily, my husband's schedule had eased up, and we brought Brodie back into our lives.

Brodie traveled with us when we'd visit family in Michigan. My father-in-law and Brodie hit it off from the start. "She's such a great dog," he'd say as he tapped her snout and handed her treat after treat.

"It's no wonder Brodie nestles up to you," my mother-in-law laughed.

When my dear mother-in-law passed away, my father-in-law was so lonely. They had been married more than sixty years. He called often to ask, "When are you visiting and bringing Brodie?"

My husband and I discussed having Brodie live with his dad. We never asked my father-in-law if it was okay; we just assumed it was. The next time we visited, we had all of Brodie's essentials with us. "Surprise! Someone wants to move in with you," we announced as we arrived.

They thrived together. Each visit, Dad regaled us with a new "doggie tale," and we watched Brodie become the healer once again.

Three years later, my father-in-law passed away. We were grateful we'd been able to help Dad through his loss. He and Brodie had been inseparable.

We brought Brodie back home. She was as sweet as ever, old soul that she was by then, with her graying snout. She had helped so many people, but she had one more important mission.

My husband's job now demanded travel as well. Luckily, someone was always home for Brodie, but our luck ran out when Bree left for Florida to start her career after finishing her master's degree.

I was stressed when we left for days at a time. I couldn't bear to leave Brodie in a kennel repeatedly.

A few weeks before Christmas, I overheard two clients talking at work. Amy was explaining about her seven-year-old son who had all but given up on Santa Claus bringing him what he wanted. As she approached my desk, I asked her about the situation.

"My son's been asking Santa for a puppy since he was four," she sighed, "but I don't have the time or patience to go through the puppy stage. I don't want to chance an older dog, not knowing if it's properly trained or kid-friendly. I wish a dog would drop from the sky, housebroken, kid-friendly, and loving. I'm worried because my son has become more withdrawn. He has very few friends. I was hoping he'd outgrow this, but it's getting worse."

I nodded as I thought about Brodie and her healing ways.

"He said he tries to be good so that Santa will bring him a dog," Amy explained. "He told me, 'That way, Mom, I'll have a real friend.'" She wiped away a tear.

"Amy, do you believe in miracles?" I asked, as I squeezed her hand.

The next week, Amy and her husband met Brodie. They were smitten with her and pleased that she still looked like a puppy. We plotted and planned excitedly, and made all the necessary arrangements. They came for Brodie on Christmas Eve.

That Christmas morning, Amy's son opened a box full of love that would forever change his life.

"It was a beautiful moment." Amy beamed at me. "It was love at first sight for both of them."

Now, it was Amy who regaled me with "doggie tales" whenever I'd see her. Her son was a new person; he was coming out of his shell. His grades had improved, and his circle of friends grew. Plus, Santa was back on his good side!

The first time Amy brought Brodie and her son to see me at work, she cautioned, "Remember, Santa brought Brodie. You can't act as if you know her." That was hard because Brodie jumped excitedly when she saw me, licked me to death and nudged to be close.

"Wow! She really, really likes you, Mrs. Feist!" Amy's son said, laughing.

Brodie happily lived out the rest of her years with Amy's family. We moved to Florida to be near our daughter, and Amy kindly kept me abreast of all things Brodie.

Having lived a long and purposeful life, Brodie died cradled in the loving arms of a grateful family. "Brodie saved my son," Amy confided.

Every time I think of Brodie, I smile. Although she was in and out of our lives, and many goodbye tears were shed, she was never truly gone. Even now, she remains in many hearts.

The day I walked into the pound and saw that sweet soul, I thought I was doing the rescuing. But really, all along, it was Brodie.

— Linda Feist —

52

Stormin' Norman

Dogs are our link to paradise. They don't know
evil or jealousy or discontent.
~Milan Kundera

My Schnauzer trained himself to become a therapy dog. Impossible, you say? Well, think again.

I rescued "Stormin' Norman the Superhero" when he was a puppy, back when I was a married woman, and before I fell off a ladder and seriously injured my back.

Six weeks after the ladder fall, I had surgery. Six weeks after that, it was obvious the back surgery didn't work. I never thought I'd be one of the 20 percent who weren't "cured" by this major surgery, but it happened despite staying immobile for months, as prescribed, and following all my doctor's orders for physical therapy, etcetera. The result was continuous chronic pain, sure to be a lifelong issue.

Norman ignored me during the first part of this so-called recovery phase. Unfortunately, my husband Gil ignored me, too. Within a short time, Gil became cruel in his complaints about how incapacitated I was. He accused me of faking it and using the pain as an excuse to get out of household tasks. I spent nearly a year on the verge of tears each day and hurting myself more by attempting to take out the trash, clean the tub, and cater to my husband's wishes.

As I struggled, Norman began to pay more attention to me, giving me loving looks and sticking close. I thought it was sweet, but thought nothing more than that. After eleven months of mistreatment from my husband, I left him.

Norman and I moved to a condo about twenty miles away. I worried that the dog would miss his sister, Della the Boxer, or his overprotective daddy, but there was no evidence of that. In fact, Norman's entire focus turned on me, the suddenly single, disabled, fifty-something woman on her own.

For the first time, I didn't have a fenced back yard. I would have to walk the dog, and I worried how I could keep up with that responsibility on the tough days. I did the best I could, but I needn't have worried. The first thing that changed was Norman's morning routine.

For chronic pain sufferers, mornings are difficult; it takes over an hour for the medicine to take effect and the stiffness to abate. Norman didn't ask to go out for that first hour as if he instantly trained his bladder to match my schedule.

My friends tried to explain the mystery of a suddenly accommodating Norman by saying he must be hearing my mumbled groans and know when I was not ready for a walk. At first, I agreed with them, based on my ex-husband's brazen complaints about my "sickening moans and groans all the time."

Then on a cold day in November, as I struggled to unload the groceries from my car, I left a few bags on the garage floor. As I put away the items I had brought inside with me, Norman dragged another bag into the kitchen, and then turned and ran for another. One by one, he brought each bag into the kitchen.

The following week, he brought the groceries inside again, and again the next week. Every so often, his canine nature took priority though. Once I found him in the garage eating a pound of hamburger meat, plastic and all. I learned to tell the grocery bagger how to double-bag and double-knot the yummy stuff, and there hasn't been a problem since.

Norman used to be independent, ignorant of all needs but his own. That's how he was raised and the nature of the breed. Now he follows me from room to room to make sure I don't need any help, like spinning the toilet paper off the roll, which he's done several times when I couldn't.

He whines until I wake from the sofa and urges me to bed. (How did he learn that sleeping on the sofa hurt me so badly?) He jumps to pick up things I drop on the floor and waits for me to take them from his mouth. (He's short, so it doesn't help much, but he certainly does it in an effort to help.) He comes to me at my desk and whines until I join him on the sofa, herding me like Lassie, somehow knowing the need to rest my back several times a day.

Schnauzers aren't prone to be "people pleasers." They're known as stubborn dogs, hard to train and control. By nature, Schnauzers are vermin chasers with traits directly opposed to those of typical therapy or companion dogs. Unlike a Labrador, Collie or Shepherd, they resist cuddling and coddling. Prior to our move, that described Norman to a tee.

Now everything is different.

The longer Norman and I live alone, the stronger is his determination to be my helper. In the last few months, he's brought my cell phone to me when it rings, learned the command "just a minute" with my simple index-finger-up gesture, and dragged the basket of folded clothes from the laundry room to the closet. He's learned when our morning walks are too painful for me and hurries to do his business on those days, leading me back home and directly to the sofa.

Stormin' Norman is always on the lookout for more ways to help. The result is an easier life for a disabled woman and an all-encompassing love for a dog that obviously loves me, too.

My superhero, indeed. He protects me from hurting and over-exerting myself, and he stands bravely to protect me from things that go bump in the night.

The story ends with good news on two fronts. Through a series of networks, I was able to see a specialist who did radiofrequency ablation on three areas of my back. My pain has been reduced by 50 percent or more, and the relief will last six to twelve months!

I also received good news from Norman's vet. Even at age eight, he's 100 percent healthy and ready to live well into his teens, as most Schnauzers do.

My friend, my champion, my Stormin' Norman the Superhero.

— Patricia Ayers —

My Very Good, Very Bad Dog

53

Cookie's Secret Life

Any glimpse into the life of an animal quickens
our own and makes it so much larger
and better in every way.
~John Muir

We live almost a half-mile from the nearest paved road, surrounded by woods and fields, with only a few homes cut into the miles of green. It was always quiet, but when we adopted our Golden Retriever, Cookie, she soon changed that. She would charge out the door every morning at dawn, pushing one or both children aside and trampling a cat or two. Then she would go roaring into the woods barking and galloping, almost prancing.

Sometimes, she would come back when I hollered, but mostly she ignored me and returned later on her own schedule, wagging her big, feathery tail. I could tell she was trying to look regretful, but her overall body language was absolute glee.

I kept threatening to track her, to see where she went all the time. But I had two small children and zero interest in getting out of my PJs that early.

Finally, one day, I saw her picture on Facebook. She was on a back deck that wasn't ours, enjoying a snack with a big guy who wasn't mine, outside a ranch house that wasn't hers.

"What is thisssss?" I asked her.

She said nothing.

The neighbor was due north, accessible only over a fence and through a vegetable garden.

It was a blow to the ego. I always wanted to get a photo with my dog, but Cookie had refused every selfie I'd tried to take with her.

The disappearances escalated. Just when I'd assume she was having a cold one with the strangers next door, she'd come loping down our long driveway from the opposite direction.

Finally, that fall, I tracked her. We have a community walking trail in the woods out back. It's a combination of our property and the neighbors' and has turned into a nice meeting place for the neighborhood dogs.

It was early, and I followed Cookie out the door on a whim, in my rattiest sweatpants, my husband's oversized sweatshirt and a pair of slippers. The grass was still wet with dew, but I was determined to follow that dog.

About five paces into the woods, I encountered another neighbor. Roger looked unforgivably dapper, as always. He turned to Cookie as if I didn't exist, a nod of respect to my state of dress.

"Greetings, Cookie," he said.

"Hello, Savannah," I countered, patting his dog's head.

We had an entire conversation through the dogs. "What is that you said, Savannah?"

"She says she loves your new house siding."

Finally, I went back inside with Cookie and accused her of taking walks every morning with Savannah but without me.

Again, she said nothing.

The very next day, I got a call from Barb, a neighbor up front. A little worry went through me. We weren't the types to call and chat.

"Hello?" I asked, quickly running through how to do CPR in my head.

But no, it wasn't necessary. "Do you realize your dog has been here all day?"

"All day?" I said, stalling. Oh, dear. The last I'd seen Cookie, she was barreling out the back door at dawn headed for Savannah. To my credit, I was so busy working that I was still dressed in last night's hiking outfit.

"Well?" Barb asked. I cringed.

What would she say next?

"Can Cookie stay for dinner?"

I heard Barb popping open a can of soft food. I stared at the day-old dry food in Cookie's bowl and hung up. Cookie wasn't losing her appetite after all, as I had feared. (Note: My neighbors had never asked *me* over for dinner.)

Finally, I had a chance meeting at the grocery store with another neighbor, Mary.

"I'm worried," she said, as we walked out to the parking lot together.

"What's happened?" I asked.

"I haven't seen Cookie in a week," she said, bracing herself for a moment. "Is she okay?"

Well, we'd been on vacation. Cookie had been gone for a week, but so had our entire family. Mary hadn't noticed that.

But before I could answer, she saw my car and its occupant.

"Oh, my Lord, you have her right here. Cookie!" she squealed. I had to open the back hatch — not to put in my groceries, but to allow Mary and Cookie a reunion.

"Now, hold on," she said. She produced a dog biscuit the size of Cookie's head from her purse. Cookie went crazy.

"Wow, thanks, Mary. See you back at home!" I said, giving her the heave-ho. The pieces were coming together. (But first I waited her out so I could go back into the store and buy gigantic dog biscuits and soft dog food, the best money could buy. It was becoming apparent that I would have to woo my own dog.)

Finally, I had my answer. My dog had a secret life. She was taking walks, eating meals and scoring dog biscuits at five houses that I knew of.

I got home and reported my findings to my husband, and we broke the news to our kids together: Cookie had another family. Several, in fact.

But they were delighted. It was like finding out we had a celebrity in our midst. And it turned out to be the beginning of something wonderful: We followed Cookie to all of the neighbors' houses after that, and the friendships blossomed for us, too. Our neighborhood that was once sprawling and separate became connected and approachable, thanks to Cookie the Golden Retriever and her secret life. I love that when I walk her now, I know everyone. Or, I should say, everyone knows her!

But if I see one of the neighbors set up a fan page for her on Facebook, I'm drawing the line.

— Kandace Chapple —

54

He Who Laughs Last Is the "Wiener"

It's not the size of the dog in the fight;
it's the size of the fight in the dog.
~Mark Twain

Combining households with my parents created some interesting dynamics, not the least of which was putting together their dog and mine. After a few weeks, my parents' Dachshund, Rowdy, and our 100-pound Shepherd, Glocken, appeared to be getting along just fine even with their size disparity, although the two rarely played together.

Wisdom usually comes with age, and as the wise old man of the pair, I suspect that Rowdy knew he would end up losing any such mismatched game. Of course, that didn't stop Glocken, who was still somewhat of a puppy, from occasionally picking on his smaller companion.

One afternoon we were outside with the dogs and Glocken bounded across the yard, holding a tennis ball in his mouth. He ran circles around Rowdy, narrowly missing the older dog each time. Finally, he hopped back and forth, stopping just short of the Dachshund's nose, and then took off running again.

Through the course of several such assaults, Rowdy stood his ground, never flinching. Instead, he gazed up at Glocken with a long, sad expression. And, as we would find out later, he was plotting retaliation.

After several minutes of jousting with Rowdy, Glocken finally grew weary. He dropped the tennis ball and ran across the yard in search of something more interesting.

Without missing a beat, the small dog strolled across the patio to the ball, lifted his back leg, and took his revenge. My husband and I looked at each other in disbelief and roared with laughter.

I'm fairly certain I saw a smile on Rowdy's face as he walked away.

— Kathy Harris —

55

No Snacks for Judy

The belly rules the mind.
~Spanish Proverb

She was a lovable little bundle of fur. A six-week-old newly weaned pup, she snuggled against my chest as I held her. I had a name picked out for her, but for some reason my sister Alice began calling her Judy, and the name stuck. Judy was a Heinz 57 variety of pet, with long ears that showed there was some hound in her.

When I wasn't in school or sleeping, we were inseparable. She was so sweet and friendly, she became a toy for every kid on the block. She never nipped or growled when they'd fold her long ears over her eyes. Short and mid-sized, she'd tolerate the little kids climbing on her back; somehow she understood that they were just playing.

Just over a year after Judy arrived, we discovered she was pregnant. When she had her litter, she became the doting mother to four little fur balls who looked remarkably like she did when she was a puppy. So she would not have more litters, my parents decided Judy should be spayed. Mom took her to the veterinarian and came back with some startling news. The vet said Judy was overweight and could not be safely spayed unless she lost weight. So it was no more table scraps or snacks between meals, just three small meals per day. But after a few weeks, her weight had not come down, not even a pound.

One day, there was a knock on our door; it was a neighbor. She hated to complain, she said, but our dog was raiding her garbage can every day, and the cans of many other neighbors, too. Apparently, Judy was having nothing to do with the diet we had put her on; she was finding her snacks elsewhere!

After surveying the neighborhood and asking all the neighbors to please put their garbage can lids on tightly every day, we figured the problem was solved.

But Judy still did not lose weight. In fact, now she was gaining even more. A quick survey of the neighborhood — again — and we were assured by each and every neighbor that she was no longer able to get into their garbage cans. But she continued to gain weight, and we absolutely could not figure out how.

Then one day I inadvertently stumbled upon the answer. I went to one of my favorite places five blocks from home — the ice-cream parlor. As usual, Judy tagged along. As I sat outside enjoying my ice-cream cone, one of my young friends came by.

"I see your dog brought you along today," he said.

"What do you mean?" I asked.

"Well, she comes by here every day begging us for ice cream."

"And you feed her?"

"Sure," he said, "we all do. She loves ice cream."

Horrified at this news, I quickly explained that we were trying to slim her down. Then I gave stern instructions to him and his friends never to feed her again.

That did the trick. Soon, she lost the weight and was spayed successfully. She remained my pet for years — mellow, happy, and a great companion.

When I think back, I have to chuckle at her cleverness. On one of our visits to the ice-cream parlor when she was a puppy, I'd given her a taste of ice cream. Once she was put on her diet and could no longer rummage through the neighbors' garbage, she remembered the ice-cream parlor and learned quickly it was where she could be fed easily — and with a delicacy, at that!

— Kay Presto —

56

I Should Have Remembered

Dogs love to go for rides. A dog will happily get into
any vehicle going anywhere.
~Dave Barry

The windshield wipers are on high as I drive up I-84 to West Hartford. Without warning, swirls of fog surround my car. Lousy weather isn't going to stop me from honoring my granddaughter at an awards ceremony this evening.

My son had told me that they'd had a new fence installed around the perimeter of their back yard to keep Sydney, their fluffy gray Bichon/ Shih Tzu mix, from wandering. The fence's white plastic gleams as I pull into their driveway. I sling my overnight bag over my shoulder, looking forward to having a cup of tea in the warm kitchen while I wait for everyone to get home.

I need two hands to unlatch the gate—one to unhook, one to pull. Once inside the house, I'm met with a fluffy bundle of love who insists on giving me his wet doggy kisses. His tail doesn't wag; it swishes. It's going double time now. Sydney may greet everyone with the same enthusiasm, but I like to think he saves this greeting for special people like me.

"Be right back, Sydney," I tell him as I go out the open door to my car. I'll need both hands to bring the apple pie I'd baked into the house, so I also leave the gate open. The pie is still warm as I carefully lift it from the back seat. I use my hip to close the car door. Back in the kitchen, I throw my dripping raincoat on a chair, fill a mug with water and stick it in the microwave.

I crave company. "Sydney, Sydney," I call walking through the downstairs rooms. No response. *That's odd,* I think as I go upstairs. *He was just here. Maybe he went outside.*

There's a March chill in the air as I search the fenced yard. Then I have an aha moment. I'd left the back door and gate open when I brought in the pie. The little stinker! He probably used the opportunity to visit his friends. I rush out to the sidewalk in front of the house. "Sydney, Sydney!" I shout as I jog up one side of the street and down the other. Every house is buttoned up tight. This family-friendly street is a few blocks long and is bookended by two roads with double-yellow lines down their middle. I can hear the cars speeding from where I stand.

If Sydney were a black Lab, I'd be able to see him, I think. But no, he's the color of fog, which is getting denser and denser. I can hear the *thump-thump, thump-thump* of my heart as panic bubbles inside me. I dash back to the house to call my son.

"Chip, I can't find Sydney," I blurt out while trying to catch my breath between words.

"Mom, I can't understand you — speak slower," says my son in his best psychologist voice.

"I CAN'T FIND SYDNEY!" I explain what happened. "Chip, which houses do his friends live in? I can go into their back yards and look there."

"Mom, calm down. No one's out today. Everyone's at work. Sydney loves to hide; look under the beds."

"Okay, but I don't think he's there. We're just wasting time."

I look under every bed, sofa, bookcase and chair. There are lots of dust bunnies the same color and texture as Sydney, but that's where the similarity ends. I call my son again. "He's not here!"

His calmness crumbles. "I'm running out to my car now, but it will be at least forty minutes until I get home."

I return to the street to retrace my steps. "SYDNEY, SYDNEY!" I don't know if I'm shaking because I'm cold and wet or because of fear.

The grandchildren's faces flash before me. How can I explain this to them? If only they were coming home right after school, then they could help me search, but that's not happening today. I look at my watch — 3:15 — and they won't be home until 6:00. By then, it will be dark.

My phone rings. "Mom, have you found Sydney yet?"

"No," I wail. The kids' faces flash before me again, but this time their mother's face joins them. Sydney is her love, and she is his. They'll all hate me forever and ever. There'll be no forgiving.

The vision of Sydney being run over by a car unnerves me. He's so small that someone might not know they hit him. "Okay, Polly," I say to myself out loud. "Pull up your big-girl pants. Get in your car and find him."

Chip calls again. "I just pulled onto 84." He doesn't have to tell me he's speeding; mothers know this type of thing.

"Be careful," I say, but he's hung up.

I return to the house. The aroma of the apple pie taunts me as I dash into the kitchen for my car keys. *I'll start on this street, return home just in case Sydney's there, and repeat on every block until Chip gets home.* I unlock my car, open the door, slide behind the wheel and pull the seatbelt across my shoulder. My hand touches something soft. GASP! SYDNEY! A little gray-and-white furry head with soulful black eyes looks up at me and yawns. I hug him so hard I fear he might pop.

He must have hopped into the back seat when I was unloading the pie, and then jumped into the front seat and snuggled up in my sweatshirt for a nap.

How silly of me to forget how much Sydney loves to ride in the car.

— Polly Hare Tafrate —

57

Shell Game

Never trust a dog to watch your food.
~Author Unknown

I came home to find hazelnut shells were strewn across the gray living-room carpet. How, I wondered, had all those shells ended up on the floor?

The shallow bowl on the coffee table still contained a number of walnuts and almonds, none of which had been damaged. However, every single hazelnut had been cracked open, and the meat extracted.

Who would break into our home and eat just our hazelnuts? Surely our Border Collie mix, Sneeks, would have scared off an intruder.

Then I looked at Sneeks. She stared back at me, trying to look innocent.

How had she even discovered that she liked just one kind of nut of the three that we had in the bowl? I imagined it started out as a game — picking up a nut, tossing it on the floor, pouncing on it — and then, perhaps, chomping down and discovering the tasty morsel housed inside that hard casing. After that, with typical Border Collie obsessiveness, Sneeks would have fixated on cracking those nuts until every last one had been opened.

Fortunately, my dog suffered no ill effects from her unusual menu choice. She'd earned her nickname Old Iron Guts with good reason.

As for me, I've continued the tradition of putting out trays of nuts around Christmas, with one caveat — serving bowls are placed well out of reach of all canine household members.

Just in case someone wants to try an encore.

—Lisa Timpf—

58

A Bad Puppy

The average dog has one request
to all humankind. Love me.
~Helen Exley

My granddaughter borrowed the little puppy from our neighbors. She only wanted to play with him for the day, she told us, and then give him back. He was a backyard-bred Chihuahua. He didn't look like his mother, father, or any of the other brown dogs they owned. He had beautiful, soft, white long hair interspersed with large and small spots of black short hair.

The next day, she borrowed the puppy again. They had sold all of the other puppies. He was the only one left for sale. He had been sold once, but the new owners had returned him within a week. He was a bad puppy, too hard to handle. He wasn't house-trained, he liked to chew on things, and his constant biting of fingers, legs, and toes, with those sharp baby teeth, was painful.

The next day, she borrowed the puppy again. We didn't want a dog, and we especially didn't want this annoying little Chihuahua. We had recently lost Sam, our wonderful, well-trained, lovable German Shepherd mix. We were still in mourning and not ready for another dog.

Then she brought the borrowed puppy home with great news. The neighbors were willing to give her the puppy for free. She was delighted. We were torn. They wanted to be rid of the "bad" puppy.

My granddaughter's pleading blue eyes won out, and we decided to give the puppy a home. But after two weeks, I was fed up. I had made no progress in training him. I have trained many dogs and had never had one so deliberately disobedient. He was not the slightest bit house-trained, had the annoying habit of chewing our shoelaces as we tried to walk, and constantly nipped at our legs.

One day, as I stood yelling "no" at the puppy attached to my shoe, my son offered to help. He went to the kitchen and retrieved two pan lids. The plan was for me to say "no" and for him to bang the lids at the same time, startling the puppy into letting go. Ready, set, "NO!" *Bang, Bang, Bang!* The puppy didn't let go; he didn't even flinch. We tried bigger lids, a spoon banging on a pan, and a horn. No reaction. The puppy seemed to be completely deaf.

We debated whether to give back the puppy. We knew nothing about deaf dogs. Was there any possibility he would ever be manageable? What if we couldn't house-train him? What if he didn't stop biting, and when he got bigger, he bit one of the kids hard enough to draw blood?

But we knew we were this puppy's last chance. So we decided to try.

We named him Toby, even though he didn't know it. I started researching how to train deaf dogs and discovered the beauty of American Sign Language. Anything one can say to a hearing dog can be communicated to a deaf dog. The first thing I taught him was the sign for "Look at me" — two fingers pointed toward my eyes. If the puppy wasn't watching, he wouldn't know what I wanted him to do. The second thing I taught him was "sit." It worked; he sat on command. We were ecstatic. There was hope.

Then we started house-breaking. I used the defecating sign for "Do you want to go out?" and the finger waggle to say, "No." He finally understood what we wanted him to do. He stopped messing in the house. With that success, many more signs followed. Some were true to their meaning. Two fingers across the palm means "Let's go for a walk." Some I improvised. The shortcut "I love you" sign means "Come here, and I'll scratch your backside." I probably shouldn't have taught him the "bath" sign because he runs and hides every time I use it.

There are only a few things we do differently because Toby is deaf. If someone knocks at the door, I tell Toby that someone is there before I jump up to open it. Deaf dogs tend to startle easily, so I let him know what is going on ahead of time. If I want him to leave a room or come in the house at night, I flick the lights on and off quickly. But most of the time he keeps his eyes on me. I think he even keeps one eye open when he's sleeping.

Once one becomes accustomed to using sign language, it's as natural as speaking. I can say anything to Toby, from "It's time for bed" to "Where's your baby?" and his favorite, "Do you want a treat?" It's so easy to communicate with him that we sometimes forget he's deaf. And he's very good at conveying what he needs or wants. Toby has the most expressive eyes I have ever seen in a dog.

Toby has become a loving cuddle bug. He has never bitten anyone, but he does like to lick. He doesn't chew on things, not even his stuffed babies. He carries them and places them around the house. He understands everything I say, sometimes to the extent I think he's reading my mind. And he is my little shadow, never far from my side.

I am so thankful that Toby came into our lives. We needed him as much as he needed us. He filled a very large hole in our hearts. We almost missed out on knowing and loving a remarkable little dog because no one understood that he didn't understand. Today, it would be hard to recognize him as the "bad" puppy he used to be. Toby is a delightful and cherished member of our family.

— Vickie J. Litten —

The Hot Dog Thief

You can trust your dog to guard your house,
but never trust your dog to guard your sandwich.
~Author Unknown

The whole family clustered around the computer screen, oohing and aahing. The face on the shelter's website was irresistible: a beautiful, white-and-liver Pointer/Hound mix with big floppy ears and the saddest, most expressive brown eyes we'd ever seen on a dog. Under the photo it said, "Jerome loves hot dogs."

Our son Patrick and his girlfriend were home for Thanksgiving weekend. It didn't take long to convince the whole family to visit the shelter. We called ahead so they were ready for us. We walked in together, five adults coming through the door at the same time, but Jerome knew which human he wanted. He walked right up to Patrick, put his paws on his shoulders and licked his face. It was love at first sight — on both sides. We didn't even need the hot dogs the shelter staff had cut up to help us get Jerome's attention.

The shelter had a waiting period, but Patrick convinced them to hurry along the process. He had to be back at his job in Philadelphia on Monday. After a quick reference check with our vet, they agreed. So on Sunday Pat packed the trunk of his girlfriend's car with their luggage — including a three-pound box of the best hometown hot dogs (the ones all locals bring back from every visit home). They made Jerome comfy on a blanket in the back seat and waved a happy goodbye as they pulled out of our driveway.

Patrick and Renee headed south on I-81 for Philly, radio blasting, and marveling at how well-behaved and quiet their new charge appeared to be. It wasn't until the Allentown rest stop, about two hours down the road, that they found out why.

Jerome had been hard at work, chewing through the back seat — upholstery, stuffing, trunk wall and all — until he reached his prize. Every one of those hot dogs was gone, and Jerome had the biggest smile on his face.

Patrick was proud of his best friend's ingenuity, and he ended up having plenty to be proud about over the coming years. We'd eagerly await his phone calls home to hear about Jerome's latest heist. He devoured whole roasts, loaves of bread and thawing pork chops, pushing the wrappers under the stove as if Pat wouldn't notice the missing meat.

In his most celebrated caper, Jerome ate an entire pepperoni pizza while Patrick was tipping the delivery driver. He closed up the box and nudged it back into the center of the coffee table as if it had been delivered empty. It was almost the perfect crime. Only his pizza breath gave him away.

In Jerome's later years, Patrick moved back to our town, and his dad and I helped care for the old guy. Because of his aching hips, Jerome had a hard time getting to sleep and wanted someone near him until he dozed off. When Pat was at work, I took to singing a lullaby with lyrics adapted just for Jerome. Each verse would have a different one of his favorite foods: "Dream of pork chops," I'd croon. Or Brie cheese, pizza, biscuits… But his favorite verse, the one that always got Jerome to doze off, was: "Dream of hot dogs, dream of hot dogs. Sleep."

Jerome lived to the ripe old age of sixteen. He proudly wore scars from a fight to the death with an opossum, lost most of his teeth, survived a congenital heart murmur and ached in nearly every joint in his body. But he never lost his love for food… or his trickster ways.

— Michele Bazan Reed —

Idle Paws

No matter how little money and how few possessions
you own, having a dog makes you rich.
~Louis Sabin

We unlocked the vestibule door leading to our apartment. There were only two doors inside, and one was ours. It led directly upstairs to our nice but basic one-bedroom-plus-loft apartment in a north shore town of the majestic and breathtakingly beautiful Lake Tahoe. Recently, we had had the good fortune to move up from the lower studio apartment, which had been rather dark and dungeon-like. We could barely afford our new place, but feared we would turn into moles if we remained downstairs much longer.

As we approached our door, we noticed a strange substance peeking out from underneath it. It was pinkish in color and had a somewhat fluffy look to it. Confused, we opened the door carefully and then, recognizing what it was, we gasped in horror.

Several weeks prior, we had broken the rules of our complex when we were won over by a little bundle of golden-colored cuteness in a box at the nearby laundromat. There was only one puppy left, and it was desperate to come home with us, or so we told ourselves. How hard could it be to hide a puppy as cute as this one? We named her Schotzi and snuck her in, along with all the necessities for a thriving Retriever mix.

She grew quickly, as did our attachment to her, but this was going to be a trial of our devotion. The pink, fluffy substance was insulation and had come from the wall of the stairwell. The stairs were carpeted, as was a strip just above the stair treads, which was then finished off with rustic wood trim. Schotzi had decided to tear off a section of the carpet midway on the staircase and rip it to shreds. Then she proceeded to dig through the drywall and into the insulation, leaving just one more layer before she would have broken through into the neighbor's apartment. That would have surely gotten us kicked out. The debris field spread from the scene of the crime down to the entrance.

After scolding her, we cleaned up the mess and then wondered how to repair her renovation project. Luckily, the apartment had come equipped with a very fancy doormat — a scrap from the carpeting. We stuffed the hole with newspaper and then cut a piece of our "doormat" to fit the missing section. Near catastrophe averted. But with a young pup, it's never that easy.

Schotzi busied herself during the day in the usual ways. I came home from work most nights to chewed-up photos and shoes — usually just one shoe from each pair. At night, she jumped in bed with me, but when Robert came home from work and began to scoot her to the middle of the bed, she would growl. It never went further than that; she just wanted to let him know she didn't appreciate the disturbance. After all, a girl needs her beauty rest.

As she got even bigger, we stopped allowing her in the bed at night, but she didn't give up without a fight. Early each morning, we would be awakened by a big brown nose peering over the top of the mattress. Next, it would be joined by two ever-growing front paws. Soon, her whole head would be propped up on the edge of the bed until she just couldn't control herself and jumped up on the bed. She was our firstborn, so it was hard to tell her "no." Perhaps we spoiled her just a bit.

Being that we were a very young married couple working in the local hotel/casinos, we barely scraped by with rent and living expenses each month. We found that furnishing an apartment was a real challenge. Previously, we had bought a cheaply made bedroom ensemble and a secondhand kitchen set from my boss. It was a white

Formica table with black legs and six matching chairs with silver glittery vinyl — yikes! We had no living-room furniture, so we were pleased to find a brown-and-gold plaid loveseat/sofa bed in the loft when we moved in. The loveseat was in fairly good shape, so we somehow got it moved down from the loft and used it as the main piece of our living-room furniture.

Schotzi enjoyed all the furniture. She would jump onto one of the vinyl chairs every morning in the hopes of sharing a bowl of Cheerios with us. And she would gladly take up the whole loveseat as she stretched out to enjoy whatever was playing on our tiny TV set.

But then, one afternoon, we returned home together and walked up the stairs to find her in the throes of another redecorating project. She stood on what was left of the loveseat, digging furiously with her front paws while ripping and shaking the upholstery with her teeth. The cushions were scattered on the floor, while bits of the mattress underneath were strewn all about.

After that cleanup, we realized that we had been going about things all wrong. Although we didn't yet have children, we knew that she was like a toddler. She had way too much time on her paws, and there was no telling what she would get into next when left unattended.

We had to make some significant changes, so every day before I went to work, I took her out into the woods behind our building and let her run until she was tired. She didn't look for ways to get into trouble when she was good and tired.

When Robert got a promotion at work, we moved into a duplex that allowed dogs. We had been very lucky to keep her hidden for the several months that we had, and that was due in part to the fact that our downstairs neighbor didn't turn us in. He was a young guy who often had his buddies over, and we didn't say a word when strange-smelling smoke filtered up from his deck to our balcony. In turn, he kept our now-eighty-pound secret.

As we gave our notice to the complex manager, we were really concerned about what to do in regards to the loveseat. It had taken everything we had to put together the money needed to move into the duplex. How on earth could we afford to replace a sofa bed? We were so relieved when she called us about a week before our move and said that if the loveseat wasn't in the best of shape, we could throw it out.

Another catastrophe averted!

—Sheryl-Ann Odell—

Where's the Beef?

I feel sorry for people who don't have dogs. I hear they have to pick up food they drop on the floor.
~Author Unknown

Reilly, my daughter's yellow Labrador Retriever, enjoys life in the country. He's friendly, playful, and intelligent, and he likes to stalk critters in their huge back yard.

Despite his active lifestyle, Reilly is a bit overweight. In fact, he's built like a tank.

Reilly watches every morsel that goes from our hands to our mouths. Drop it, and we don't stand a chance of beating him to it. It's gone in one gulp.

Sometimes, he clamps his jaws onto the rim of his wide-mouthed cheese-ball jar. His hope is that someone will drop doggie treats in his jar. Then he will drop the jar on the floor so that the treats bounce out, and he pounces on them fast as lightning. He loves this game!

If we're preparing dinner and ignoring him, he carries his jar into the kitchen and drops it with a loud plop onto the hardwood floor. He hopes that someone will add some treats to his jar. Reilly's hungry, you see. He's always hungry.

One day, Reilly disappeared, and my daughter Erin didn't know where he went. He isn't allowed to leave the yard, and usually he doesn't. But he did that day. Erin was worried and walked to neighbors' homes looking for him. No Reilly.

Sometime later, the big dog was back... and not empty-handed.

In his huge mouth was a fragrant roast beef, still warm. Erin felt lightheaded. Whose dinner was this? Where did he get it? What would people think when they went outdoors and found their grill empty and their roast gone?

Nobody seemed to know a thing about it. One big yellow Lab knew, of course, but he wasn't talking.

"Oh, Reilly, what have you done?" my daughter said. To this day, not a single neighbor has reported the theft. It's still a mystery.

— Louisa Godissart McQuillen —

Under Georgia Red Clay

Accept the challenges so that you can
feel the exhilaration of victory.
~George S. Patton

One Saturday morning, I took our Irish Terrier, Martha, and our Westie, Lewis, on a walk in our neighborhood. We lived in a new development with lots of construction and new roads being built. That day, I walked to the side of the neighborhood that still had no houses. It was peaceful and quiet; one could easily walk for a half an hour without seeing another soul.

Martha, her usual boundless self, ran and jumped along the newly paved road without a care in the world. Lewis stuck right by my side. I felt calm and happy. It was a beautiful March morning and I was thinking about how my body was beginning to change. I was fifteen weeks pregnant with our first child.

Along the side of the road where a sidewalk would eventually be, the construction workers had put up long strips of black tarp, about three feet high. These were in place to keep the dirt and clay from blowing into the road. I was enjoying the moment when suddenly Martha leapt over the tarp — Irish Setters are quite the jumpers! I pulled her leash to draw her back, but no Martha. I pulled again, and still no Martha. Finally, I walked over to the curb and peered over the tarp.

My Very Good, Very Bad Dog | 195

And there, hidden from street view by the black plastic, was a long four-foot deep trench that had been dug for utility cables. It was only about ten inches wide, and much to my horror, Martha had jumped over the tarp and right into that narrow but deep space. The more she struggled to get out, the deeper she sank as the Georgia red clay poured in on top of her.

The situation was not good. Sensing my panic, Lewis barked and skipped back and forth frantically. I pulled again at Martha's leash, desperate to get her out, but it was useless. She was stuck firmly, and I only succeeded in pulling her collar over her neck. I screamed for help, but in that isolated area, no one heard me. The more she thrashed, the worse her predicament became. It wouldn't be long before she was completely buried in red dirt that was coincidentally the exact same color as her fur.

After a few minutes, Martha stopped moving. I had already realized that being completely covered in such a confined space, she would suffocate. Although I was sure she could not be saved, I decided I had to do something drastic. Leaving her to die alone was not an option. Lewis stayed close as I maneuvered my body into the trench behind Martha's rear end. Then, almost covered myself, I leaned sideways pushed my arm and hand under Martha's rump.

It was one of the saddest and strangest moments of my entire life. But just as I began to raise her heavy body with my arm, Martha slowly moved her head. Even though she was weighted down by pounds of fresh dirt, Martha was still alive. Slowly and carefully, I used all the strength I could muster in this confined space to push her body upward. And it seemed as though she understood not to fight or panic as we worked together to move her inch by inch to the top of the trench.

When I finally pushed her the last few inches to safety, Martha clamored back to solid ground. I pushed myself out carefully and watched with enormous relief as Martha eagerly shook off the red dirt blanket that covered her from head to toe. I reattached Martha's collar, and she was her usual carefree self before we had even walked another block.

I love to tell Martha's story to my daughter. I suppose a lot of things in life turn out the same way. One minute, it seems like sure doom, and then disaster is averted by some miracle. Why does an adult dog with the temperament of a child end up in a hole covered in dirt one minute and live to see the next? Maybe Martha had more stories to tell. She never did grow up, but she lived sixteen glorious years full of mishaps and adventures, which was a miracle in itself.

— Rebecca Edmisten —

Two for the Road

Not all those who wander are lost.
~J.R.R. Tolkien

On a crisp November day, while suffering from a massive head cold, I dragged myself out of bed to check on my dogs in the back yard. Sliding open the glass door, I called, "Scamp! Moto!" and waited calmly. *They must be at the front gate,* I mused. I peeked around the corner of the house since I was clad only in my oversized pink T-shirt. To my horror, the gate was open and they were gone.

I dashed into the house, pulling on my clothes as I headed for the door barefooted and with uncombed hair. All cold-induced drowsiness was forgotten as panic and adrenaline kicked in.

Driving slowly up and down every block near my home, I questioned gardeners, a mailman and a jogger I passed. No one had seen my Shepherd/Chow mix or my Norwegian Elkhound in the past three hours. I knew the time because my pool cleaner came at 9:00 and left by 9:30, and I always kept the dogs in until he left. I'd never had a problem with Bob locking the gate behind him, but this time he must have replaced the lock without snapping it shut. When I heard him leave, I assumed the gate was secured as usual and let the dogs out.

The last thing I'd heard was the dogs barking the way they always do when someone passes the house. Their barking soon stopped, and I rolled over gratefully for another nap. At this point, they must have jumped up against the gate, forcing it open.

Having had no luck finding them by car, I returned home and printed up signs. Armed with twenty-five hastily made fliers and plenty of tape, I drove even farther from home, posting them on nearly every block leading back to my place.

My friend Bill joined the search, and we recanvassed the area before going to the animal shelter to see if they'd been picked up. No such luck, but we posted their descriptions and my phone number should they be sighted or brought in. At 3:30, I paused for the first moment since I'd made my grim discovery. Tears flowed as I imagined what my dogs—who were never out of the yard without me and a leash—were going through.

Scamp is a clumsy two-year-old. He looks like a German Shepherd except for his long, soft fur and disproportionately short, stubby legs. When he walks, he sashays his hips hula-girl style. I found him as an abused stray when he was six months old, and he always follows me around with a combination of trust and adoration. I'd rescued him from what must have seemed like a friendless world, but now he was back on the streets wandering aimlessly, possibly hit on a busy street nearby.

Moto, on the other hand, is a mature eleven-year-old. Though he was once a pound puppy, he now carries himself with a regal air. He's calm and even-tempered; only Scamp's never-ending friskiness seems to try his patience. If he tries to keep up with Scamp, he usually ends up collapsing on the grass. At this moment, I prayed he didn't collapse in the middle of a street.

Having failed in my initial search, I returned home again to check my answering machine. I was overjoyed to hear a man named Richard saying that the dogs were at his business having a snack on the patio.

I called Richard back and he explained that he'd found my phone number on the dogs' tags. Suddenly, those five-dollar tags were worth a million to me.

"Where are they now?"

"In our east lot. One of my co-workers put them in her pickup so they wouldn't wander off."

"I'll be right there!"

The three-mile drive to Butterfield crossed two busy intersections and a freeway overpass. I prayed my dogs were unharmed.

When I arrived, I had to deal with the lady at the front desk. She was singularly unimpressed by my plight or my mission to pick up my dogs. Finally, she buzzed Richard, but he was away from his desk. "Can't help you," she said, dismissing me while she typed something on her computer.

No Richard? No dogs? I had to force myself to remain calm. I hurried out to the parking lot, spotting a number of pickups and having no clue which one they were in. I kept walking around, and suddenly I spotted Scamp. He ran up to me, tail wagging and muzzle pressing against my palm when he reached my side.

I hugged him tightly and then looked around for Moto, but he was nowhere to be seen. As quickly as Scamp had appeared, he broke away from my arms and began running up the aisle of parked cars. Stopping behind a dark blue pickup, he barked twice Lassie-style for me to come. I obeyed and was rewarded with the vision of an exhausted Moto resting his head on his front paws as he lay across the front seat.

He perked up when I called his name, but my eagerness to reach him was thwarted by two locked doors. Frustrated by the fact that Richard was away from his desk and I didn't know who owned the truck, I wondered how I'd release Moto.

My ever-logical friend reminded me that both dogs had been in the truck when I called. If Scamp got out, so could Moto. Then I realized that the sliding-glass window behind the seat was open.

Bill and I continued to talk to Moto, and he wagged his tail excitedly. Next, he stared expectantly at the door, waiting for us to let him out. Finally, Bill enticed him to stand and squeeze his rather rotund body through the now fully opened rear window. As he came through, Bill lifted all sixty-five pounds of him out of the truck bed and handed him to me for a gentle parking-lot landing.

Scamp slobbered kisses on Moto's face as we led the daring duo to my car. Just then, a pleasant-faced man walked over to us.

"Great! You found them!" he beamed.

"Richard?" I asked. When he nodded, I thanked him repeatedly and asked for his and the pickup owner's full names so I could send them something. Though he said it wasn't necessary, I was relentless in my desire to reward them for their kindness.

Safely home at last, we walked through the front door with Moto and Scamp jockeying for the front position; the phone was ringing. It was a little girl who attended the Christian school about a mile and a half away. She'd noticed one of my flyers on her way home and wanted to tell me she'd seen my dogs at lunch. First, I thanked her for calling, and then I told her my dogs were now safe at home. Then I asked what Scamp and Moto did at her school. "They ate lunch with us. They really like peanut-butter sandwiches and cookies."

Between their snacks from the office workers and lunch with the kids, I figured they wouldn't be very hungry. Indeed, they only had eyes for their large water bowl and soft bedding.

I'm sorry they got out, and I'll be ever more vigilant to assure that it never happens again, but I'm more than impressed by Moto and Scamp now. They not only managed to safely navigate busy streets and charmingly mingle with kids and office workers alike, but they did so without injury or missing a meal.

—Marsha Porter—

Resilience and Forgiveness

64

A Gentle Healer

There is no psychiatrist in the world
like a puppy licking your face.
~Ben Williams

I brought Sasha home when she was six months old — a tiny bundle of white fluff. She stood a bit taller than a typical Bichon Frise, and her soft white coat, gentle manner and happy nature made her the best dog for our family.

When Sasha turned three years old, I started working out of the basement of our home, counseling women who struggled with issues related to child abuse and rape. Many of these women had difficulty speaking. They often sat in front of me, on the edge of their seat, as if they were prepared to run out. Most looked uncomfortable, and they frequently repeated they couldn't think of anything to say.

During one of these sessions, I became aware of Sasha standing on the top step, peeking through the railing at us. My client hadn't noticed her, and I had to fight to keep myself from laughing. I watched as she moved down a step and squeezed her head through the banister to peek out at me again. After a minute, she pulled her head back in and gingerly stepped down one more stair. I stood up and told her sternly to go back upstairs. My client turned around and, seeing the dog, begged me to let her come downstairs.

Nodding, I called Sasha to come to me. She scooted down the rest of the steps, ran and jumped into my lap. My client broke out in a huge smile and asked if she could hold her. I lifted my wiggling, excited pup onto her lap. The dog settled down, positioning her body so that she faced me. A few strands of wispy hair hung over her big brown eyes, which seemed to be saying, *I can help this woman. I can help her talk.*

And that's exactly what she did. As the woman stroked the dog's soft white fur, something amazing happened. The client started to relax, and then she began to talk. Over the next few years, I had Sasha attend every counseling session. She proved her expertise in helping every client feel comfortable enough to tell her story.

My unlikely counseling partner taught me the therapeutic power of dogs in helping people who are damaged by abuse and trauma. She became the tool for their healing. Somehow, as the people preoccupied themselves with touching and stroking the dog, they were able to calm their fears and anxieties enough to disclose the shame and pain that had kept them stuck. And when they cried, Sasha instinctively pushed her head into their chests and even licked away their tears.

Her unconditional acceptance and gentle support worked wonders. The power of dogs to help people heal and recover from trauma is powerful. Their presence can make a huge difference in the person's ability to open up and let go enough to move forward in recovery. I am grateful to have had the experience to co-partner with Sasha, making a difference in the lives of so many women.

— Nikki Rottenberg —

65

Mitzie Has Arrived

We derive immeasurable good, uncounted pleasures,
enormous security, and many critical lessons
about life by owning dogs.
~Roger A. Caras

Before she came to our home, Mitzie had food, water and shelter, but not the love and attention this little Yorkie/Pom deserved. She lived in an outdoor dog lot that, over the years, she shared with various other dogs. For a while, she even shared it with a goat. That's what the first few years of her life were like.

The day we got her, she was alone in her dog lot. Her owner had told us all we had to do was open the gate and pick her up. But when my husband walked up to the gate, she ran into her doghouse. When he went inside the lot, she backed herself as far inside the doghouse as possible and growled. My husband knew the best thing to do was walk away.

When he came out of the lot, I went over to the gate and started talking to Mitzie in a calm, encouraging voice. In less than five minutes, she came out of her doghouse and walked hesitantly over to the gate. I gave her a treat, and her tail started wagging. I put my hand through an open area of the fence and slipped a collar with a leash attached to it around her neck. When I opened the gate, she leaped into my arms.

From that point on, she wiggled with excitement through each step of her new adventure. That experience taught me that sometimes

I have to trust the outstretched hand that wants to lift me up and take me to a new or better place, whether that place is a physical location or a state of mind. Mitzie's willingness to trust me led her to a better place where she receives the love and pampering she deserves.

Before joining our household, Mitzie had a much-needed visit to a dog groomer. It's amazing what a bath, blow dry, fancy bows and pedicure can do for a little dog's appearance and self-esteem. She came out of the dog salon fluffy, perky and proud.

Her next adventure was a stop at the vet's office for a check-up and vaccination update. She was sweet, friendly and cooperative — a real show-off. As we were driving home with this new addition to our family, I wondered how she would adjust to living indoors and to our other pets. As soon as we pulled into our driveway, we heard the usual chorus of barks that always greet us when we arrive home. All that noise didn't bother Mitzie one bit. She was excited and eager to continue her new adventure.

When we opened the door, Mitzie pranced confidently into the house with an attitude that declared, "I have arrived!" An onlooker would never have guessed the age of this frisky little dog. At six or so years old, she was as bouncy and lively as a puppy. Immediately, Mitzie claimed her bowl and bed. She did so with such confidence that she instantly earned the respect of the other pets. Mitzie fell right into the household routine. At "potty time," she'd rush out the door into our fenced-in yard with the other dogs. She was often the first to return to the door and would bark loudly to announce her arrival. She learned quickly that a bark would get her a free ride on the recliner footrest, a lift up to the "big" bed, or a little extra attention.

From the day she arrived, Mitzie soaked up all the love and attention we gave her. Quickly, she discovered the pleasure of belly rubs and snuggling. After years of living outdoors, she suddenly became a "prissy-missy" and didn't like getting her feet wet on rainy days. Relaxing in the recliner with my husband and snoozing beside me when I read are two of her favorite things to do. When we have visitors, Mitzie is an enthusiastic greeter. She always becomes the center of attention.

Typically, I approach a new adventure or opportunity with hesitancy.

Mitzie's attitude that proclaimed, "I have arrived," taught me the importance of exuding confidence each time a new adventure, opportunity or challenge comes my way. Confidence generates respect.

Unlike some of the dogs we've rescued, Mitzie didn't need an adjustment period. She very clearly demonstrated the art of adaptability. Immediately, she began enjoying her plush bed, treats, specially prepared meals, new playmates and lots of individualized attention. Change isn't always easy for me, so I got a refresher course in adaptability from her.

From the day of her arrival, Mitzie became, and remains, my shadow. Since she's not lacking in confidence, I interpret her devotion as an expression of gratitude. I'm sure that, as time goes by, I'll learn a lot more life lessons from Mitzie. At one point, I considered developing the diva frame of mind that Mitzie has mastered so perfectly, but then I decided one diva in the house is enough.

— Veronica Bowman —

Hazel's Resilience

*Because of the dog's joyfulness, our own
is increased. It is no small gift.*
~Mary Oliver

One sunny June morning I was on my way home from working a twelve-hour night shift at the hospital. I was driving down the highway when I saw people gathered around an injured dog.

I pulled over to help. It was a Pit Bull and she was injured. When she saw me, she started scooting toward me using only her front legs, as her back end was evidently injured severely.

I got a blanket from my trunk and placed it on the floorboard of my back seat. With a little help from some of the bystanders, we lifted her into my car.

I called my husband and said tearfully, "I have an injured dog in my car. What should I do?"

He advised, "Let's see if she has a chip, and we'll go from there."

So, off to the vet we went. She did have a chip, and her name was "Hazel." I was so relieved that I would be able to find her owners and help them get this girl fixed up. To my surprise, even after multiple phone calls to the phone number associated with the chip, multiple phone calls to vet offices in the surrounding areas, and Google searches of the owners' names, I was not able to contact her owners.

My husband and I decided to find out the extent of her injuries and what could be done for her. Hazel stayed at the vet for the remainder of the day and had X-rays, ultrasounds, and lab work done to figure out what was wrong with her. The vet called that evening and told me, "We assume that she has been hit by a car. Hazel has a broken pelvis in four places and a large blood clot in her bladder. She is covered in fleas and ticks, and has multiple deep lacerations to her right hind leg. The pads on her paws are rough and hard, which indicate that she has been in the elements for a little bit, and she is heartworm-positive."

I was devastated and didn't know what to do. I knew her vet care would be quite costly. After discussing her treatment options and prognosis with my husband, we decided to have her treated. We started a GoFundMe page for Hazel. Within hours, we had almost $1,000 for this sweet girl, all with the help of our family, friends, and even strangers who had come across her story. In total, we raised $1,790 for Hazel over just a few weeks. The money helped us pay for all of her medical care except the heartworm treatment. One week after I found her, she was able to come home from the vet with us, to a new life with a loving family.

We have now had Hazel for nine months, and she is a completely different dog. The deep lacerations on her leg have healed after doing wound care twice a day for the first two months we had her. She is no longer covered in fleas and ticks. The pads on her paws are soft. Hazel did not end up needing to have surgery on her pelvis because she healed without it after three months of restricted activity.

When we first brought her home and for several weeks, she could not walk without assistance. Now she can run and keep up with my other three rescue dogs. She has also been treated for heartworm and will be retested in a few months to determine if treatment was effective. One would never be able to tell that she has gone through such a traumatic experience.

In spite of the pain and trauma she went through, Hazel is the sweetest and most loving dog I have ever met. She runs to greet us at the door when we come home, snuggles on the couch with us, and smothers our faces in kisses multiple times a day.

She is a wonderful role model for faith, trust, and resilience, and she continues to inspire me on a daily basis.

—Abigail Smith—

67

Hope on Three Legs

If I could be half the person my dog is,
I'd be twice the human I am.
~Charles Yu

There are two types of people. There are those who, when they see a huge, white three-legged dog ambling down the street, offer up a sad smile and an "Awww... poor guy." Then there are those who shake their heads in amazement and say, "Wow, he's really incredible, isn't he?"

I used to be the former. Any disability in an animal made me want to avert my eyes. And then our dog Polar, a Great Pyrenees, was diagnosed with osteosarcoma. Bone cancer. Front left leg.

The diagnosis stunned me. The recommended treatment even more. Amputation. Then chemotherapy. An expected survival of six months, maybe a year if we were lucky. It seemed draconian. Lopping off a leg? Really? That's the best modern veterinary medicine can do?

I drove home from the vet clinic in a daze. The thought of losing Polar was, well, unthinkable. But amputation? Polar was a giant. How would he manage? Or perhaps, more to the point, how would *I* manage?

Later that day, with my head still reeling, I called a dog-loving friend, sure she would agree that amputation was barbaric. Instead, she shared a story I hadn't heard before about her old dog, Cassius, a Boxer who had been diagnosed with bone cancer. They had amputated his leg, and he'd lived another full — and active — year. "A year is a long time for a dog," she reminded me.

Another friend pointed me in the direction of an online group of pet owners whose dogs had bone cancer. I read their triumphant stories. And their tales of heartbreak. My mind began to open.

My family, including three young kids, gathered round and watched online videos of celebrated tri-pawds, as they're called affectionately. We saw amputees leaping to snatch Frisbees out of the air, swimming, and napping contentedly in the shade. Big tri-pawds and small. Front amputees and back.

In the end, the three-legged ambassadors on the Internet swayed us. We also wanted to show our children that when life throws you a bad diagnosis, you throw everything you can right back at it. Besides, Polar seemed in no hurry to say goodbye.

The morning I picked up our new amputee from the vet clinic, he jumped into the back of my car — less than twenty-four hours after surgery. Optimism surged.

It was short-lived. The pain meds wore off. He cried in his sleep. I fretted constantly. My online group saved my sanity more than once, offering up a blend of comfort and been-there-done-that advice.

I took my cue from our other two dogs who gave Polar the full-body sniff when he returned home and then pretty much settled back into their routine. His devoted sister Kira collected dog toys from around the house and dropped them at his head. Polar slept surrounded by rubber bones and chewies. Kira gave him twenty-four hours to get over it, and then began badgering him to play with her, no matter that he was missing a leg.

After a few weeks of healing, Polar seemed unconcerned about what he'd lost. Sure, he got tired more easily on his walks. Sometimes, he tripped and fell. But he was still our Polar. Loyal. Smart. Affectionate. Big.

For six months, we drove two hours for Polar to have his chemotherapy. He was X-rayed and declared cancer-free. We knew that bone cancer had a nasty habit of resurfacing, but we'd reached our six months. Each day after felt like a bonus. We reached one year. The months melted into more years.

Then, one gorgeous summer evening almost four years after the initial diagnosis and a week after Polar's eleventh birthday, we noticed he was favoring a back leg. Always the stoic, he never emitted even a tiny cry of pain.

But the vet confirmed our fear. The cancer was back. This time, amputation wasn't an option. Not for an eleven-year-old, three-legged dog.

And so we made the final appointment—and then cancelled it and made another for a week later. Saying goodbye always comes too soon.

We savored those final two weeks. We told him over and over again what a good boy he'd been, and what an inspiration he'd been to so many. This three-legged giant who seemed not the least bothered by what he was missing had taught the rest of us not to be so bothered by it either.

Polar reminded us daily to focus on what we had. A warm bed. A tree to snooze beneath. A family.

Polar wasn't a "poor guy." Nope. He was worthy of the awe he inspired. "Wow," indeed.

—Leslie Garrett—

68

The Mayor

*Blessed is the person who has earned
the love of an old dog.*
~Sydney Jeanne Seward

Two veterinary students loaded our six-year-old Newfoundland, Buster Brown, onto a dolly and wheeled him from the parking lot into the state-of-the-art Iowa State University veterinary clinic. It was their first day out of the classroom and in the examining room, and they had an assessment checklist that went from nose to tail. Buster was happy to comply: he let them look in his ears, run their hands over his entire body, and stretch and bend his legs and feet.

The problem was that Buster had torn both rear cruciate ligaments (like the ACL in humans), an unfortunately common problem in large breeds. He was completely lame in his back legs, and so big at 140 pounds that it had become a real challenge for my husband Roger and me to help him get around.

After examining a series of X-rays, the vet explained that Buster would need two TPLO (tibial-plateau-leveling osteotomy) surgeries to help him regain control of his back legs. The surgeries were expensive — but that was not what bothered me.

"If he can't have a good outcome, I don't want to put him through this," I told the vet.

"He should be able to walk, swim, do what he likes," she said. But first he would need to have surgery on one leg, spend six weeks in recovery, and then go through the whole process again.

That sounded like a long time in dog years, and little did we know that there would be many setbacks along the way. When they shaved Buster's leg before the first surgery, they found he had a skin infection. This meant they couldn't operate. We had to take home a lame, shaved dog, and try to get the infection cleared up with a special shampoo. Then, post-surgery, he developed two separate internal infections that had to be treated with two different rounds of antibiotics.

During this time, Buster was not very mobile. He barked when he wanted water brought to him, and we would bring it. He barked when he needed to go outside, and we would use a beach towel as a sling to lift his back end so that he could get out the patio door and into the back yard.

Before his injury, Buster usually walked about two miles with us each morning. One of his favorite loops followed the main thoroughfare of our small town of Storm Lake, Iowa. When we passed Bedels Pharmacy, the pharmacist gave him biscuits at the drive-up window. When we passed Johnston Autostore, where the door was often propped open to let in the breeze, Buster would step inside just far enough to make the motion-sensor bell ring. "Hey, Ralph!" the guys behind the counter would call, even though they knew his name was Buster. Satisfied with this greeting, Buster would walk on.

Buster befriended everyone. Once, a little boy of about six got out of a minivan right next to Buster. Before I could react, Buster was licking the remnants of *elotes*, a Mexican grilled-corn treat, from the little boy's face. Fortunately, when his mother looked over and saw what was happening, she laughed.

"Buster," I said as we rounded the corner, "there is such a thing as being too friendly, you know."

Now, when we walked down the main strip without him, people poked their heads out of pickup trucks, a waitress ran out of The Pantry café with her order pad in hand, and mechanics looked up from engines. They all had one question: "Where's Buster?"

Buster was at Iowa State in physical therapy — walking on the underwater treadmill, doing range-of-motion exercises, and working on regaining his balance. After his second TLPO surgery, I was anxious on the ride down to the clinic, thinking, *Poor Buster, we need to bring him home!*

"How is he?" I asked the veterinary technician when she took us back to the examination room.

She laughed. "We call him 'The Mayor,'" she said. She explained that when they walked Buster down the hall to get him to practice using his leg, he insisted on stopping at every single door, waiting for the person in the office or exam room to say "hello" to him, pet him, shake his extended paw, or give him a treat.

"He's made quite a number of friends," she explained.

I didn't understand the full extent of this statement until we brought Buster back in for a post-surgery check-up. People came from all over the facility — rehab, surgery, lab — to see our dog. "Hey, it's Buster!" "Hi, Buster Brown!" "Buster's here!" "How are you doing, buddy?"

I had been so worried about how Buster would handle the ordeal, but he was the one who pulled us through with his winning personality. I know he didn't want to be in pain, and he certainly didn't enjoy being in recovery from surgery. But I should have realized that he would put the best spin on the situation, making friends among the locals, shaking hands, and collecting donations, as any good politician would.

— Gwen Hart —

69

Finding the Way

*The one absolutely unselfish friend that man can have
in this selfish world, the one that never deserts him,
the one that never proves ungrateful or
treacherous, is his dog.*
~George Graham

The alarm on my watch went off—it was time. That delicious curl of excitement and nerves unfurled in my belly. I'd been a police K-9 handler for five or six years by then, but always reacted this way when it was time to track a suspect. It didn't matter if it was a training scenario, like this was, or a for-real track, I got geeked up. Ranger, my police dog, and I both loved finding bad guys who would otherwise get away. We relied on each other, and others relied on us.

I let Ranger out of the patrol car and pulled his tracking harness from the equipment bag. He trotted over and nosed it, and then began spinning in circles. He got geeked up, too. I put the harness on him in accordance with our little ritual—right foreleg first, then head, then left foreleg, clicking the belly band into the top-line buckle, and then snapping the thirty-foot line onto the d-ring on the back-strap. The ritual was important. The snap of the line buckle signaled "Game On."

This was our scenario. Another officer had attempted to stop a stolen car twenty minutes earlier. The driver had pulled behind a nearby abandoned manufacturing plant in a light industrial area and then fled on foot. Our job was to find and arrest him.

Ranger and I walked up to the open driver's door of the "recovered steal." I fed out the line so he could move freely, and I hung back to keep from getting in his way. He knew his business. He sniffed around the door and seat, and then backed out, ducked under the door, and took off around the front end of the car and into the large parking lot north of the building. Dogs with four legs outpace humans with two legs so to avoid being a literal drag on Ranger while he worked, I swung into my more-than-a-jog, less-than-a-run tracking pace.

Ranger was a big, handsome German Shepherd whose intelligence and good nature sparkled in light, reddish-brown eyes. He was a traditional black and tan, but the tan on the inside of his legs and on his chest was very light. A scattering of black-tipped hairs in these areas kept the color from sliding into cream. At ninety-five pounds, he outweighed most other working dogs by twenty to twenty-five pounds, yet he moved with grace and power. That strength was now channeled into his excitement for the track. He pulled me forward in a somewhat straight line, nose about six inches off the ground, head occasionally shifting back and forth—all his usual signals that he was on the track.

We had crossed about a third of the lot when he veered to the right and began pulling harder. Normally, he only did this when he found the person at the end of the track, yet I was skeptical because as training tracks went, this one was rather short so far. I reminded myself of the first rule of tracking: *Don't second-guess the dog. You've no idea what he's smelling. Let him work it out.*

By now, it was nearly dark. Ranger headed into a grove of tightly packed trees along a riverbank. We scrambled up the bank where he turned right and made for some low bushes. Lunging through them, he stopped abruptly, but didn't bark or growl. He ignored me when I called his name, so I moved up the line hand over hand and came up behind him. As the near-dark and bushes concealed his face, I grabbed the flashlight from my belt. I brought up the light, and the edge of the beam glinted off glossy black fur trimmed with a jagged streak of white. I panicked and shouted, "Out! Out!" Obediently, Ranger spit out the skunk, and it toddled off into the darkness.

I pulled him away from the area to check him out. Getting downwind of him was unnecessary; he reeked of skunk stink, especially around his head and chest. Ranger shook his head a few times, wrapping strands of drool around his muzzle. He stood there looking up at me forlornly, smelly and dripping drool, and then blew it all off in a sneezing fit. Knowing water would only make things worse, I dry-wiped his face and tongue. His eyes looked okay, and his breathing settled down after a few minutes.

Ranger had been tracking for years, but I was worried an experience this bad would put him off it. I had no idea if he would be willing to track given his discomfort or even if tracking was possible with the way his sense of smell was contaminated. On top of that, the track itself was now over an hour old, and much of the area was asphalt parking lot and roadway — difficult surfaces because they held so little scent. Wanting to salvage what we could of the training session, I took Ranger back to the last place where I was sure he was on the original track. When his head-shaking, drooling, and sneezing subsided, I cast him there and told him to track. His stink wasn't the only reason I held my breath.

Ranger milled around for a bit, and then took off in the same general direction as the original track but about fifty feet downwind of it. That was okay; it made sense given the conditions. My relief was short-lived, however, as he began the first of countless loop-the-loops and backtracks. For thirty minutes, he spun and turned, dragged me over to bushes and away, across rock-filled parking lot medians and sidewalks only to re-cross them farther on.

Ranger's behavior and body language were so different that I gave up trying to read him and let him pull me along wherever he wanted to go. Frustrated and worried that we were just going for a walk, it took me some time to realize that although we repeatedly covered the same ground, there was a small segment of "new" ground each time, and those segments added up to a consistent direction of travel.

A third of a mile from the start, Ranger left the commercial area and crossed into a field. So clueless was I that I stumbled and almost fell when he lunged forward and began barking. The "suspect" jumped up out of a shallow gully and surrendered.

I was amazed at what Ranger accomplished that night and grateful for the example he set. He knew what he wanted and refused to let an obstacle discourage him. He used his determination and what ability was left to him to work out the path he should take. He adapted and persevered until he found a way to his goal and, in the process, he improved himself.

— Suzanne M. Kurth —

Good Golly Miss Molly

Dogs are miracles with paws.
~Susan Ariel Rainbow Kennedy

"**G**ive it three weeks," the vet told us, "and then we'll see where we're at." He had just diagnosed our thirteen-year-old Pug mix Molly with vestibular disease, better known as "old-dog disease." We'd sat up with her the entire night before while her eyes darted back and forth, and she panted and vomited. She held her head at an odd angle and walked into the furniture when she could walk at all. Her tongue hung out of her mouth. We thought she'd had a stroke.

Two days earlier, she'd been prescribed antibiotics and cough medicine, and I was sure a bad reaction to the medicine had caused what was happening to her now. The vet assured me that wasn't true. It was just something that happened to old dogs.

From the day we'd adopted her eleven years before, Molly had been energetic, strong-willed, and loud. She tore around the yard and barked, jumping up on the gate when a stranger approached or an unfamiliar dog passed by. Her junkyard dog persona was all for show, though. She was really a cuddly lapdog with her own spot on the sofa.

Now, she couldn't bark, couldn't walk without falling down, and couldn't eat. Our family of four took turns sitting with her, hand-feeding her, and getting her to drink. We had to hold her up when she went out to the bathroom, and hold her back when she came in the house and tried to jump up on the sofa like before.

In addition to her physical limitations, we realized she was now blind in one eye. We worried we wouldn't be able to provide the constant care she now needed, but more than that we worried about her quality of life. Was she in pain? Was she even aware of what had happened? What kind of existence was she going to have now that she was an old dog and had all the ailments that went with it?

One week in, during a follow-up visit, the vet commented on how severe her head tilt still was. He said it wasn't a good sign. The best news he had for us was that her condition was not life-threatening, but it was life-altering. He was right about that.

Molly was part of the family, so we cared for her with love. We kept her alive and comfortable, but we'd lost our dog just the same. Over the next few days, I carried her outside and laid her in the sun when I thought she'd like that, and brought her into the shade when I thought she'd had enough. It was heartbreaking to watch the chipmunks she used to scold scurry right up to her now, when she either didn't notice or couldn't react.

She couldn't be left alone because she was unsteady on her feet, making it a real possibility that she might hurt herself. The only person we would leave Molly with was my mother, but looking after a dog that needed this much care was a lot to ask of anyone, so we cancelled our summer plans and stuck close to home.

Over the next few days, we noticed Molly starting to adapt. Her head remained so tilted she couldn't walk a straight line, yet she maneuvered around the furniture using an improvised crab walk. She still couldn't eat or drink without our help, but she could tell us when she was hungry or thirsty by pawing at her food and water bowls.

One day, we brought her outside to lie in the sun while we did some yard work. She showed a marked improvement by being able to sit instead of lying down. She closed her eyes and lifted her face to the sun. She seemed content, so we all turned our backs to return to the weeding. We were all stunned when Molly barked a few minutes later — first once, as if she were trying out her voice, then again and again as she remembered how to do it.

She stood up and tried to run, but fell down after a few steps. That didn't stop her. By the end of that day, she had mastered trotting. It wasn't in a straight line, and more often than not she ended up in the bushes, but it was apparent that she was struggling to regain some independence.

At the three-week mark, she could eat and drink on her own, go out to the bathroom without help, and walk without falling over. But her head was still almost perpendicular to the floor, and her tongue still hung out. She could no longer get up or down from her spot on the sofa, and stairs were off limits. She was still blind in one eye. The vet told us this was it. She was as good as she was going to get. This was life with an elderly dog.

We were happy she had recovered as much as she did, and that she seemed in good spirits. But we missed our old dog—the one with all the moxie and spunk. I felt sorry for her, especially because it had all happened so fast. I imagined the same thing happening to me or one of my loved ones and getting that this-is-the-best-it's-going-to-get diagnosis.

Luckily, one thing that hadn't changed about Molly is that she never listened. It wasn't for a lack of training. It was and still is more about her strong-willed nature. She always knows what we want her to do; she just doesn't often comply. This time was no different. She defied the vet by continuing to improve and adapt. I watched her calculate how to get from point A to point B knowing she couldn't walk a straight line. I watched her measure and test until she could jump up and reclaim her spot on the sofa.

She didn't care how many weeks it had been, or who said she wasn't going to get any better, or how old she was. She continued trying and challenging herself until she could do exactly what she wanted to do. It was as if she'd begun a rigorous physical-therapy regimen all on her own. She made an effort to get better.

Eight weeks after her initial diagnosis, she is no longer blind in one eye. Her head tilt is almost completely gone. She chases fireflies on warm summer evenings, barks at fireworks, and jumps up on the gate when strangers walk by. She eats her food and ours. And if we sit in her spot on the sofa, she lets us know.

She can't talk, but when my husband and I were discussing our aches and pains recently, along with our dismay at how much mail we get from AARP these days, I think she chuckled. Then she jumped down off the sofa and went outside to chase some chipmunks.

— Tracy Falenwolfe —

I Remember Mama

*Dogs love company. They place it first
in their short list of needs.*
~J.R. Ackerley

As the Controller for a local, nonprofit animal-welfare agency, I don't usually have much contact with the thousands of pets that come through our doors each year. I am somewhat of a cat aficionado, though, and I do enjoy visiting with them. Dogs, on the other hand, are too heart-breaking for me to visit on a regular basis. I avoid the kennels as much as possible.

Occasionally, though, we have a very special dog brought in, and that was the case one winter when a little eight-pound Chihuahua we called "Mama" arrived. We did not realize that her presence would forever change each of us.

Mama was brought in by a man who explained that he had found her abandoned. When her paperwork was completed, she was escorted to her assigned kennel. Since she was so small and elderly, we tried to make her comfortable by giving her a small dog bed and a blanket. Mama stood in her new living quarters, quietly taking inventory of her new situation. As if trying to express appreciation for this small kindness, Mama went to her bed and lay down.

Within days, Mama's sunny disposition and easygoing, take-life-as-it-comes attitude had won the hearts of the kennel staff. "Have you met Mama yet?" I overheard the kennel manager say as I was passing in the hall.

"Who is Mama?" I asked. I was escorted to the kennels and introduced to this sweet little lady.

"*This* is Mama," she said, smiling broadly. "Mama, say hello to a new friend." Mama looked up at me, threw back her head and began an enthusiastic little yowl that ended with a yip. Funny thing, she seemed to be smiling at me.

Eventually, every staff member knew Mama, and she thrived in her new surroundings. She even helped out! When small dogs first came in, we put them with Mama so she could calm them down. Mama welcomed each new roommate in her sweet, straightforward manner. She was extremely nurturing and paid close attention to each new charge. Without realizing it, we had given Mama a regular job, and she accepted her new duties with happy dedication. It was as if she wanted us to know that she would do her very best to make the new dogs feel safe and at home while earning her keep.

Mama hadn't been with us very long when a lump was discovered on her lower neck and upper left shoulder area. The veterinarian took X-rays and did a biopsy. The news wasn't good. Mama's lump was a slow-growing, malignant tumor that was inoperable. Mama didn't appear to be in pain, and her appetite was very good, so we made her comfortable, realizing at the same time that Mama would be considered non-adoptable.

The fact that she was elderly and terminal didn't dampen Mama's good spirits and love for life. It was decided that Mama would make our facility her new "forever home." As long as she was not in pain or suffering in any way, she would stay with us. Our staff members already considered her a family member and visited with her often, taking her on outings to various departments in the facility and outdoors to the grassy pen. Mama loved everyone she met. It was obvious there were no strangers in her world, only friends she hadn't met yet.

Those new friends included three volunteer groomers, whom I refer to as our "Angels in Aprons." Every Thursday, these three wonderful ladies arrive at ten o'clock and check with staff members to find which animals need their attention. Grooming is not just limited to dogs and cats. They have clipped and bathed badly matted and dirty guinea pigs and assisted in grooming a great horned owl. Even a pot-bellied pig named Lulu enjoyed an afternoon at their spa.

Mama held a special place in the hearts of these ladies. They brought lunch for her every Thursday. Bite-sized pieces of hot dogs were thoroughly relished by Mama, who spent the lunch hour with her groomer friends. Her affection for the ladies was obvious, and they knew how much Mama enjoyed getting out a bit.

Six months after Mama moved in, a lady came to the adoptions counter and asked about adopting the little Chihuahua in Kennel #4. She was told that Mama's condition was terminal, even though Mama seemed happy and was not suffering. Most people would have moved on at that point, but this lady was not discouraged and asked to visit with Mama. She was escorted to the visiting room, and Mama was brought on a leash to meet her. They were left alone for some time, and when the lady came out of the visiting room, she announced, "I'd like to take her home with me."

The little dog we all assumed would never leave the kennels had found her "forever home" with her new best friend. The staff was both overjoyed and mystified. Only Mama understood that a good attitude and hard work can resolve a difficult circumstance.

A few weeks after Mama went to her new home, I telephoned her adopter to inquire as to how they were getting on together. The new owner explained that she was the perfect pet for her, and that she had previously had two other dogs. She went on to say that Mama sleeps in her bed with her, and she calls her "Baby." The little Chihuahua never causes a nuisance, is not displaying any signs of suffering or illness, and still maintains a healthy appetite.

I have encountered many animals in my career at the facility, but none is more notable than Mama. She used her talents and positive outlook on life to make a difference to all the humans and dogs she encountered.

— Cheryl Wright —

It's Never Too Late for Love

My dear old dog, most constant of all friends.
~William Croswell Doane

Oscar entered my life at a point when my life was in flux. I was changing jobs and I had also lost my white Husky, Lady Bear. After seventeen years, her arthritis became so disabling that she could no longer walk and was suffering terribly. My neighbor and I had taken her to the vet and I had held her while she passed.

I had no desire to take on another dog after that. Lady Bear still filled my thoughts. Plus, I still had many cats to support, so I threw myself back into work.

Then one rainy Saturday morning, I heard a horrible ruckus in my driveway. I ran out to see two medium-sized dogs barking and snarling at something under my car. I'd pulled out the car because I had planned to go shopping that day. Immediately, I assumed they had cornered an animal, so I pulled out the garden hose and gave them a good wet-down.

They took off and I went to see if it was a feral cat, or even a raccoon or opossum that was hiding under my car.

What I found looked like a large ball of mangled, tangled hair that appeared to be spattered with blood. I pulled some old towels from the garage and tried coaxing the animal out of hiding, still not quite knowing what it was, but pretty sure that it needed a lot of help.

After only a few minutes, I saw that it was a very dirty dog with long, matted and tangled hair. He was covered with chunks of mud, dried leaves and things I couldn't even describe — plus the oozing red stuff all over his fur. He focused one beady eye on me, decided I was safe, and slowly scrabbled out from under the car. Then he rolled over on his back. I couldn't tell how badly he might be hurt and didn't want to hurt him further, so I wrapped him in the towels and put him in the back seat of the car. After running back to get my purse and lock the house, we headed to my vet.

My vet took the messy bundle from me and soon we discovered that it was an extremely old dog. The red all over him was not blood; it was rancid sweet-and-sour chicken that the dog had probably foraged from a garbage bin somewhere. He had no broken bones or bites from the other dogs, but the vet told me he was very old, had a bad heart, wheezy lungs, one blind eye and only six teeth left in his mouth. His pads were thick as if he'd been on the pavement for quite some time. Possibly, he was a throw-away dog. He had a deep area around his neck that indicated he had worn a collar for many years, but that collar was long gone, and he had never been tattooed or chipped.

"We can wash him up and get him looking a little better, but I truly suggest that you have him euthanized. He is very old and not in the best of health. If he has the perfect home, he probably has six to seven months left in him… and that's just a guess," my vet said. "It would be the kind thing to do."

"Wash him up and give him his shots," I replied. "If he fought this hard to stay alive in his condition, he deserves to live those last few months in comfort. If he gets worse, I'll bring him in."

I named him Oscar after Oscar De La Hoya, the boxing champion. I figured the little guy with his one-eyed "Popeye" stare and one of his six good teeth peeking out of his undershot jaw still had a lot of fight in him. He turned out to be a Shih Tzu mix, but he had the heart of a Pit Bull.

Thus started my life with a crabby, absolutely adorable, and also absolutely untrainable, hairy monster. He dug holes in the carpet. He chewed the door moldings. But he adored the cats and was a complete "love bunny" to me and anyone who visited. The comment was always the same: "He's so darn ugly, he's cute."

I knew that we were meant to find each other. Nothing could replace Lady Bear, but keeping up with Oscar? Well, no time to mourn the loss. There was too much to do in the present. He did most of his shenanigans when he didn't get attention, so I let him into my office while I worked on my writing. He would jump into the old chair in the corner, curl up, lay his shaggy snout on crossed paws and watch me with his one good eye.

We went for walks and gathered with the cats to watch TV at night together. I got him a nice dog bed and put it in the kitchen. The kitchen was best for him because he couldn't make it through the night without making a mess. It was easier to put down newspaper in the kitchen than to scrub carpets every morning.

By the end of the first year with me, he had gone blind in his other eye as well, but still managed to navigate the house and back yard. My oldest cat, Ringo, had taken a shine to the shaggy little guy and acted as a Seeing Eye guide for him, keeping him away from the rosebushes.

The second year, Oscar preferred being inside with me. He was like my shadow, following me around with his nose on my leg. I could tell he was slowing down.

I never had to make that visit to the vet as I'd promised, though. Almost two years to the day that I'd found him under my car, Oscar passed away peacefully in his sleep in his little dog bed in the corner of the kitchen. I woke up and found him with his favorite toy between his paws.

Was it stupid of me to waste so much time and money on a dog who I knew was on his last legs? Some may say so. But whatever kind of strife that little dog had experienced in his younger life, at least he went on to his next life from a place of love, peace and happiness. I hope somebody will be as kind to me when I'm looking for a place to live out my last days. Oscar taught me that love knows no age.

— Joyce Laird —

73

Ol' Spanky

None are as fiercely loyal as dog people. In return,
no doubt, for the never-ending loyalty of dogs.
~Linda Shrieves

T he Terrier mix I'd been spotting along Sweet Run, West Virginia's Route 75, was growing thinner by the day. Every morning, my husband Mark and I stopped on our way to work at the VA hospital to try to lure him into our car. But even the remains of a T-bone steak didn't do the trick. That dog was terrified of us. The moment we would open the car door and call for him, he would vanish into the nearby woods.

Then we started delivering a sausage-and-double-cheese pizza to him every evening on our way home from work. We'd simply drop it on the shoulder of the highway, and when we'd disappear, he'd return to make fast work of it.

One evening, we noticed a man working under the hood of a rusted, old truck in a nearby gravel driveway. "Know anything about the mutt that wanders the roads?" I asked. "I'm a nurse, and from the looks of him, he's pretty sick. If he doesn't belong to someone, I'd like to have my vet check him out."

The middle-aged man tipped his ball cap in my direction. "We call him Ol' Spanky around these parts," he said. "Don't reckon the fellow has a real home. He just showed up about six months ago, and all of us here in Happy Hollow have sort of been taking care of him."

His comment had a familiar ring to it. I knew from working with patients that if everyone is taking care of a patient, that patient is probably falling through the cracks. Accountability is much better if a patient is under the care of one particular nurse.

But there was no doubt about it: I was madly in love with the shaggy sweetheart. So I asked the man if it would be alright if I tried to get Spanky to go home with me so I could get him a good look-over, starting with the fat ticks all over his filthy body. The guy was delighted.

Finally, one evening, Mark and I were able to coax Spanky into the back seat of our car with a MoonPie — admittedly not the healthiest treat for a dog. But we nurses have our ways. As we drove off with Spanky, he barked loudly out the car window. The guy yelled back at us: "You know what they say about Happy Hollow! You come in happy, and you go out hollering."

When I took Spanky to visit Dr. King, she fell in love with the shaggy stray on the spot. Still, her diagnosis was disturbing. Spanky had advanced heartworm and the cost of his care would be $1,500 — money I didn't have. And there was no guarantee he would survive the regimen in his weakened condition. Dr. King locked eyes with him. "You've been fighting for your groceries lately, haven't you, bud?" Then she kissed a patch of smelly brown-and-white fur. From then on, Spanky was the gentlest dog ever.

Dr. King went on to remark that she'd seen a lot of strays in her day, and she felt certain this one was simply separated from his owner. "Tell you what," she said. "I'll patch up Ol' Spanky, and if his original owner comes around, my services will be a gift. If not, I'll give this little doll baby to my brother's children. They've been looking for a dog, and I just know this one would be great with kids."

That's all it took to make me re-evaluate my bank account. It was like I was at an antiques auction, and there was a bidding war. Everyone there wanted the same farm table with the original blue milk paint.

"Well, if it's okay with you, I'd like to pay for Spanky's medical care and take him home with me," I told her.

She grinned. "I kinda figured as much. You've got yourself one fine dog."

Spanky didn't just survive his heartworm and dietary treatments;

he thrived. And he also became the most loyal dog ever. Still, I couldn't help but worry about his original owners. What if they surfaced one day and wanted him back?

I wrote about my love affair with Ol' Spanky in *Guideposts*. The magazine is a favorite at veterans' hospitals, and mine was no exception. Our patients adored that story and passed the publication around the inpatient wards.

One day, another nurse telephoned me from her unit. "The most amazing thing happened, Roberta," Lisa said. "One of my patients handed me a little brochure called *The Guiding Light*, and it had a story in it you wrote. Of course, I couldn't wait to read it on my break. Well, you know that dog in the story? I think he's my dog. He looks just like him, and he got lost when we were camping about six months ago, just like the stray in the story. He's been so dear to us through the years and gotten us through some really rough patches. My kids were crazy about him. We called him Buckwheat."

The next day, Lisa brought in some pictures. I shared them with my sister, who is known to be rather cynical. "Compare these pics, Reb," I said. "I'd like to know how likely you think it is that this is actually her dog." Lisa had gotten the name of the magazine wrong, so I was hoping she was wrong about the dog as well.

Reb scratched her chin in deep thought. I figured she would say, "Not a chance in this world." Instead, she said, "I'm sorry, but I'd say it's about 99.9 percent certain, Roberta."

When I asked Mark the same question, he said, "I know you don't want to hear this, but you've got to give him back."

I couldn't get over the irony that the two names for this dog were Spanky and Buckwheat, the names of two children on the old TV show, *The Little Rascals*.

I was inconsolable. Lisa was nice about it, but she desperately wanted her Buckwheat back. And I adored my Spanky.

The following day, I was teaching a skills class to the nursing staff. Lisa was in the front row of the classroom. I tried not to look at her. Then I finished up teaching about ten minutes early, and an idea came to me. My eyes took in the rows of students, especially Lisa. "As you all know, I always say a story is the shortest distance between two hearts. Well, Lisa and I have a little drama going on about a sick dog that's now doing great. You all want to hear it?"

"Yes!" came the group's enthusiastic reply. At the conclusion of my story, Lisa raised her hand. "And I have an announcement to make. I've done a lot of thinking and soul-searching about this. The dog now belongs to Roberta. Forever and ever."

Spanky lived in my care for seventeen years. He saw me through a serious illness and several major surgeries, the deaths of my parents, and my divorce. When the two of us moved to a 100-year-old log cabin together called The Leaning Log, my beloved Spanky taught me how to begin life anew.

— Roberta Messner —

Canine
Comedy

74

The Unwavering Trust of a Dog

We never really own a dog as much as he owns us.
~Gene Hill

We've all heard stories about remarkable dogs separated from their owners while traveling, who then manage to trek hundreds of miles home many months later. Well, that was not our Prissy.

Prissy came to us as a puppy, a little black Pekinese mix with the cutest face. She had a distinctive under-bite, which always made her look like she was up to something. And most of the time, she was. As cute as she was, Prissy had one major flaw — she couldn't even find her way home from the mailbox.

We spent half our time hunting for that dog. We live on twenty-six acres in a rural community of northwest Georgia — mostly woods and a small lake. She loved that lake, and spent most days patrolling the water's edge for frogs. If we went canoeing without her, she would swim out to us and we'd have to drag her over the side, sopping wet.

Prissy didn't always stay by the lake, though. She liked to explore. Consequently, it became an almost weekly ritual to look for her somewhere in the far-flung community. We rescued her from a boot camp for troubled teens, a neighbor's house six miles away, a neighboring farm where she was being chased by two 800-pound mules, and even once from fifty feet up an oak tree. She had gotten there by chasing a squirrel up a fallen pine tree that was leaning against it.

Prissy was smart but she never paid attention to where she was going. She would just put her nose to the ground and start following a squirrel, rabbit or stray cat. When she finished her mission she would have no idea how she got wherever she ended up. We even had to rescue her from the neighbor's house at the end of our own driveway.

After a while, most of our closer neighbors knew her. Consequently, she never really "had" to find her way home because she would just go to the nearest front door and cry and whine until they let her in, at which point they would see her tag. They'd call, and we'd drive over and get her. If we weren't home, they would just load her in their car and bring her home.

However, one time when she wandered off, no calls came in.

She had been missing for about fourteen hours, and we had not been able to find her on our property. None of our neighbors had seen her, so we decided to search by car. We drove up and down the surrounding roads calling out to her, driving slowly and checking house to house if the houses were back from the road a bit.

After driving several miles in the surrounding area, we became discouraged and decided to head home to regroup and figure out what to do next. Then, I caught a glimpse of something black in the road up ahead. It was about a quarter of a mile off, and I really couldn't tell what it was from that distance. But as my husband drove toward the black object in the road, I was terrified. "Oh, my… What if that's her and she's been hit by a car?

As we got closer, I started praying that it wasn't her because the black object appeared to be right in the middle of a road with a fifty-five-mile-per-hour speed limit! But the closer we got, the more I knew it was her. She was just sitting there on the yellow line with traffic whizzing by her on both sides. My heart sank.

"Oh no, oh no. She's been hit by a car, and she's too injured to move!"

Before we even got to her, I was crying. We finally stopped by her side and I flung open the car door, prepared to carefully pick up her broken body and rush her to the vet.

Instead, she jumped up, ran to the car, and hopped in! She had a look on that little face that I recognized from all the other times we had retrieved her: "What on earth has taken you so long? I have been sitting here for hours!"

Baffled but relieved, we gathered her up. Hugs and wet kisses mixed now with tears of joy, and we headed home.

She simply had an unwavering faith and trust in what she knew to be true. Every time she couldn't find her way home, we would magically show up in the car. Of course, she had no clue that people were calling and telling us where to find her. I suppose after hours of us not coming, she decided to go where the cars were and just sit down and wait.

She was smart enough to go to a road to wait for us. With those kinds of problem-solving skills, one would think she'd have gotten a little sense of direction, too. But as we say in the South, "Bless her heart," she never did.

— Andrea Peebles —

75

Ruger, the Frog Prince

A well-balanced person is one who finds
both sides of an issue laughable.
~Herbert Procknow

One night when my husband and I got home from a day of errands, we let our six-year-old Labrador mix, Ruger, and our older Lab, Bear, outside to stretch their legs and relieve themselves. As we were unloading the car and getting our daughter out of her car seat, we noticed Ruger ran to the back of our property, near the swampy pond behind us — a common event for him. With the whole family in the house now, it was getting dark, so I stood at the side door and called for the dogs.

As usual, Bear was the first one in, slow and obedient. Then I heard Ruger, running a million miles per hour, heading straight for me. Right as he was coming out of the darkness, I noticed he was shaking his head from side to side like a maniac. I couldn't tell why he was doing that, or if something was wrong. Next thing I knew, he ran up the steps into the kitchen and gave his head one last shake as he came to an abrupt stop. It all happened so fast, I almost didn't notice the object that flew off his head.

He stood there, proud of himself for finally flinging off whatever had been on his head. And there, in the middle of our kitchen floor, was a frog! Yes, a huge tree frog had ridden into our kitchen on Ruger's head! My husband and I burst into laughter. I can only imagine this poor frog, holding on for dear life, trying to survive the ride of its life.

The frog was safely transferred back outside, and Ruger was known as my Frog Prince from that point on.

— Taylor Reau Morris —

76

Game of Chance

A dog will quickly turn you into a fool, but who cares.
I'm a fool for my dog and proud of it.
~Author Unknown

It was a typical weekday evening. My husband and I sat in our recliners watching television. Our dogs, Chance and Zarita, played with their toys on the floor in front of us.

Chance was a tall, handsome dog with a long, dark red coat. He came from a Golden Retriever rescue group, but looked more like an Irish Setter. He was six years old when we adopted him and, weighing over 100 pounds, had a little weight to lose.

Zarita is my little fawn-colored Chihuahua. Even though she weighs only five pounds, she has always ruled the roost. We got her as a puppy and now, at twelve years old, she is on her fifth big companion. Two were already in the winter of life when she arrived at six weeks of age, and we adopted the other three as adults or seniors.

Watching Chance and Zarita chew and shake their toys vigorously, I turned to my husband and said, "I have an idea. Take the bear into the other room and hide it while I hold Chance. We'll see if he can find it."

Mark didn't roll his eyes but I knew what he was thinking. With a dramatic sigh, Mark reached down, picked up the ratty gray bear and walked into the other room. After he returned and sat down, I released Chance. He ran into the other room and was back in a flash with the bear in his mouth. My jaw dropped, "I can't believe he found it so fast!"

I was amazed. Maybe our big, goofy boy was highly intelligent.

We tried the game again. Mark went into the other room and hid the bear in a new place while I had Chance sit in front of me. Mark sat back down, and I told Chance to get the bear as I pointed to the doorway. He trotted into the next room and was back in two seconds flat with the bear clamped securely in his jaws.

I could hardly contain myself as he proudly carried the gray bear over to me. Taking the bear, its fur wet with fresh drool, I praised him profusely. "Good boy!" and "You're so smart!" I rubbed his long, silky ears and kissed his forehead. I looked over at my husband and asked if he could believe Chance could do that. "Not in a million years," he replied.

My thoughts went to all we could do with this newly discovered talent. We could be a search-and-rescue team and save lost children. We could enter tracking competitions and win trophies. This was wonderful! My dog was smart. No… my dog was a tall, red, gorgeous genius! We could be famous!

Mark was equally amazed, although not quite as enthusiastic as me.

We continued playing the game and, no matter how many places Mark hid the bear, Chance returned it to us within a matter of seconds. It's not that I thought Chance lacked intelligence, but I had considered him to be average. As far as I knew, he had no special talent.

As he sat in front of me, accepting all my praise with a perplexed look in his eyes, I looked down toward the floor and noticed a pair of round eyes gazing up at me. There she sat, shivering with anticipation of the "ooohs," "ahhhs" and kisses that were surely coming her way. Zarita. My little princess. She waited quietly at my feet.

I narrowed my eyes at her as a disturbing thought came to mind. Where had she been, and what had she been up to as Chance demonstrated his astounding abilities? She always seemed to have a lot going on behind those expressive brown eyes and in that tiny Chihuahua head. I had a sneaking suspicion that a big letdown was about to occur. Her erect ears were rotating front to back like radar antennae, and her active eyebrows let me know that her little pea brain was working overtime.

I looked at Mark. "Where was Zarita when you went to the other room?"

"I have no idea."

I picked her up. "Hide the bear again, but this time I'm going to hold her."

After he hid the bear, I told Chance, "Find the bear." Blank stare. "Get the bear." Nothing. Finally, he ran into the other room, but came back empty-mouthed. "Get the bear." He left and came back with a snake. I got up, Zarita in my arms, and went to the other room. Chance followed. He didn't search for the bear; he just watched me intently. Hoping for a treat, I suppose.

I put down little Miss Smarty Pants to see what she would do. She just ran around my feet, looking up with expectation in those big, round eyes. Just as I suspected, she had been following Mark because he had her favorite bear, and she watched where he hid the toy. Chance went into the other room to see what she was doing, not because he was following my command. When he got into the room, she was already there with the bear. What a team!

Disheartened, I plopped back down in my recliner and went back to watching whatever sitcom happened to be on at the time. My dream of Chance and me forming a renowned tracking team had been dashed for the time being.

— Debbi Mavity —

77

Slow Learner

Sometimes when you get in a fight with a skunk,
you can't tell who started it.
~Lloyd Doggett

Our grand-dog Roxie is a sweet-natured, chocolate Lab, but she's not very bright. The runt of the litter, she's small for her breed and rather timid. She defers to most dogs, even her cousins — two very yappy Chihuahuas. The only species she won't kowtow to is squirrels. I blame my son-in-law for this. He gets her wound up by yelling repeatedly, "Roxie! Squirrel! Look! Squirrel!" She then goes crazy, barking and charging the patio doors.

Only one squirrel visits my daughter's yard. On the other hand, we have eight bird feeders and four suet holders on our decks, so we have in excess of twenty squirrels dropping by on any given day. Since we frequently dog-sit Roxie, providing Grandma/Grandpa daycare and accommodations for overnight and extended stays, this is problematic. Whether she's upstairs or downstairs, she parks herself in front of the French doors leading out to the decks and barks nonstop. Very annoying!

Roxie can't differentiate between a bushy-tailed squirrel, persona non grata as far as she's concerned, and the neighbor's cat. The cat has little patience for Roxie. She doesn't like being barked at and expresses her displeasure by hissing, arching her back, and swiping her paw, claws extended, over Roxie's tender snout. The cat wants to be left alone, but Roxie has yet to get the message.

Lots of other small, furry creatures visit back yards in our area of upstate New York. None of them resemble squirrels, but Roxie can't seem to tell the difference. One night when she was home at my daughter's house, she went out to do her business and spotted something scurrying across the lawn. Roxie gave chase, thinking it was a squirrel. That was a huge mistake! The squirrel wasn't a squirrel, or even a cat. It was a skunk! A very irritated one! The skunk took umbrage at Roxie's behavior and sprayed her. Roxie was stunned. None of the squirrels had ever done that before! She began snorting, yelping, and whimpering. My daughter called me in a panic, asking for advice as to what she should do.

There are a couple of skunk-odor removers on the market, but it was after 10:00 p.m. and stores were closed. I told her to drench the dog in tomato juice; she did, but Roxie still reeked. My daughter found a better solution on the Internet. She mixed a quart of 3 percent hydrogen peroxide, 1/2 cup baking soda, and 1 tablespoon of Dawn dishwashing detergent in a bowl. Putting on a pair of rubber gloves, she massaged the mixture into Roxie's fur and let it sit for ten minutes, being careful not to get it in the dog's eyes, nose, or mouth. Then she rinsed it out and repeated the process again, and again, and again, until the smell was finally gone.

A smart dog would have learned her lesson, but not our Roxie. Two months later, she met up with the skunk again, this time at 2:00 a.m. when she went out for her middle-of-the-night constitutional. The skunk was minding its business, but Roxie, as usual, wasn't minding hers. Roxie barked and lunged at the skunk. Bad move on Roxie's part! She couldn't seem to get it through her head that there were serious consequences for threatening or annoying a skunk. Roxie got sprayed again! A fresh batch of "skunk stink remover" was mixed up, and my daughter and son-in-law worked until 4:00 a.m. trying to get their malodorous canine smelling normal again.

I'm embarrassed to say that it happened again six weeks later. The definition of insanity is doing the same thing over and over again and expecting different results. It could also be the definition of stupid. Roxie wouldn't leave the skunk alone, and she was paying the price.

We were beginning to think the skunk had a vendetta against our grand-dog. My daughter lives in a large development with lots and lots of back yards. But for some reason, the skunk preferred hanging out in theirs. A few weeks later, in early September, my daughter was startled by a small animal peering through her patio door. At first, she thought it was the cat, but it was the skunk coming to call! She freaked out, grabbed the dog, and locked her in the bedroom where she couldn't threaten the skunk. The last thing they wanted or needed was to have the skunk spray their house. The skunk hung around a few minutes, and then got bored and moved on.

A few weeks later, my son-in-law noticed the dog walking back and forth on their side of the fence. It looked like she was on patrol. Then my daughter realized there was something on the other side of the fence walking with her — a furry black critter with a white stripe running down its back! They were afraid to whistle or call in Roxie, fearing the skunk would be startled and spray. They let the scene play out, and after about fifteen minutes, the skunk and Roxie, who hadn't barked once during their walk, went their separate ways without incident. My daughter and son-in-law breathed a sigh of relief. Roxie had made a stinky friend.

It's all well and good that Roxie made friends with their skunk, but we have our own skunk. He lives under the shed a few feet away from our house. He's an ornery little cuss! A few times every summer, when the windows are open, we can smell him, or rather, his spray. He's easily aggravated. We had to remove the suet feeders from the downstairs deck because the skunk and the neighborhood raccoons were arguing over ownership. The skunk won, leaving our deck reeking!

The last thing we need is for Roxie to enter into a love/hate relationship with our skunk. When she stays overnight, we make sure we know what's roaming the back yard after dark. We don't want her meeting up with our cranky polecat. Not with her history! We turn on the floodlights, and my husband, a former infantry officer, reconnoiters the yard with eyes peeled, making sure the skunk is nowhere around. Once he's sure it's safe, he hustles Roxie out the door. As soon as she's done her "business," he hustles her back in. We're not taking any chances. We don't want Roxie to have a "close encounter of the skunk kind" at our house.

My daughter has given us an emergency de-skunking kit to keep at our house, too. Now we're prepared for any eventuality—just in case Roxie has a relapse!

—Mary Vigliante Szydlowski—

78

The Mayor of Fox Den Road

Why does watching a dog be a dog
fill one with happiness?
~Jonathan Safran Foer

Two years after our beloved Wheaten Terrier passed away, it seemed our Miniature Schnauzer might again like a sibling. We selected a dog breed that had been on my radar for more than twenty-five years: a Petit Basset Griffon Vendéen (pronounced "Puh-TEE Bah-SAY Gree-FOHN VON-day-uhn"), also known as a PBGV, Peeb, or simply a Petite.

It's an unusual hound breed. When strangers stop and ask what type of dog he is, they often respond to his very long name by saying, "Wow, fancy." But the elaborate name of these canines belies their down-to-earth nature and appearance. He's short and long-bodied, like a Bassett, and has scruffy, wiry hair all over his body. Long ears, eager eyes, and a pronounced nose give him a distinct face. His fanlike tail never stops wagging, perhaps why they are known as the happy breed.

So, who couldn't use a little happiness in their lives? Eagerly, we welcomed our first PBGV and named him Milo.

Our surprise came on his first night home. Around 4:00 a.m., Milo whimpered from his gated area in the kitchen. My husband and I woke but stayed still, hoping he'd go back to sleep. Suddenly, a deep sound rumbled from the kitchen.

"I think that's our puppy," I whispered to my husband.

"Either that or there's a lighthouse sending us a warning."

On the second low, deep cry from the pup, we rolled out of bed to soothe our new family member's worries. It seemed that Milo had found his voice.

And boy, oh boy, does he like to use it! During our daily walks in the neighborhood, Milo has taken on the role of town crier.

"Hear ye, hear ye," he'll bellow in a gentle howl to any approaching man or beast. "It is I, Milo. Friend to all, foe to none."

As he got older, he took his self-appointed role more seriously. His howl — always friendly — grew louder... and louder... and louder. Once-quiet strolls with my dogs along our residential street are no longer discreet. In fact, I'm pretty sure he's turned me into a neighborhood spectacle. Everyone within a certain radius knows when we're outside. I can hear him in our house when my husband is out walking him.

Milo adores the neighborhood kids. Upon seeing them, he'll howl for their attention no matter how far away they're playing. If neighbors are getting out of their car, Milo will stare at them, wagging his tail, alerting them to his presence with a gentle howl and a smile.

I always feel self-conscious at the amount of noise we make. I typically wave, smile, and yell something like, "Vote for Milo."

Don't get me wrong. I always say "hello" to my neighbors, even stop to talk with them. Lovely people, whose company I enjoy, surround me. But I also realize they may not want a huge fuss made over them every time I pass by their house.

For a while, I tried to get Milo to be a little quieter. "No, shhh," I'd say as firmly as possible with a gentle tug on his leash. But after a few times, I stopped. I'm not sure he even heard me over the sound of his own voice. Besides, I felt terrible about the idea of cramping Milo's style.

Then one day, a neighbor came outside to get her mail as we walked past her house. She got her standard loud greeting from Milo, but she approached us this time.

"He's so sweet. He makes me feel so special when he says 'hello' to me."

She talked to us for a minute, and then we continued on our walk. But her words stayed with me and, quite honestly, made me feel ashamed. I'd been missing the big picture. Every single time Milo howls his loud "hello" to someone, while I cringe, others smile back at us. Nobody minds his noise. Milo makes others feel special.

And it isn't just the people on our street. At the dog daycare he attends a few mornings a week, he's earned quite a reputation.

"Some dogs have just a few friends," an employee at the center shared with me. "Milo is friends with everyone, though. He even gets the dogs who don't want to play to play with him."

Sometimes, I wonder how I missed the gift Milo brings to my world. I know how special he makes my entire family feel. Mornings, he greets us with a sleepy version of his world-famous howl. If one of us returns from running an errand during the day, we can't stop smiling as he runs up to us upon our return, singing his exuberant song of joy. Those greetings are probably the best part of my day. In fact, I regret the way I missed the obvious when it came to Milo's public displays toward others.

Now as I walk through the neighborhood with Milo, I've learned to embrace his inner town crier. I wave to my neighbors with a smile, chest puffing with pride that I'm lucky to have found such a lovable addition to our family — a dog whose single mission in life seems to be to make others smile.

And one thing is certain: If Milo ran for public office, I'm pretty sure he'd have a landslide victory.

— Sharon Struth —

79

The Three Musketeers

A door is what a dog is perpetually
on the wrong side of.
~Ogden Nash

Although we had gotten each dog at a different time, by the time they got older it felt like they were the Three Musketeers — always together, having fun, and getting into mischief, including one Fourth of July some years back.

We were at the lake visiting my mother-in-law. We had brought all three dogs so they wouldn't be alone back home when the fireworks went off. They were all terrified of fireworks.

So we loaded Brandy, the Springer Spaniel, Coco, the chocolate Lab, and Stardust, the Golden Retriever, into the van for a day at the lake. After swimming, boating and fishing, we decided we put the dogs in the laundry room to have their supper while we watched the fireworks. It was plenty big enough for the three of them. They'd had fun romping in the lake, and we anticipated a relaxing evening watching the sky light up with fireworks while they slept in the laundry room. The house was far enough away from the lake; we thought they might not even notice the noise.

After watching the fireworks, our youngest daughter, Shiloh, decided to run up to the house to check on the dogs.

"Dad, Dad!" she yelled as she ran back. "Come quick!"

"What is it, honey?" my husband said as he started running toward the house with the rest of us right behind him.

Try to imagine our shocked faces when we beheld what looked like a giant rathole in the laundry-room door. The dogs were all lying in there looking very innocent, as they had scurried back in when they heard Shiloh enter the house. All these years later, I still can't figure out how exactly they did it.

The Three Musketeers are all gone now, and all we have are memories of them. But none are as memorable as how they celebrated the 4th of July by chewing through that laundry-room door.

— Donna Collins Tinsley —

80

The Amazing Invisible Dog

Dogs act exactly the way we would
act if we had no shame.
~Cynthia Heimel

For simplicity's sake, I always referred to Sneeks as a Border Collie although she actually boasted mixed parentage. Her Border Collie heritage was dominant in terms of appearance, intelligence and many other traits, but her muddied pedigree included some variety of Terrier. The Terrier lineage endowed Sneeks with a stubborn streak, which led her to challenge me on occasion. Despite our mutual attendance at obedience class, this occurred with disconcerting frequency, particularly when it came to those commands that Sneeks preferred to tune out.

"Come" happened to be the command that most often caused Sneeks' defiance. Standing stock-still to see if I could find her became one of her favorite ploys. This ruse worked particularly well at night if she was standing in a dark area. I had to point straight at her and say sternly, "I see you," before she would walk forward, wagging her tail good-naturedly as if to say, "Okay, you caught me this time."

I read somewhere that dogs can see moving objects better than stationary ones. Unfortunately for Sneeks, she never did figure out that human vision doesn't work quite the same way. She always seemed surprised and a trifle disappointed when her magic stand-still tactic failed to fool me.

I'll have to admit that, several years ago, Sneeks almost had me convinced that she was invisible or, at the very least, a hairy Houdini. At the time, we were living in a house with a fenced section of yard, which Sneeks kept escaping somehow. No matter how hard we looked, we couldn't determine her method of egress, and she timed her escape attempts carefully so we didn't catch her in the act.

Alas for Sneeks, through complacency or sheer bad luck, her secret was revealed. One afternoon, we heard a banging noise coming from the vicinity of the metal shed. A few seconds later, Sneeks popped out from behind it — into the open yard. Upon investigation, it became clear that a gap between the shed and the fence — a gap that we'd thought would be too narrow — was her escape route. She was managing, with some effort, to squeeze between that seemingly impassable space between shed and fence, causing the banging noise by flexing the metal and perhaps hitting it with her tail as she wriggled through.

When Sneeks saw us staring at her, she paused for a moment. Then she heaved an enormous sigh, spun back in the direction from where she'd come, and retraced her steps — banging against the shed the whole way.

After that episode, a couple of well-placed stakes made the gap so narrow that even a snake would have had difficulty negotiating it. Sneeks found herself foiled — for now.

Good as she was at hiding, Sneeks usually forgot one important thing: her tail. One hot August afternoon, I was looking for her and, not surprisingly, she was ignoring my calls. I happened to glance over at a low shrub and noticed a long, black, furry appendage with a white tip — a dead give-away to the dog lurking in the cool shade of the shrub. She probably credited me with X-ray powers for managing to find her that day.

Sneeks was so proud of her abilities, that in her old age, when I caught her snoring on the forbidden couch in the basement I would just tiptoe past. I didn't want her to know that her Houdini-like skills had diminished.

I was in the basement the other day, and I saw that couch, now unoccupied. For a moment I wanted to believe that Sneeks was still around somewhere, still being our amazing, invisible dog.

—Lisa Timpf—

Eleanor's in the Room

Every survival kit should include a sense of humor.
~Author Unknown

I was new to this family and was both excited and nervous to have been invited to dinner. I had been dating my boyfriend Steve for a while, but this was my first time being invited to his family's gathering and I wanted to make a good impression on everyone — especially my hopefully soon-to-be mother-in-law. From everything I'd heard from those who knew her, she ruled the roost. Her word was law. She didn't take any guff from anyone — especially someone who was younger and didn't know anything... like me! Okay, you could kind of say that she was a bully.

We arrived right on time for this party. Chalk one up for us. I brought her flowers. Chalk another one up for me. We said "hello" and she hugged me. A terrific sign! We made small talk and then she pulled me over to one side of the room and in a very low, conspiratorial tone whispered to me, "Whatever you do, don't give any food to Eleanor. She is extremely overweight and has been put on a very strict diet by her doctor. Any deviation from what she is allowed to eat will make her sick. She'll try to make you feel sorry for her and she is very persuasive but please don't give her anything. She's fine."

Then she turned and started talking to someone else. She hadn't given me any clue as to which person out of all these people Eleanor was. Then another person came over to talk to me. We chit-chatted for a minute or two and then, as she turned to go, she said, "You were told not to feed Eleanor, weren't you?"

"Oh yes," I answered but before I could ask which person Eleanor was, the woman turned away and started talking to someone else.

The room was full of people. All strangers to me. And pretty much a bunch of chunky strangers at that! No skinny-minnies here. From what Steve had told me, this was a family that liked to cook and liked to eat. And none of those low-fat, no-taste dishes for them. They liked their food tasty and full of calories. You didn't use a butter or cream substitute when you cooked in this family.

And they all kind of looked alike. Well, they were all related so looking alike should have been expected. If only they had been wearing name tags it would have made my life a lot easier. But they weren't, so the only clues I had were that Eleanor was female and fat. Young? Old? Tall? Short? Blond? Brunette? No clue. And everyone seemed to be holding plates full of appetizers and munching happily on them. I checked to see if anyone had just a carrot stick or a lettuce leaf on her plate. Nope.

I started working the room to find the elusive Eleanor. My boyfriend was of no help; he was outside with a group of his male cousins playing a fast game of basketball. Inside, I introduced myself to each person hoping to meet Eleanor. I couldn't find her. Was she off in the kitchen scarfing down forbidden foods?

And then, suddenly, a new female relative appeared. There was no doubt about it… Eleanor had entered the room. She was obese and she was the only person in the room without an appetizer plate, so I thought she was following her doctor's orders. I watched her closely. She was very animated and social but didn't seem to stay that long with any one person. Then I noticed that when she talked to people, she always took something off their plates. Doctor's orders be damned! I was glad she hadn't made her way over to me yet. I didn't know what I would do if she tried to take food off my plate.

Soon it was time for all of us to take our dinner plates and stroll down the buffet line. The aromas coming from the steaming platters of food were amazing. These people knew how to cook! Everything looked delicious. I took a little bit of everything and found that my plate was piled high with food. Eleanor took a lot of everything, so her plate was not only piled high, it was spilling over.

I wound up sitting across from Steve so I couldn't quietly ask him about Eleanor and why everyone else had let her eat appetizers right off their plates.

Just at that moment I heard someone call, "Eleanor, come." I turned to look at the audacious Eleanor and saw a very plump, fluffy, white dog enter the room. Oh no!

A few years later, after Steve and I had married and plump, fluffy Eleanor had passed on, I told the story at a family gathering. Everyone was hysterical. And now, many more years have passed, but if you want to make a family member laugh, all you have to do is whisper, "Don't feed Eleanor!"

— Bea L. Montecarlo —

82

In Full Flour

What do dogs do on their day off?
Can't lie around — that's their job!
~George Carlin

After returning home from the store with a week's worth of groceries, I put all the perishable items away, everything except a five-pound bag of flour that I left on the dining-room table. Needing to get back to studying for my BSN degree, I secured Aero, my son's Weimaraner, in the den/kitchen area. Just before leaving the room, I looked at the flour and decided it would be okay. The flour wouldn't smell like anything interesting to the dog.

After thirty minutes of studying, I returned to the kitchen, and I think my scream could be heard for miles. It looked like there had been a snowstorm. Flour covered the entire kitchen floor and the blanket the dog had removed from the couch. He had found gloves and other clothing items to add to the mix, which gave the area the look of a crime scene. There was not an inch of surface area not covered with a fine dusting of flour. White paw prints on the couch and all over the floor led to the sofa, where the dog was perched looking down at the mess. He had this "I don't have a clue what just happened here" look on his face. Oddly enough, he didn't have a speck of flour left on his soft fur or paws. He had licked them clean or rubbed them off on the couch.

I was so angry I had to walk away for a while. I think I was still mumbling when I left the room to calm down. After several minutes of alone time, I returned to the kitchen. I was still angry, but realized cleanup had to start sometime. I snapped a quick photo so I could prove to my son what a mess his dog had made. I also paused long enough to post the snapshot of the mess on my Facebook account.

Then and only then did I begin to see the humor in the situation. My Facebook account lit up, logging hundreds of hits almost instantly. Everyone was making fun of my situation, and even writing captions for the photo. The funniest one said, "Hey, look, Grandma, I don't know what happened in here. It just exploded, and I am lucky to be alive."

I learned from this experience, where dogs are concerned, it is not wise to make assumptions about what they may or may not find appealing. They can make a toy out of even the simplest household items. It also taught me how important it is to pause a moment and see the humor in life, and not take everything so seriously. What seems to be just flour may, in fact, be a fun toy in the right (or wrong) paws.

— Tammy Collins Gibson —

83

It's a Dog's Vacation

If you want the best seat in the house,
you'll have to move the dog.
~Author Unknown

I t used to be that when our family headed south for March break, the only things we had to worry about were finding our passports and getting to the airport on time. But now, thanks to Oreo the Portuguese Water Dog, we have another concern.

Since his momentous arrival as a puppy the summer before last, nothing has been quite the same. A kitchen that hadn't seen baby gates in years quickly became a three-gated fortress. And a backyard fence that had more holes than Swiss cheese had to be secured on all fronts.

But as time passed, we all adjusted to our new Oreo-filled life. Except for me. From tripping on dog toys to stepping in dog pee to writing frequent, three-figure checks to our local vet, I was finding it hard to warm up to our new four-legged friend.

So it came as a bit of a surprise to me that when we were preparing for last year's spring break getaway, I started to worry about how Oreo would fare in our absence.

Luckily, my wife Cheryl had taken extra pains to ensure that Oreo's week would be as trauma-free as possible. Rather than book him into a standard kennel, she discovered a doggie resort out in the country that featured a large fenced-in play and exercise area.

For sixteen dollars a day, Oreo would be boarding on the main floor of a country farmhouse with seven other canine guests. Instead of spending his week in a wire cage, he would get to spend it "free range" with some new friends.

Still, I couldn't help thinking that the separation would be hard on the dog. But it turns out that my fears were misplaced. Instead of worrying about how Oreo would make it through the week, I should have been more concerned about how I would do.

Our one-week stay at an all-inclusive, five-star, newly renovated, over-hyped Caribbean resort got off to a great start. But then I developed a nasty case of bronchitis two days into our stay and spent much of the holiday hacking, coughing and whining. At least I could lie in the sun and nurse myself back to health. But what about poor Oreo?

In retrospect, I shouldn't have been wasting my worry on Oreo. He was having the time of his life.

The day after we got home, Cheryl drove out to the "resort" to pick up the dog. According to the resort owner (who doubles as the "concierge"), Oreo spent most of the week playing with another puppy his own age. Since the dogs had the run of the main floor of the house, he also warned her that Oreo might have picked up some bad habits.

When Cheryl got home, something wasn't right. Although Oreo was happy to see us, he seemed tired and listless.

Once again, I worried about the poor pup. Maybe the week away was too much for him. It seemed as if he was slipping into a depression.

By the next day, it was clear that my concern was once again misplaced. Oreo was back to his old self. He hadn't been depressed; he was just exhausted. He'd had so much fun playing with his new pals all week that he needed a rest from his vacation.

And that's just what I needed — a rest from my vacation. A few days lounging on the sofa would surely help me shake my Caribbean chest cold and get me back to normal. The only trouble was that one of those bad habits Oreo picked up at the "resort" was sleeping wherever he wanted to, including on the sofa.

Based on last year's experience, I'm thinking that maybe this year we won't go anywhere for March break — except for Oreo. He can return to the doggie resort, and I can get my sofa back, at least for a week.

— David Martin —

Chapter
9

Always the Protector

84

A Miracle Named George

Faithful friends are gifts from heaven:
Whoever finds one has found a treasure.
~Author Unknown

It was Monday, July 20, 1998, about 1:00 p.m. I was standing in the doorway of my room at The Seeing Eye in Morristown, New Jersey, anxiously waiting to hear my instructor call my name. All sorts of questions ran through my mind, and in the forefront was the fear that I was making an awful mistake. A guide dog when I had been afraid of dogs all my life? Crazy!

Each time a name was called, a few seconds would go by, and then I would hear a person and a dog walk quietly past my door. I wanted to bite my nails. I probably cracked my knuckles a time or two. I shifted from one foot to the other and sighed so many times I could have filled a balloon with all that hot air. Finally, shocking me out of my own thoughts, I heard my instructor say, "Shannon!"

I don't remember responding, but in seconds I was seated in a chair in the lounge, my instructor standing beside me.

"Shannon," she said, "this is George."

Two huge paws touched my knees.

"Down, George," my instructor said, and the dog obeyed immediately.

We were taken back to my room where the door was closed, leaving us alone. I petted him, he put up his paw to shake, and he sat so nicely, as if to say, "I'm a good boy, I promise."

However, after several minutes, George got bored with me and went to the door. He whined, crying out for the lady who had trained him.

I was at a complete loss as to what to do next. "Okay, God, you got me here. Now, what am I supposed to do?"

Sometime later, my instructor took George and me on a walk outside. George wore the harness and leash, as well as a second leash that my instructor held in her competent grip. It felt like I stumbled around that path instead of walked, and I kept stepping on poor George's feet, but he never stopped and neither did I. Still, I was worried. If this stumbling around was what I could expect, maybe this guide dog thing wasn't for me.

From the beginning, we were taught to feed, water and care for our dogs without any sighted assistance. We were also taught how to use a plastic bag in order to pick up after our dogs when they left their droppings at our feet. Cleaning ears, brushing teeth, grooming, feeding, watering, and giving pills were all things we had to master before we left the school. Sometimes, it was easy, and sometimes it was not, but there was always a can-do atmosphere.

One day stands out in my memory. My confidence was still shaken and I was still thinking this was a mistake. Our instructions were simple: Take the handle of your dog's harness and walk down the sidewalk. The instructor would be right behind us, watching our every step. No need to worry.

I stood there at the corner and took a deep breath. Quite literally, my instructor was asking me to put my life into the hands — ahem, paws — of a dog. Could I do it?

I hooked George's leash around my wrist, lifted the leather handle and took another bracing breath. "George, forward."

Suddenly, this seventy-eight-pound dog started pulling me down an unfamiliar sidewalk. Several times, I cracked my toes on the uneven surface and protruding tree roots.

"Toes up, Shannon!" came the voice of my instructor.

"Oh, Lord," I whispered, frantically. "What on earth am I doing?"

Swerving around trees and overhanging branches, George and

I flew down that Maple Street sidewalk. I had never walked that fast in my entire life. I was barreling along, and my feelings were ranging between terror, amazement and joy. And then...

Without warning, George stopped, and for a moment I just stood there in awe. I heard the traffic in front of me and my instructor's words, "You did it!"

I did it! I had walked down an unfamiliar sidewalk at a pace that most sighted folks would call running, and I was still alive to tell the tale. I had... Wait! I was forgetting something... someone. Right then and there, I knelt down on that hot sidewalk and hugged that big Labrador/Golden Retriever mix. I, who had never hugged a dog in all my nineteen years, threw every reservation aside and wrapped my arms around him. "We did it, George! You did it!

For the next eight years, I was covered in dog hair. I did not feel like a disabled person. George and I went to school and work; walked in ten-degree weather; trudged through snow; splashed through rain and mud; went to grocery stores, concerts, and restaurants; visited elementary schools; took a plane to visit a friend in Savannah, Georgia; slept side by side on the floor to the sound of audiobooks; shared pizza after a long week of church camp; and spent many happy hours just enjoying each other's company. Many times, George led me up a church's aisle to the piano, where he lay quietly while I played and sang.

Looking back, I know I could have done some things differently. Not all my decisions back then were the best ones, but George never stopped loving me, and I never stopped loving him. Some said that having a guide dog wasn't worth the clean-up, but they never knew how much we meant to each other. George retired as a guide dog in August 2006, but he lives on in my memory, reminding me every day to give up my own control and trust in God no matter how rough the sidewalks get.

— S.J. Wells —

85

Barely Awake

Protecting yourself is self-defense.
Protecting others is warriorship.
~Bohdi Sanders

Deep, low growls disturbed my sleep. Opening my eyes, I realized I was safe in my own bedroom, even as the growls morphed into snarls and then barks. "Shut up, Jack. Go back to bed," I muttered, too groggy with sleep to yell. I rolled over to look at the open balcony door. It was a breeze-less night and the sheer curtains were hanging there, not moving. Jack was between that sliding door and me. His ears were raised in sharp points.

We had recently moved to Colorado from Texas, trading our farmhouse for a townhouse. Colorado nights were cool, making it a joy to sleep with open windows rather than air conditioning. Neighbors were close, with forty-five units situated snugly together in what had once been an apple orchard. In spite of so many people living in such close proximity, the townhome complex was respectfully quiet, especially at night — or it had been until Jack began barking loud enough to raise the dead.

My real problem at the moment, however, was not the dead, but the living. What were my neighbors going to say about this early morning wake-up call? I didn't want to start our new life with enemies instead of friends. I could only imagine explaining to my husband Kevin why everyone had developed an intense dislike for us while he was away on a business trip. We were about to be labeled "those people with the annoying dog."

In the six years since Kevin had found Jack in a dumpster, the dog had never acted this crazy. Jack looks like a Kelpie, an Australian sheep dog, and certainly has the temperament of one. When Kevin found him, he was a painfully skinny puppy, having both worms and mange. With proper care, he soon filled out to a healthy weight. The only thing that didn't change about him was his tail and ears. Those were full-size even on the puppy version of Jack. With those big, pointed ears and thick tail on his scrawny little body, he looked more like a cartoon drawing of a dog than the real thing.

Like any working breed, Jack's a busy guy during the day, herding anything that needs it, from small children to baby deer. At night, though, he sleeps like the hard worker he is. The vicious, snarling dog before me that night was not someone I knew. He was no longer a herder. He was ready to attack.

Hoping to silence his crazed barking, I climbed out of bed. As I ran downstairs, Jack was on my heels. I didn't stop running until I was outside in our small, fenced back yard. Turning quickly, I stepped back inside the kitchen before Jack could follow. Now that he was securely locked out, I could further investigate the cause of his outburst.

I retraced my steps through the townhouse, going out the front door this time. My balcony was directly overhead, so if there was a reason for his barking, I would find it. Standing on the front steps in my pajamas, the rashness of my decision struck me, along with a terrible odor. As my hand flew to my nose, I whispered, "It smells like a zoo out here!"

As foolish as I felt standing outside barely dressed, there was no one to witness my embarrassment. I'd expected at least to see a family of raccoons. That might have caused Jack's barking. All was quiet, though, except for the gentle sound of rustling bushes.

Wait, why was I hearing rustling in the bushes? We no longer had any bushes; they had all been cut a week earlier when the complex was painted.

I looked up at the tree that was touching my balcony, swaying gently in the breeze. Except there was no breeze. I recalled that the sheers in my bedroom had been quite still.

And then I put it together: the swaying tree, the smell, Jack's barking.

My life didn't flash before my eyes, but news stories did. I had seen footage that showed what happened when a bear got into a house. Worse than property damage, I'd heard of people getting mauled occasionally in a bear encounter.

With a pounding heart and bear-fueled adrenaline, I forced myself to slip quietly back into the house, locking the front door behind me. With one entry secured, I raced to the kitchen to let Jack in. Together, we charged up the stairs to my bedroom.

The gray, pre-dawn light gave me a clear view of the room — the thankfully bear-free room. Bounding to the sliding door, I slammed and locked it. Jack quieted at last as I slumped to the floor. He accepted my seated position as an invitation, crawling into my lap and covering my face with kisses of forgiveness.

Now that I was certain the townhouse was bear-proof, my thoughts turned to my neighbors. I dressed quickly while I tried to determine how to prevent more early-morning bear encounters. While I was dressing, my stinky friend wandered away. Had he given up now that he couldn't come inside the townhouse and possibly peruse my kitchen? Jack had sounded like quite a beast. Did all that barking and growling deter him? I would never know why the bear left, but I did know he could come back.

The story of Jack's intelligence and heroism spread like wildfire, with my own actions adding some humorous kindling to it. As funny as my pajama-clad escapades were, we all took our safety and the bear's seriously. A bear that repeatedly finds food in populated areas will eventually be put down. Residents became more diligent about trash and any other smells that might attract bears, as well as more cautious about late-night or early morning walks.

It was not our last bear sighting, but there weren't many more. The only amenity the bear sought in our complex was food, and there was no reason for him to join our community without it. Besides, it might not be the best hunting ground. After all, we are guarded by a sheep dog in wolf's clothing.

— Linda Kinnamon —

86

Buddy Barked

You see, sometimes in life, the best thing for
all that ails you has fur and four legs.
~Mark J. Asher, All That Ails You:
The Adventures of a Canine Caregiver

Yorkies bark, and Buddy was no exception. But he only barked for a reason and rarely for long. He was never one of those dogs that yapped if a breeze ruffled his ears or another dog barked three blocks away. If someone came to the door or he saw a squirrel, Buddy would become his most fierce self, barking and lunging as much as a little Yorkie can lunge. But he would always stop on command.

One night, though, Buddy began to bark about ten o'clock. He slept in the same room as my son, so I called out, "Quiet, Bud!" Instead of getting quiet, he became louder, more insistent, barking faster and faster. It was his on-the-job bark, and I could not imagine why he kept barking so fiercely. I wondered if we had a mouse in the house.

I got up and went into my son's room. Buddy was on the bed and barking at Brendan, right into his face. I turned on the bedside light and saw the problem immediately. My son was on his back, breathing shallowly, with his eyes rolled back. When I tried to pull him to a seated position, he was limp and unresponsive. He slid off the bed and onto the floor.

Buddy had stopped barking and was now on the floor next to Bren, frantically licking his face. I grabbed my cell phone and dialed 911.

The dispatcher had me run down and open my front door so the EMTs could come right in. Buddy didn't leave Bren's side.

Buddy never once barked or growled at the emergency personnel when they arrived and worked on Bren. He seemed to step back out of their way, but hovered nearby.

As they raised up the stretcher to wheel it through the front door, I turned to Buddy. "Good boy, good boy, thank you!" I hugged him for a moment, crying all over him. "If I'm not back soon, I will send someone to let you out. Good, good boy!"

Then I shut him in Bren's room. I was going to follow the ambulance to the hospital and had no time to waste, but I still had to thank Bud for waking me up. What might have happened if he had not?

At the hospital, Bren opened his eyes and spoke to me. He was transferred to Cardiac Intensive Care and in the morning he had a pacemaker implanted.

I was in the hospital for a couple of days but Buddy was still at home. I had called a friend, and she went to the house to stay with Buddy, feeding him, letting him out, and reassuring him that his people would be back soon. She reported that he seemed depressed, not his usual bouncy self. Most of the time, he perched on the back of the couch, looking out the window and waiting.

When I brought Bren home, Buddy was ecstatic, wiggling with joy and jumping. Bren was exhausted, and all he wanted to do was go to bed and sleep. He was instructed to be as still as possible to allow time for his heart to heal. He had to sleep on his back. Buddy jumped up on the bed and promptly lay across Bren's chest. I pushed him off, trying to get him to lie next to Bren as opposed to on him. Bud was having none of it. I would push him off, and he would wiggle back up and on. I was afraid this was painful for Bren and was thinking about taking Buddy out of the room entirely. But Bren wanted Buddy.

"It's okay, Mom. He can stay there. It doesn't hurt too much, and I want Buddy with me." I was not sure about this. What if Buddy somehow jostled Bren and moved those wires in his heart? What if, as the medication wore off, it became painful to have this pressure on his chest? But Bren wanted him, and Buddy was not moving, so I decided to let it go, figuring Buddy would move over to his usual spot beside Bren in just a little while.

That was not what happened. Every time I went in to check on Bren, Buddy was right there, stretched across his chest. When I went in at 6:00 a.m., our usual wake-up time, he finally jumped down and Bren sat up gingerly.

"How are you, son?"

"I'm better, Mom. Buddy stayed on my chest all night. If I tried to push him off, he crawled right back."

Bren got up, had breakfast, and began his healing journey. And Buddy? It seemed he only needed that one night to reassure himself that Bren's heart was not going to stop again. He resumed sleeping in his normal location at the foot of the bed. And he never, ever barked at night again.

— Jude Walsh —

87

A Dog Knows

*Our perfect companions never
have fewer than four feet.*
~Colette

I pulled my running shoes from the closet, the telltale sign that good times were about to happen. My rambunctious Irish Setter began to dance circles around my chair as I bent down to tie my shoes.

"Come on, bag of bones," I said. "You may not need exercise, but I do."

"Woof, woof." I had to shush her or my toddler and baby would wake up before I could slip away.

Brandy's almond-shaped, dreamy brown eyes looked up expectantly at me.

My brother's words echoed in my head. "You shouldn't go running in that park at the same time and same route every day. There have been some nasty reports I don't even want to scare you with."

I'd waved my hand, dismissing his worry. "Has volunteering as an auxiliary cop turned you into a worrywart?"

"No, seriously, Sis. With the densely populated woods and secluded trails, it's dangerous. There have been reports of rape."

I shook off his warning as I tugged the second shoelace tight. Popping up, I snapped the leash onto Brandy with determination, and quietly closed the front door behind us. These few precious moments alone would be the only break I got all day, and I wasn't about to give them up. The call of nature and the serenity I found off the beaten track beckoned, and I reasoned that I had my dog and God. What more protection does a girl need?

I breathed in the fresh morning air and gloried in the lemony sunlight spreading across a cloudless sky. There was a glow lighting up the tips of the distant mountains, and I smiled at the blessing of another day. My warm-up walk picked up speed, but not before I stopped to breathe in the fragrance of one of the lilac bushes that grew in glorious abandon by the road. I started with a slow jog and was into a full run by the time I reached the entrance to the park.

Brandy, well trained in the etiquette of what to do and not do when I was on a serious run, loped at my side. She knew that she would get the opportunity to sniff and explore during my cooldown, but not during the running part of the excursion.

The trails opened before me. Once again my brother's words came to me, and once again I shrugged them off.

"We're not going to let fear spoil a perfect day, are we, Brandy?" She looked up at the mention of her name but kept in perfect stride.

The gathering sunlight dimmed as the trees closed in around me, and a nervous shiver prickled up my spine. Unexpectedly, Brandy missed a beat. The perfect cadence of dog and owner running in sync faltered as she pulled back on the leash. The hackles on her neck rose, and the hair lifted in a wave along her backbone to her tail. She growled a deep, throaty warning, so unlike her usual lovable self.

I stopped. "What is it, girl?"

Brandy strained on the leash.

A whisper carried on the morning breeze brought words to me. "There she is!"

Brandy broke into a snarl before her bark took on a ferocious tone.

A chill spread through my bones. A man's voice talking to someone else could only mean one thing—there were two of them.

Like a jackrabbit, I turned with a snap of the leash and ran as if my life depended upon it. Brandy flew alongside me. That park entrance never looked so good. I kept on running. My lungs were on fire, and my legs felt like lead by the time I crashed through our front door. I sank into the nearby chair with sweat and tears mingling. My head fell into the soft fur of my beloved dog, and I wept in relief.

"Good girl, Brandy. Good girl. I love you, girl. I love you."

Her tongue hung out of her mouth as she gloried in the attention.

Joshua, my toddler, waddled his way down the hall toward us.

"Mama run?"

I laughed through the tears. "Oh, and how, baby, and how."

I gathered him onto my lap in a tight hug with Brandy sneaking in a good-morning kiss all the way up his tiny face.

Joshie giggled, and I lifted a prayer of thanks. Both God and dog had done their job, despite my foolishness.

I did not allow fear to have the final word. I kept running, but my routes were varied, and the park was off limits at 6:00 a.m.

With my beloved Brandy, my faithful companion and protector, ever at my side, I continued to enjoy the sun, the run and the fun. As body, mind and spirit melt together in harmony, there is no better way to start the day.

— Blossom Turner —

Springing into Action

Gratitude; my cup overfloweth.
~Author Unknown

My three children played peacefully in the back yard. This alone should have put me on alert, but the setting was so serene that I hung our clothes to dry in the soft breeze and enjoyed the unseasonably warm September afternoon. Our home was nestled amongst the dry oaks and Manzanita trees of the Northern California foothills. We had only a handful of neighbors within a half-mile radius, so our property was quiet and private. There were no fences or barriers between houses, only smiles and friendly waves as we passed each other's homes on our walks.

It was a good place to raise our children: four-year-old Andre, two-and-a-half-year-old Yvonne, and fourteen-month-old Philippe. From the clothesline I had a clear view of the kids. Philippe was so cute, wearing only a diaper as he peered intently into the grass looking at bugs or something. He was always the curious one.

Our dog Jessie was always present yet unobtrusive, a constant participant in all the family activities. She lay fast asleep, warming herself in the sun. She had been with us from an early age, reared several litters of beautiful Springer Spaniel pups, and was loved by all. Her temperament was docile and kind. Her only irritating trait was her propensity to wander away from the house when I wasn't looking and come back with a pack of male suitors trailing behind her. But this day, she was to prove her worth.

Having hung all the towels and pillowcases from the first load, I ventured into the house to grab a pile of wet sheets from the washing machine. The air was dry and warm, and I knew we'd all have fresh-smelling sheets for our beds tonight. As I wasn't in the habit of leaving my children unattended, I returned quickly to my clothesline duty. The afternoon was so tranquil at first that I didn't notice that Jessie had moved from her slumbering position. When I did notice her absence, I exclaimed annoyingly, "That dog! She's off again, and we don't need any more puppies!" I looked around for her but couldn't find her. I knew she'd return eventually.

I resumed my laundry responsibilities, took a quick survey of the kids and saw, to my horror, that Philippe was missing. As he grew, he would prove to be an adventurous, inquiring soul, and that day was the first indication of his fearlessness. To my knowledge, no car had driven down our road, no passers-by had walked the usual paths close to our home. I began to yell his name, trying to stay calm. I needed to keep my head about me.

I put Andre and Yvonne in a secured place, sternly instructing them to stay put until I brought Philippe home. I sprinted up and down the street, calling his name. There was a water ditch close to our home that the county used to transport water to adjoining houses. I ran along it, but no Philippe.

I went back home to check on the other two and call the police. This was in the days before cell phones. We lived so far back into the woods that it would take a good twenty to thirty minutes for help to arrive, so I needed to make that call right away.

As I lifted the receiver to my ear, I glanced out the window that overlooked the back yard. There, coming from the direction of the water ditch that I had just checked, was my almost-naked little boy toddling along. He was so far away I could barely make him out, but it seemed that he would stop from time to time to investigate some treasure along the way.

Strangely, every time Philippe would stop, he seemed to be pushed forward. And there she was, our Jessie deliberately pushing him from behind with her nose. She had been roused when he wandered off and left her spot in the sun to follow him and bring him back. I am convinced she saved my son's life. To this day, he loves Springers. In fact, he has one now that watches over his own children.

As I ran toward Philippe with tears streaming down my face, I didn't know who to hug first: my son or his rescuer. I picked up Philippe in my arms and inspected his little frame for any bumps or bruises. Jessie knew by my embrace and continual affirmations that she had won a place in my heart and at the family table, albeit on the floor, from that day forward. A steak that night was her reward. The whole ordeal spanned maybe fifteen minutes, but it felt like an eternity. Jessie was a valued family member for many years after that, and when we speak of her today, it is always with gratitude.

— Michelle J. Nunnes —

The Accidental Hero

Dogs have a way of finding the people who need them,
filling an emptiness we don't even know we have.
~Thom Jones

"Where are we going, Mom?" my siblings and I asked from the back seat of our woody station wagon. Mom just smiled like she had a big secret.

Finally, she stopped the car at a place called the Humane Society. "Where are we?" I asked.

Mom smiled again. "You kids have been begging for a dog. Let's go pick one out."

After much happy dancing, we went inside to choose our pet.

My siblings and I looked around, searching for the cutest, friendliest-looking dog. But Mom had a different idea. "Which dog has the least time left?" she asked the volunteer quietly.

The volunteer pointed at a small, fuzzy dog with big, floppy ears. Mom studied the dog. "Is he a Beagle? He's got Beagle ears, but he's fuzzy like a Terrier."

The volunteer smiled. "We've been calling him Teagle. It's a cross between Terrier and Beagle."

Mom nodded and then turned to us kids. "What do you think of that little guy?"

To be honest, there were cuter dogs in the shelter that day. But every time one of us tried to show one of them to Mom, she just directed us back to the Beagle/Terrier mix. "I really like that one," she said about 100 times.

Finally, it became clear that when Mom had told us to choose our pet, she meant that we had to choose the one she liked. And clearly, the one she liked was Teagle.

Years later, Mom agreed that there were cuter dogs in the shelter that day. "But he was the one who needed us the most," she said.

Turns out, we needed Teagle, too.

One day, about six months after we'd gotten Teagle, my siblings, the neighbor kids, and I were playing hide-and-seek in our basement. At first, everyone tried to coax Teagle into hiding with them, but he was too rambunctious and gave away our hiding spots. But we discovered that he was actually very good at finding people.

It was my turn to be "It," so I enlisted Teagle's help. Together, we found everyone but my older brother, Mike. We wandered around the basement, calling his name. "Sniff him out, Teagle," I said.

We were just about to give up when Mike came flying out from behind some old boxes, crying and waving his hands in the air.

"What's wrong?" we asked him.

"Wasp nest," he screamed. "I already got stung once."

Earlier that summer, Mike had wound up in the emergency room after being stung multiple times. He was allergic, but we hadn't known until that day. It had been scary watching him swell up and gasp for breath. None of us wanted it to happen again.

"Go upstairs and get Mom," I told him. "And don't you come back down here!"

As we devised a plot to get the wasp nest outside without being stung, Teagle took matters into his own paws. He started barking and then ran behind the boxes where Mike had been hiding.

We watched from afar as the little dog picked up a wasp between his teeth and shook it. His huge ears flapped in the air with his vigorous movements. After shaking the wasp, he'd toss his head and throw it on the ground. If it moved, he'd pick it up and shake it again. If not, he'd find another wasp to shake. "Teagle is killing the wasps!" we said. "He knows Mike is allergic, and he's saving him!"

By the time Mom came downstairs with the insect spray, Teagle had killed most of the wasps. And he'd solidified his place as a hero in our family.

That was the first time I watched Teagle kill a wasp, but it wasn't the last. In fact, he had a thing for killing all kinds of insects. Over the years, I watched him shake a housefly, a bumblebee, and more spiders than I care to think about.

While deep down, we knew that Teagle couldn't have really known about Mike's allergy, my siblings and I bragged about that incident every chance we got.

"Your dog plays fetch? Well, our dog saved my brother's life," we'd say.

Teagle might not have been the cutest dog at the shelter that day, but he was the best dog there.

We saved him. And whether he meant to or not, he saved us, too.

— Diane Stark —

The Dog Who Cried Wolf

*Most owners are at length able to teach
themselves to obey their dog.*
~Robert Morley

You know how the story goes. A young lad runs in from the pasture, claiming that a wolf is ravaging the flock. When the good people of the village march off to check, Canis lupus is nowhere to be seen. Worse, there's a significant lack of evidence to suggest he was ever there. And thus the shepherd becomes "the boy who cried wolf." The villagers tire of the game and ignore the boy. Then, of course, one day the wolf really does visit.

I thought of that story often when it came to our Border Collie Sneeks. She may have been a herder and shepherd genetically, but she yapped with similar intensity at visiting family members, squirrels, or falling leaves. We learned to pay no heed to her annoying barking.

One particular night, long after the sun had set and the rest of us had sought our beds, Sneeks shattered the silence with a series of strident yips. Despite several exhortations to "Be Quiet," the baying continued. I will admit, not to my credit, that the requests for silence became progressively less polite — to no avail. Finally, the woofing wound down, seemingly of its own accord.

The next morning, grumpy from interrupted sleep, I gave Sneeks the proverbial cold shoulder. That is, until I looked out the front window and noticed that at some point in the night, person or persons unknown had absconded with our minivan.

Sneeks and I exchanged glances as I processed this new information. Even in its sleep-deprived state, my brain made the connection: Sneeks's frantic barking was intended to alert us to this calamity.

That incident did nothing to temper Sneeks's vocalizations, but it did alter my behavior. After that, when Sneeks barked in the night, no matter what the hour, I did her the honor of checking for the reason.

After all, I had no desire to endure her smug look a second time.

—Lisa Timpf—

No Joking Around

*A dog judges others not by their color or creed
or class, but by who they are inside.*
~Author Unknown

My friend twitched uncomfortably as the powerful dog moved purposely toward her. I knew it was wrong, but I couldn't help enjoying a moment of perverse pleasure. The tentative smile on my friend's face was frozen somewhere between terror and disbelief as the huge red Doberman stood above her.

Joker, my Doberman Pinscher, was the third dog I had trained and shown in AKC obedience trials. I love the large working breeds and the teamwork required to win the obedience titles. I also enjoyed the competition and camaraderie at the shows. It was fun to watch the different breeds and the diverse crowd. And there were all those amazing doggie personalities.

When you arrive at an obedience show, you first stake out your spot, with canopies, blankets spread on the ground, and your food supplies and chairs. The day that Joker frightened my friend we were at a trial and we set up next to each other. She was showing her Siberian Husky, and even though Huskies can be a challenge to train, my friend was terrified of Doberman Pinschers for some reason, regardless of how well trained they were.

When my "Killer Dog" walked over to her, her first reaction was terror. But then he stretched his huge muzzle across her neck and snuggled close, nuzzling her chin. "Watch out… he's going for your throat!" I teased. And then she got it. She smiled, rubbed his head, and scratched behind his ears. He was in doggie heaven, and she was quite pleased with herself for making an unexpected new buddy. She could see that we can't judge a book by its cover or a dog by its breed.

When anyone came to our house, Joker sidled up to them to initiate petting. If they ignored his request, he'd back up and try to sit on their feet or lap. If they still failed to comply or stopped petting him too soon, he'd raise a big paw and swat them. Our family agreed that our Doberman would sooner escort a burglar around the house than attack him.

But then, when Joker was around three years old, he proved us wrong.

Joker liked to ride in the back of the camper shell of my old Datsun pickup. His large, handsome head looked impressive stuck through the boot in the cab, resting on my shoulder.

Late one evening, I parked my little truck in a local fast-food parking lot and left Joker in the camper as I went inside to pick up our chicken dinner. I waited my turn, listening to a chatty older gentleman in line irritate a few impatient customers.

It wasn't until I walked out of the well-lit store and got into my truck that I realized how dark it was where I had parked. As I rummaged through my purse for my car keys, a shadowy form appeared next to my slightly opened window. I gasped, and my body jerked under Joker's muzzle as a hand reached toward the opening and a raspy voice growled, "Hey, you in there!"

I didn't even have time to lock the door before the explosion came. My docile Dobie gave a ghastly roar as he catapulted his body through the boot over my body, snarling and gnashing at the window. With foam flying off his teeth, he looked like something out of a Stephen King novel. Then I heard a familiar chatty voice say outside, "Lady, you forgot your keys." This, of course, accounted for my not finding them in my purse.

"Hello, doggie," the friendly man crooned cluelessly as he attempted to push his fingers through the space in the window toward the flashing teeth. I composed myself enough to mutter, "I wouldn't do that if I were you."

I did get my keys back and a fresh respect for my previously unappreciated hero. It was clear he would be quite formidable in an emergency, but he was always sweet and discerning in his approach to family, friends and acquaintances.

My valiant protector has been gone for quite a while, but his regal form and smiling face are still etched on my heart. When I recognize my tendency to judge circumstances, situation or people in a superficial manner, I remember my friend's initial perspective and my own regarding this great dog's character. I've learned that one can't judge a man by the way he looks or a dog by the size of its teeth or bark. The true character of man or beast can be seen in what they do and is established when one looks through their eyes into their soul to see the size of their heart.

—Valerie J. Frost—

92

His Chance to Save Me

One of the most enduring friendships in history —
dogs and their people, people and their dogs.
~Terry Kay

It was a sunny September day in northern Iowa. The sky was blue, the fields were green, and the air was fresh. At the time, we were living on an acreage about twenty-five miles from the nearest city and seven miles from the closest small town.

I was going out to feed the animals. After I was done laying out hay and chicken feed, I decided to ride around on one of our newest mares. She had been with us for about two months and got along great with our other four mares. She had a calm temperament and enjoyed getting attention, so I thought nothing of it when I saddled her up. We did some light trotting around the fenced-in pasture.

About twenty minutes into my ride three deer jumped the low end of our fence and headed across the pasture to a densely wooded area. They spooked my mare, and she took off at full speed. I used all my strength to pull back the reins and stop her, but the right rein snapped! I flew off her, and landed on my left hip, cracking my head on the ground, too. I blacked out.

A few seconds later when I opened my eyes I was being dragged on the ground toward the fence gate. I looked up and saw the mare standing about fifteen feet away. Then I locked eyes with my dog,

Chance. He was pulling me by my shirt out of the pasture. I tried to stand, but couldn't. My left hip wouldn't bear any weight. So I used my right leg to help move me along while Chance kept dragging me. My head was throbbing and I was seeing black spots. My whole left side felt like it was on fire.

Chance was persistent as he dragged me toward the gate. He wanted me out of the pasture where the five horses were roaming. Once we made it to the gate, I was able to use the bars to pull myself up and open the door. It was exhausting and took all of my strength, and I slid back to the ground once I was on the outside.

Then Chance started howling. He was a seven-year-old Pit Bull who I'd had since he was five weeks old and I had never heard him howl before. He was so smart to do that. Had my husband heard him barking, he probably would have ignored it and thought he was just barking at the goats or something routine. But my husband, who was in the garage, heard the howling and knew that something was different. He came running to Chance's aid.

At the hospital, we learned that I had fractured my hip and suffered a severe concussion. I had physical therapy for eight weeks, and I still suffer from migraines and occasional leg pain.

Had Chance not been there to pull me out of the pasture, who knows what would have happened? He had always been my shadow, but that day he was my angel and hero, and I will be eternally grateful that he was there for me.

—Ashley Bell—

93

Oso Concerned

Even dogs know how important it is to hear
somebody else breathing.
~Benjamin DeHaven

I came home sick on the last day of school, just before Christmas break. Mad at the bad timing, the weather, my students coughing in my face, and the whole world, I crawled into bed. I made some Theraflu tea with lemon and curled up under my comforter with a book. I drifted off, only to be jolted awake by Oso, our fifteen-year-old Chow Chow, who was barking.

"What do you want?" I asked groggily.

Oso stared at me. When I got back to sleep, he started barking again, and again, and again....

This happened the following night, and then again on the night after that, and the night after.

During the day, things were quite different. My pal with the furry tail dragged his arthritic legs around the house, his beautiful brown eyes fixed on me. No barking, no whining, no running up and down the stairs.

One particular night, in desperation, I even took down a large painting from the wall to block the stairs to my bedroom.

I drifted off. Next thing I knew, there was a loud barking again by the door. The painting was no match for Oso.

I decided that desperate times called for desperate measures, put in earplugs, adjusted a pair of headphones on top of them, closed my bedroom door, and went to bed, determined to catch up on sleep. I drifted off momentarily, only to wake up again, startled by the same loud barking, scratching, and bumping at the door.

"What do you want?" I cried out, blowing my stuffy nose.

My guess was that Oso was suffering from separation anxiety. I had always kept my bedroom door open before his barking started. So, I came up with a new strategy of sleeping on the couch in the living room. It didn't work the way I had planned. It just gave him access to lick my face and bark directly into my ear, his bad breath catapulting me into a sitting position.

"God, why is this dog keeping me up at night?" I whined.

Over time, my sinuses and headache got better. Strangely enough, Oso's wild running and barking tapered off as well.

One night, I realized that Oso used to act in a similar manner before I was diagnosed with sleep apnea. His crazy behavior around my bed was actually the main reason I went to see a sleep doctor a few years before.

And then it hit me. Oso had been waking me up every time I stopped breathing. My Guardian Angel overcame his own arthritic pains—even jumping over that painting and running up the stairs—so he could keep me breathing.

— Nadia Ianakieva —

Chapter
10

Miracles Happen

94

Lost and Found

Where there is great love, there are always miracles.
~Willa Cather

When my cell phone rang early on the last morning of our weeklong vacation at Disney World, and I saw the dog sitter's phone number pop up, the bottom dropped out of my stomach. I punched the button to answer and heard a distraught but restrained voice on the other end of the line.

"He's *what*?" I screeched.

"Lost," she said. "I'm so sorry. He must have slipped out when my daughter took out the trash. We looked into the night and this morning, but now I have to go to work."

Sleep? Work? How could she consider doing anything except searching for the eight-pound Miniature Poodle she was tasked with protecting? The dog we had fallen in love with on Petfinder.com three years earlier. The dog we had driven from Alabama to Tennessee to retrieve. The dog who we knew needed us when we saw that he sat alone, away from the other dogs, at the rescue shelter. He became our baby, our responsibility, and we had failed him.

Sensing that the sitter was not going to be any further help, and knowing that time was of the essence, I disconnected and huddled with my husband to concoct a plan. Lee would try to reschedule an earlier flight home. I would e-mail my best friend and ask her to blast a "lost dog" e-mail message with Grant's picture to our entire neighborhood and school district.

Despite our attempts to catch an earlier flight, we still had the morning to wait. Our original last-day plan was visiting Epcot. So we took our two school-aged children to the park. What else were we going to do? While the kids amused themselves, my husband and I sat on a bench feeling dazed. Other visitors probably wondered how faces could be so glum at Disney World.

At the airport, I bought *90 Minutes in Heaven* to distract myself, and I devoured the entire book on the return trip. A book about a miracle kept my attention and instilled a little hope — not an easy task when I was imagining catastrophe hundreds of miles away.

Meanwhile, back in Alabama, angels abounded. My group of friends, called "coffee girls" for our Tuesday morning coffee dates, did more than send e-mails from the comfort of their homes. They printed flyers from the photo I had transmitted and posted them in the neighborhoods near where both we and the pet sitter lived. I wrapped myself in that love, and it held me together.

After an agonizingly long day of feeling helpless, we arrived home. I was torn as to what to do first. It was 2007, so I wasn't familiar with sites that instructed owners how to find lost pets. And social media was so new that it was not a viable option for sharing our lost-dog plea. So we started working in the only way that made sense to us: We printed more flyers. I bought poster board, duct tape, and the fattest Sharpie I'd ever seen. My fax machine hummed as it contacted myriad veterinarians' offices, the Humane Society, and animal control. My husband started canvassing the neighborhood around the dog sitter's house. I manned the phones.

Going to bed that night was one of the hardest things I have ever done, but I knew our chances of finding Grant in the dark were slim, and we would need energy for the next day's search.

We worked from dawn till dusk the next day. Angels in the guise of more friends helped us go door-to-door. There had been several sightings of Grant, but no one could catch him. People told us tales of coyotes and dog thieves that made us shudder. Where was our little guy? We continued moving through neighborhoods, handing out and posting flyers.

Another night fell, as did more tears.

On Sunday morning, the third day, I took the children to church for some normalcy — again feeling guilty — while Lee kept looking. After church, the kids and I rejoined the search. We had worked our way a mile from the dog sitter's house in several directions. We had heard stories of Grant darting this way and that. We had endured several false leads via phone calls. By 4:00 that afternoon, we were at a loss.

The family returned home to regroup. We wondered what to do next. More flyers? More knocking on doors? Which direction should we drive in this time? Then the really tough question — could Grant have even survived this long? Lee and I stood in our study, hot and sweaty from walking neighborhoods in Alabama's late May heat, with flyers, markers and poster board scattered all around us, staring at each other silently.

The phone chirped, shocking us out of our reverie.

A fisherman at a local creek had found Grant and called the phone number on his tag. He said that Grant was too tired and weak to run away, so he had been able to catch him. We rushed there, praying for this to be the real deal. We knew right away it was. Grant looked noticeably thinner and was covered in mud and bugs, but his distinctive spring collar in shades of purple, though caked in dirt, was visible. As he recognized us, his tail wagged. As we realized he was healthy, our hearts soared.

The fisherman refused the reward money, so we donated the amount to the local Humane Society in his honor. Ten years later, I cannot remember his name or face, but I will never forget that he took the time to get involved and reunite our family.

Gone for three days. Found miles away. Grant had crossed over a major four-lane highway and knew to drink from the creek. He had avoided cars, predators and bad people. His collar and tag had stayed intact. Friends who assisted us made Grant a celebrity in our small city as people across town talked about seeing the large quantity of flyers posted. And the fisherman phoned at the exact moment when Lee and I were deciding whether to give up the search.

We may have been at the most magical place on earth the preceding week, but that feeling could not compare to the sense of community the angels provided us and the euphoria of Grant's miraculous rescue. That day, little Madison, Alabama was truly the most magical place on earth.

—Jennifer Poff Cooper—

95

Harry

Death leaves a heartache no one can heal.
Love leaves a memory no one can steal.
~From a headstone in Ireland

"Harry," my dad proclaimed with a wry smile. "We can get a dog, but his name must be Harry." To this day, I'm not sure if that ultimatum was intended to dissuade my younger brother and me from wanting a dog. Fortunately, neither my brother, at that time a kindergartener, nor myself, a wise second-grader, cared much about names. So Harry it was. Harold Tanqueray Kluxen, to be exact.

A perky Cairn Terrier and Toto look-alike, Harry seemed to sense from the start that my dad brought him into our family. Dad had named him (sight unseen), chosen him from the litter, and drove him to our home — a quivering fur ball wrapped in a thin beach towel held tightly by my brother in the back of our Volvo station wagon.

Perhaps Harry even realized that Dad was responsible for keeping him in our family despite all the things he chewed. Whatever the reason, it was clear to any observer that Harry and my dad had a special bond — wrestling nightly and sharing scraps of pepperoni at cocktail hour. Much to our giggling delight, my brother and I spent many evenings nibbling our own pepperoni slices while we watched Harry grab an old washcloth with his razor-sharp puppy teeth as Dad pulled him gently across the linoleum kitchen floor on his round pink belly. As far as cheap entertainment goes, that was hard to top in our book.

In addition to roughhousing with one another, Harry and Dad were also walking companions. Each night before bed, my dad would pull on his coat, attach Harry's worn red leash, and trudge up and down the hilly road alongside our home. They always followed the same route, with Harry marching dutifully in my dad's footsteps. Harry's silver rabies vaccination tags would jingle loudly as he looked up at my dad with an admiration reserved only for his best friend.

One night, Harry even indulged my dad by walking up and down the hill without his leash attached. After a long day of work as an overstressed, underpaid attorney, Dad, too exhausted to see straight, missed connecting Harry's leash to his collar. Rather than sprint away when he reached the outdoors, as he would have done for anyone else, Harry played along with the charade by walking his usual route in my dad's footsteps, limp red leash scraping along the ground behind them both.

I was eleven and my brother had just turned ten when a car accident took our dad from us. In a one-car accident with no witnesses, our trusty station wagon, the one that had brought Harry to us, flipped over on the side of the road while my dad was driving home from a haircut. The accident severed Dad's spinal cord and inflicted life-threatening injuries that led to his removal from life support only days later. Our world turned upside down.

Given their special relationship, it should have come as no surprise that Harry felt the loss just as strongly as the rest of our family. His sagging tail and cocked head each night, at the time he would have wrestled with my dad on the kitchen floor, gave us a glimpse into how much Harry missed our patriarch. My mom did her best to fill the void. I can still picture her pulling her bulky snow pants on her tiny frame to take Harry on his nightly trek up and down the hill. Sometimes, she would return with a tear-stained face. If it were possible to see Harry's cheeks under his coarse brown fur, I imagine his face might have looked the same. However, special connections, like the one shared between my dad and Harry, are powerful and, as I would come to learn, can transcend even death.

One night about a year after my dad passed away, I lay quietly in bed, alone with my thoughts. The lights were out, and my mom and brother were already sleeping. It often took me a while to drift off. As my mom used to say, I had trouble "turning off my brain," and still do to this day. So I stared at the white ceiling, my fingers tracing the soft silky edges of my Care Bear blanket.

Then I heard it. Footsteps. Downstairs in the kitchen. Faint at first, but then growing louder. Strangely, the sound did not make me fearful; I did not suspect an intruder. I just held my breath and continued listening. A jingle followed — the tags on Harry's collar! He had been asleep on my mom's bed, his nightly post since my dad's passing, but had jumped down with a thud to investigate. I waited, grateful for Harry's reaction, which suggested (at least to me) that I was not imagining the sound of footsteps.

The mix of footsteps and Harry's jingling tags continued for several minutes, moving throughout the entire downstairs, before they turned toward the staircase. Intrigued by the mystery and feeling an odd sense of comfort, I peeked out from my room. In that moment, I experienced the most reassuring of sounds and sights. The footsteps continued up the stairs and throughout the second floor, moving slowly from bedroom to bedroom. Directly in their wake was Harry. Tail wagging and eyes bright, he followed right along with each step of our ghostly visitor, in the exact same way he had on his nightly walks with my dad. In that moment, I knew that Harry had recognized something I could not see — his best friend coming back to check on us all.

This scene repeated itself several times in my adolescence. Each time that Harry joined my dad for his nighttime patrol, I was thankful for the reminder that death does not break the bond with those closest to us.

— Samantha LaBarbera —

96

The Golden Rule

A dog has one purpose in life: to bestow his heart.
~J.B. Aukerly

I had a class of sixteen behaviorally disordered preteen boys. You could cut the angry vibes with a knife. Even in my youthful determination to stand firm on the classroom rules, I needed help. One Friday, hoping to change things up, I brought my Golden Retriever, Bonnie Jean, to school.

Her effect was immediate. Manuel, who wore a permanent scowl and never uttered a kind word, opened two angry fists to greet my golden girl. It was a subtle yet miraculous transformation. B.J. swaggered straight for Manuel as my students and I collectively held our breath. With tongue hanging and eyes wide with anticipation, B.J. thumped a paw on Manuel's knee. The boy reached out, roughed up her ears, and smiled. We all looked away. No one ever commented on the sweetness of that moment, but Manuel was never again quite the bully he wanted us to believe he was. B.J. had exposed his childlike soul.

Mr. V., my principal, dropped in one Friday making his usual rounds. Up until then, B.J. was our class secret. When she romped over to welcome him into the class, Mr. V. asked, "And who is this?" Before I could respond, B.J. jammed her broad, wet nose into his lap. The end of my career at that school flashed before my eyes. Sixteen jaws opened. Mr. V. pushed B.J. away gently, laughed, and then turned around and walked out of the room. He never mentioned my dog, but from that day forward, B.J. was a permanent member of our class.

Another school year, I had a particularly challenging student. B.J. was a miracle worker. Poor Jeff didn't have one friend. He was on the verge of a crisis intervention. With his head down, Jeff would slink in and out of the shadows of dark hallways, trying to hide his awkward, overweight body. Until he met B.J.

It was the second Friday of that school year, and I was already seeking professional help for Jeff's depression. However, as soon as Jeff saw B.J., he dove to the floor to be nose-to-nose with her. He began to giggle and then exclaimed loudly, "Look, Miss Escallier, her eyebrows go up and down in opposite directions!" All of my students left their seats and plopped onto the floor to see for themselves.

Sure enough, B.J.'s eyebrows did teeter-totter, something I had never noticed before. Jeff didn't seek shadows quite so often after that day. He even made a friend because of their mutual admiration for my golden girl.

That May, Jeff brought in his own puppy to show the class. As he reached into the basket to lift out a little, furry mutt, he announced, "I decided to name him B.J.!" The class beamed with pride. And B.J. continued to make Jeff laugh until he left us much thinner and more confident, ready to face high school.

Now, twenty-five years after that success with Jeff, my mind wanders back to that May afternoon watching B.J. sleep after a full day of kid care. My exact words return to me. "Come on, girl, it's late," I said as I packed up piles of paperwork and closed down my room. B.J. yawned, stretched and followed me to the door. When I reached down to scratch her ear, I said, "Are you ready to do this again tomorrow?" She sat and raised a paw, and we clapped hand to paw in a high-five. We were quite the team, I thought, thinking about Jeff's transformation.

B.J. passed away about five years after I left the middle school to teach high school. She stayed alive long enough to lead me to my future husband, making sure I wouldn't be lonely.

My students from those B.J. years, now middle-aged adults, often see me around town. Invariably, they retell B.J. stories and remind me how much her love guided them through some hard times. Truth be told, I wouldn't have succeeded with many of my Special Day Class students without her.

—Jeaninne Escallier Kato—

97

Satchie's Gift

The gift which I am sending you is called a dog,
and is in fact the most precious and
valuable possession of mankind.
~Theodorus Gaza

"Y ou're telling me what?" my husband Chris said, half-distracted as he rang up a customer at his shop.

"I found our next dog. Can you take off work this Saturday?"

"It's my busiest day."

"Satchie told me we have to get this dog."

Satchie was our first dog, a Shar-Pei of Westminster lineage. She had died a year ago, and the sorrow was still palpable. Chris didn't even question the fact that I was communicating with her from the Great Beyond. I had spoken with most of our dearly departed loved ones, furry or otherwise.

"Okay," he said. "I'll do what I can."

We had Satchie for twelve years, or more accurately, she had us. We became her dedicated servants, feeding her homemade food, taking her for long hikes, and showering her with as much love as she could bear. She was my first baby, but a year after we brought her home I was pregnant. I was labeled high risk and sent to bed for five months with complications. Satchie sat vigil on the edge of my bed, just out of reach, but always watching over me.

Ten years later, she stood in the hallway, peering into the kitchen where Chris and I were chatting. Chris, whom Satchie had wrapped around her little paw, walked over to massage her neck and belly. In an instant, the expression on his face changed. Underneath her wrinkles, he had felt tumors. It was lymphoma. We spent our savings and countless hours on her care, giving up weddings, travel, and time from our careers. When she could no longer walk more than a few steps and began refusing food, we knew it was time to let her go.

She died in my arms at the vet as I sang her the alphabet, her favorite bedtime tune. Steeped in grief, I felt no sign of her after she passed. And then a few weeks later, it started. She would come running up to me in my dreams, her tongue wagging, drool sliding down her chops, as I kneeled to meet her. She buried her head in my chest as I rubbed her ears, and then, as quickly as she had appeared, she was gone, leaping like a doe across a lush meadow.

A year after she passed, I had a different kind of dream. Satchie was cuddling a male, brown Lab puppy. I asked her, "Why are you cuddling a dog? You don't like to cuddle." She responded, "He is not as smart as I am, but he will learn."

It wasn't as if her mouth was moving and she anthropomorphized into a talking dog. I can't even describe the sound of her voice; I just understood her message intrinsically. But how would I ever find this new dog? Besides, I had been looking for a female, preferably a Shepherd mix, per my son's request.

That morning, I turned on my computer to search rescues, and there he was. He was the first dog on the rescue's webpage, and only an hour away! I called up to inquire. Bailey Breeze was still available, but I'd have to go through a screening process. I almost shouted, "It's okay! My deceased dog already screened us for Bailey." But then I thought that might not be the best approach.

Three grueling days passed, and then a phone call came. We could meet Bailey at an adoption event. I pleaded for them to allow us to come directly to the shelter before he could be scooped up by someone else at the event, but they refused. With no other recourse, I convinced my husband to take off from work and come with us to rescue our new dog before someone else did.

I ran into the event like a lady on fire, calling to the workers, "I need to see Bailey." Puppies in playpens jumped and barked, begging for attention. "We don't have a Bailey," someone said. But I tried again, describing the dog, asking the worker to call the manager, and he said finally, "Oh, you mean Breeze."

Bailey Breeze was cautious. He was affectionate, but not rambunctious. The workers offered us other, more active dogs, but my family agreed that we were there for Bailey.

As we played with him and strolled around the store, we noticed he had an odd walk. We called our vet. We called the shelter's manager. We solicited advice from anyone passing by. The words "hip dysplasia" were thrown around. My husband turned to me. "We cannot afford another dog with special needs right now. I'm sorry." He was right. As much as I wanted Bailey, we didn't have it in us to care for another suffering dog. I took Bailey into a quiet aisle and sat down, holding him to my chest, explaining why we couldn't take him home. "I'm sorry," I whispered.

My son stood over me. "Look, Mom, look at his leash!" I had been holding his leash for an hour, but I hadn't noticed. Right there on the leather tab was the name Remington—my son's name! This was no coincidence. Bailey was our dog, and we were taking him home. My husband and I came to an agreement: We would take Bailey to our specialist, get her opinion, and then decide.

Three days later, the results were in: Bailey's hips were fine. He just walked with a lilt! I knew that somewhere along the way, Bailey had met Satchie. Whenever we mentioned her name, his ears perked up.

Satchie had picked the perfect dog for us. And she was right: He is not as smart as she was, but he's learning.

—Aileen Weintraub—

98

Hell's Bells

All God's angels come to us disguised.
~James Russell Lowell

I was a sophomore at the University of Alabama when I decided to get a puppy. I thought it would be easy; I grew up with dogs, so why not get one of my own? When I was back home in Florida for Christmas break, I adopted an adorable Golden Retriever puppy against my parents' wishes.

Well, it didn't take long for me to realize that my parents were right. My adorable puppy was a full-time job, and I was in way over my head.

I named her Bella and took her back to school to live with my three roommates and me. She was a wild puppy, so misbehaved, and I began to feel like I couldn't handle her anymore. As a college student, I had a very busy social schedule and was definitely not ready to be a dog mom. At times, she would frustrate me so much I would sit on the floor and cry. I'd yell at her, "Why do you do this to me?!" I called my parents for help, but they insisted that I learn from this decision.

Bella was such a handful that she earned the nickname Hell's Bells. In time, though, she taught me how to be a better dog mom, and I taught her how to be a better dog. We became best friends and did everything together. Bella went wherever my social calendar took me: parties, tailgates, restaurants, bars, friends' houses, even dates! We loved spending time together and went for daily runs and summer swims.

By the time I was a senior, Bella and I had an unbreakable bond.

She was truly my best friend. She had met all my friends and a ton of people at school. Sometimes my friends would walk into the house without knocking just to stop by and hang out with Bella and me.

Bella grew up to be a beautiful eighty-five-pound Golden Retriever. I would hear comments that she was the largest Golden people had ever seen, or she'd be mistaken for a male because of her muscular build. Despite her intimidating size, she was a complete goober. Everyone loved Bella and she loved everyone back, including other dogs.

I worked at the local college bar not far from the house. One night, I was running late. Bella and I had been with friends down the street when I realized it was already 9:00 p.m. We had to rush home so I could make it to work by 9:30. I ran through the front door and jumped in the shower. Bella followed me into the bathroom and lay in her usual place on the bathroom floor.

Then I heard my front door slam open. It was so loud that I thought it was odd. My roommate was flying back into town and was supposed to be home at 10:00 p.m., but it was earlier and she wouldn't enter the house like that, or she would have called if her plane had landed. Nonetheless, I turned off the shower and yelled her name. No answer.

Bella was crouched facing the bathroom door, growling, foaming at the mouth, with the hair raised on her back. Instantly, I knew something was seriously wrong. I had never seen her like that before. Someone was in my house, and I was in danger.

Naked and soaking wet, I felt helpless and terrified. Bella charged suddenly through the bathroom door. I heard a struggle in the living room, crashing of furniture, a man yelling, and then the front door opening again. Bella went barking after him. I jumped out of the shower, got dressed quickly and called 911.

Then I went outside to call Bella. She came back unharmed, and I noticed that the intruder had deadbolted the door behind him when he entered. When Bella attacked him, he couldn't get out fast enough and ripped the door from the frame! The fact that he had locked the door behind him sent chills down my spine. As the police asked questions and searched the house, Bella stayed by my side the whole time.

The police found a man hiding behind a house down the street with a broken forearm and blood on his shirt from something that looked like a dog bite. Bella identified him for the police; she went nuts when she saw him again. The police could not detain him just on the word of a dog, but when he was searched further, they found drug paraphernalia on him. As his injuries were consistent with my story, they arrested him.

Bella was my hero, and I am so thankful for her courage that night. I cannot imagine what would have happened if she hadn't reacted so quickly and bravely. She was such a goofy Golden Retriever, but that night she was strong, fierce, and brave. I often think she was an angel put in my life for that very moment.

— Kelley Knott —

99

The Last Goodbye

Things that were hard to bear are sweet to remember.
~Seneca

I stared into the darkness of our motel room, trying to calm my racing heart, while jumbled thoughts and images swirled through my head. What had just happened?

My husband Bracey and I were back in my hometown, where we had traveled for the funeral of my fifty-six-year-old brother. We had made the twelve-hour journey from our home in Tennessee to West Virginia to bury him in the family cemetery. The funeral had been yesterday.

That same day, we received a phone call. My husband and I were at dinner and missed the call, but there was a voicemail. It was from the veterinarian's office where we had boarded our three pets, telling us that Scooter, our fourteen-year-old Shepherd mix, had thrown up twice. They had given him something for nausea and another medication because he seemed to be in pain. They promised to call "if he continued to decline."

Bracey and I debated about driving home to Tennessee that night. But we had both spent the past two weeks at my brother's bedside in the nursing home with my sister, and we were exhausted.

"Dr. Scott's office won't even be open when we get back," my husband pointed out.

I wavered at this point, debating what would be best. I really wanted to see Scooter again with my own eyes, to make sure he was all right. He loved Bracey, had accepted him after our marriage nearly five years ago, but he was my dog, fiercely loyal and protective of me, and I was worried about him.

Scooter had shown up on my doorstep fourteen years earlier, a two-month-old puppy who was throwing up balls of foam that came from his lungs. An X-ray revealed that he had been shot with a pellet gun. Dr. Scott had been unable to remove the pellet from Scooter's lung because of its proximity to his heart, but he and I nursed him back to health with several months of antibiotics.

I had worked for a local veterinarian for several years in high school and college, but had never met another dog with Scooter's intelligence. For one thing, his vocabulary was incredible; he could pick up the meaning of words or commands after hearing them only a few times. He was so smart that my husband and I had to spell some words, like "w-a-l-k, "c-a-r r-i-d-e" and "p-o-p-c-o-r-n."

It was the same way with hand signals. Scooter learned to "kiss" my cheek or the tip of my nose when I tapped them with my index finger; I didn't have to say the word. My favorite command, however, the one that never failed to impress family and friends, was when I would command him to "scoot back." I would do it by making a shooing motion with my hand, and he would step back a few paces and sit down facing me. My son used to tease him by making him "scoot back" all the way across the room until his back was up against the wall. Scooter would protest loudly but would obey.

I loved Scooter as deeply as it was possible to love anyone, and I marveled at his unconditional love for me. It was the deepest, most profound love I had ever experienced in my life, and his devotion to me was unflagging. Even Dr. Scott said that he had never seen such a deep bond between a person and a dog as what he witnessed between Scooter and me.

I was still feeling uneasy about the phone call from Dr. Scott's office, but in the end, fatigue won out. Reluctantly, I agreed to stay one more night in West Virginia and go home in the morning. It was a decision that we would come to regret.

In the middle of the night, I had a dream. In this dream, I found myself staring into the dark motel room, wondering what had awakened me, when I suddenly became aware of Scooter standing by the bed, looking at me. Why was Scooter here in West Virginia? Was I imagining things? No… It looked like Scooter, and yet…

He looked different, I realized. He looked beautiful, so young and healthy, no trace of white on his muzzle. His reddish coat had a golden glow that I could see quite clearly in the darkened room. But when I looked at his face, I could see the tears shimmering in his brown eyes.

And I heard, in my head, a voice that I knew without a doubt was his voice.

"I'm sorry," he said through his tears. "I really wanted to wait until you got back, but it's my time to go. I just wanted to say goodbye."

And then, as suddenly as he had appeared to me, he was gone.

I stared into the darkness, trying to stifle my sobs so that I wouldn't wake my husband. I kept telling myself that it was just a bad dream, brought on by the stress of the past few weeks and my worry about Scooter. But my heart was telling me otherwise. My beloved Scooter was gone.

I looked at the glowing dial on my watch. It was 12:45 a.m. EST, which meant that it was 11:45 p.m. back home in Tennessee.

The next morning, Bracey and I packed hurriedly to return home. I showered and dressed quickly, unable to shake the feelings of unease and the need to hurry. I drove first and found myself constantly checking the time on the dashboard clock, calculating how long it would be until the veterinary clinic opened. Three hours into the trip, right after my husband and I switched places so that he was now driving, my cell phone rang. It was the veterinarian's office number on the screen.

I burst into tears. "I can't take this call," I told my husband, letting it go to voicemail.

It was Dr. Scott telling me that Scooter hadn't made it; they had found him gone when they opened the clinic this morning. It was fortunate I wasn't driving because I totally lost it. I sobbed uncontrollably as I called Dr. Scott back to tell him that Scooter had come to tell me goodbye. We made arrangements to have him cremated so that he could stay with me.

An autopsy showed that Scooter had thrown a blood clot a few months prior, which had killed off half of his stomach tissue. In addition, he had an aortic aneurysm, which was ready to burst at any time. In short, Scooter was living on borrowed time, and there was nothing we could have done to change that. Unfortunately, we were gone when time ran out for him.

I continue to grieve the loss of both my brother and Scooter, whose deaths will be forever intertwined. But I have come to realize what an incredible gift God gave me, both when He first gave me Scooter, and when the bond we shared was strong enough to transcend time and space in order to enable him to come and tell me goodbye.

—Jan Hopkins-Campbell—

I'll Take a Mulligan

Until one has loved an animal,
a part of one's soul remains unawakened.
~Anatole France

T hey found her on Christmas Day. She was running up and down the streets in the pouring rain, her ribs poking out noticeably. The police officer who found her managed to usher her into the patrol car, where she sat silently in the back seat staring forlornly out the window. Ultimately, she wound up at the local animal shelter and was given nourishment and protection within their walls. A seven-day hold was placed on her in case someone showed up to claim her.

On the sixth night, one of the employees posted a picture of her on their website, letting everyone know that she would be up for adoption the next day. I just so happened to be scrolling through social media at that exact moment. My breath stopped at the sight of her. Something called to me that could not be explained.

Earlier that year, we had lost one of our beloved pets, a Boston Terrier. We were still broken and healing, and really weren't in the market for another dog. We weren't certain that we could truly love another one so soon.

But that face. She appeared to be staring at me through the surface of my phone, and I quickly took a screenshot of her, determined to share her picture with my family when morning arrived. I was certain that they would be just as moved by her as I was.

I hardly slept that night. The anticipation of rescuing this precious soul kept my heart racing. I worried that someone else might adopt her before we had the chance. Fortunately, once I showed her face to my loved ones, they agreed immediately.

The name assigned to her at the shelter was "Mulligan." How incredibly fitting for this precious creature since the name means "to be given another chance." In the deepest part of our souls, we knew that chance was going to be within the confines of our home.

Now, we are rescuers by nature and have taken in many forsaken dogs over the years, but something was different about Mulligan. From the very beginning, we recognized that fate had brought her into our lives. What if the police hadn't stopped, or they had taken her to another shelter? Why was I scrolling through social media that late at night when I was normally sound asleep? And, before I forget to mention it, she was a mixed breed with the surprisingly familiar face of a Boston Terrier.

We took her home that day, our hearts mending with each kiss. We were over the moon with happiness. The addition of her to our household caused a constant discussion of unexpected gifts and blessings as we marveled at the amazing way she fit in. People sometimes wonder aloud after rescuing an animal if it is truly us rescuing them, or if they are actually rescuing us. I have to say resoundingly that it is most definitely both. But perhaps this lesson wasn't truly understood until she not only healed our hearts, but fiercely broke down some thick barriers and helped heal the hearts of some dear friends as well.

Years ago, one of their daughters was unexpectedly and brutally attacked by a dog, leaving scars on her face. Our relationship with them started to falter due to our love of dogs and their inability to be around them for fear that something else "bad" might happen. We were saddened by this rift between us.

When they heard about Mulligan, who was part American Bulldog, a fairly large breed, it was obvious that weren't comfortable visiting us. But on their first visit after we brought Mulligan home, she seemed to understand. She stayed still and quiet as their youngest daughter approached her. Her parents yelled for her to stop, but it was as if the girl were on a mission. Mulligan was gentle with her, and the girl wasn't afraid. Her parents relaxed, and our friendship was back on track. Mulligan had indeed given that family a second chance at being around dogs, at friendship, and at fully participating in the world without fear.

— Jenny Filush-Glaze —

On Eagles' Wings

If there is a heaven, it's certain our animals are to be
there. Their lives become so interwoven with our own,
it would take more than an archangel
to detangle them.
~Pam Brown

My Australian Cattle Dog Bandit and I had been together for ten years — since he'd found me when he was a puppy. He leapt out of bed each morning eager to greet the day. Every time we went outside, he brought me a ball. If I sat at the computer for too long, he bopped me with a toy rubber chicken. By example, he taught me to be a positive person, not to take myself too seriously, and to give each day my best shot.

Bandit was whip-smart and competitive in obedience, agility, and versatility events. He'd even won a cattle-herding contest! Over the summer, we'd spent many hours training for a tracking test. But in September, Bandit, my strong, intrepid Cattle Dog, couldn't start a track. Something was terribly wrong.

Bandit was diagnosed with multiple myeloma, a blood and bone cancer. The veterinarian prescribed a daily chemotherapy pill that Bandit would take for the rest of his life. We continued our regular walks, and with medication and good nutrition, he did well.

The vet said that eighteen months was the average survival time after diagnosis. I gave Bandit the best quality of life I could afford while he enjoyed living. Every day, we played ball, and he ran and played with my other dogs, Chase and Cayenne, on long, leash-free walks. Although Bandit had lost muscle mass from the disease, he still looked strong and healthy.

Then the eagles came, with their striking white heads and bold brown feathers silhouetted against a bright blue sky. I first noticed one perched high in the cottonwood tree across the road. Later that day, two eagles sat in the tree by our garage. It was February, and the river was frozen, so I thought they'd moved inland to find food, evidenced by the pheasant whose feathers Bandit had found and the dead rabbit left by the drive.

A month later, I would understand a greater reason why they had come.

On the first morning in March, all three dogs barked wildly. Outside, a bald eagle was circling. That afternoon when we went for a walk, Chase took off running full speed across the field, looking up and barking. There was the eagle, flying in a straight line! What was up with all these bald eagles?

As Bandit aged and his head became whiter, he looked like a bald eagle, too, with his reddish brown body and white tail. As his medications made him have to "go" more frequently, he led me outside more often. On cold, clear nights, looking up at the stars, I pondered the vastness of the night sky and wondered where Bandit would go when his body failed him. He'd begun staying out longer, even on below-zero nights, spending time alone, separating more and more from our little pack. Yet I had never felt closer to him.

As the disease progressed, Bandit's tail hung low, and he struggled to climb the stairs. He had such a tremendous spirit and determination to live that he must have hidden a lot of pain. But it began to show, and painkillers weren't helping much. One night, Bandit couldn't lie down comfortably and stood for most of the night. His pain was becoming unbearable, even for a stoic Cattle Dog.

Tests indicated that Bandit's kidneys and immune system were failing. The vet was surprised because Bandit looked so good on the outside. That night, even with a new pain medication, he stood and panted, clearly uncomfortable. Sleeping on the floor with him, I dreamed that we were out for a walk. A man was calling Bandit toward the railroad tracks. I said, "Hey, don't call my dog onto the tracks. That could be dangerous!" Then I realized it was God calling for Bandit.

The next morning, Bandit ran outside and grabbed the ball. Ignoring his pain, he wanted to go for a walk. I opened the gate and was amazed as he charged up the hill. He brought the ball and fetched it a few times with gusto. He rolled in a patch of dirt, and then surveyed the landscape, taking it all in for one last time. Bandit saved the last of his energy for love, fun and enjoying life. He was ready to cross over.

Given how much Bandit was hurting, I had to tell him how much I loved him and say goodbye. It wouldn't be right to ask one more thing of him. That afternoon, we went to the vet, who set Bandit free from that once-powerful and still-handsome body, to let his spirit fly free. And fly he did, I have no doubt.

Once Bandit passed on, I learned the significance of the ever-present eagles. That afternoon while driving across town, thinking about Bandit, I saw a large bald eagle in a tree by the road. A few minutes later in a busy suburb, another bald eagle flew low over my truck, comforting me greatly. The next morning, an eagle was circling high in the sky over our front field, the sun catching the white on his tail every time he looped around. I felt Bandit's unmistakable presence and let out the gut-wrenching sobs I'd been holding in. Suddenly, three eagles were circling, and then five! I knew then that Bandit was soaring high, free from pain, and these majestic birds were his messengers.

That afternoon as the dogs and I headed up the hill, I felt Bandit's presence. The bald eagle was circling! The following evening when we climbed the hill, the lone eagle winged in a straight line down the length of the field, as if checking in to say "hello." Grateful to see him, I felt energized and wanted him to stay.

A week after Bandit crossed over, I again felt his strong presence up on the hill. Three eagles circled and ascended toward the sun. As we continued to walk, I turned and saw a lone eagle behind us. He flew so close that I could almost touch his yellow feet with their sharp talons. He turned a tight circle directly above me, drawing out my tears yet again. I should have been frightened, but I felt Bandit's spirit and wasn't afraid. The eagle retreated, flying straight down the field, leaving me breathless.

During the next year, eagles were ever-present, visiting me in the most unusual places. They were bold and striking, just like Bandit, and they had come to help with his transition. Magically, they flew over the highway just above my truck when I was driving 60 miles per hour. How did they get the timing just right every time?

A year after Bandit's passing, I found a long white feather, an eagle's tail feather. I sensed it was a goodbye gift, and shortly afterward, the regular eagle visits ended.

I'm incredibly lucky to have known Bandit. In the years we shared, he influenced my life more than any other being. I'm grateful for the eagles' presence during Bandit's transition. I always believed that dogs go to heaven. Magically, Bandit showed me that sometimes they fly there on eagles' wings.

— Jenny Pavlovic —

Meet Our Contributors

Patty Ayers retired from a career as an advertising writer with an unending need to write. A recovered alcoholic with twenty years of sobriety, Patty published the shocking and inspirational story of her life. You'll find her short stories and motivational writings in a variety of literary journals and blogs. Learn more at facebook.com/curlywriter.

Lucy Barrett grew up in Albany, NY. She is an outdoorswoman, educator, and avid reader.

Brenda Beattie is a retired letter carrier from the United State Postal Service. She is also the Chaplain of Branch 203 of the National Association of Letter Carriers. She is now living the dream in Bradenton, FL. She loves walking the beach, biking, and writing. She has recently published her book, *Finding Sacred Ground In The Daily Grind*.

Connie Beckman resides in the beautiful state of Montana with her husband and their four cats and dog. Now that Connie is retired she enjoys writing about her faith, their four-legged family members and the wondrous adventures of growing a vegetable garden. Read her blog at www.conniescatholiccorner.com.

Ashley Bell studied child psychology at Upper Iowa University. She has three children and is a stay-at-home mom. Ashley enjoys spending time outdoors, at museums, and with her family.

Jill Anne Berni is excited to be a contributor to the *Chicken Soup for the Soul* series for the fourth time. She is a history buff, animal lover and an avid reader. She lives in Mississauga, Ontario with her loving husband Fred and their two dogs, Max and Maggie. Learn more at www.jillberni.com.

Veronica Bowman is a poet and writer. She and her husband share their country home with their much-loved rescue dogs, cats and chickens. She enjoys reading, gardening and cooking.

Kandace Chapple is the editor and publisher of *Grand Traverse Woman* magazine. Her essays have been published in *Motherwell*, *Writer's Digest*, *Literary Mama* and others. She loves to mountain bike on Northern Michigan trails, hike with Cookie, and spend time with her husband and two sons. Visit her at www.kandacechapple.com.

Gwen Cooper received her B.A. in English and Secondary Education in 2007, and completed the Publishing Institute at Denver University in 2009. In her free time she enjoys hiking and backpacking with her husband and Bloodhound rescue in the beautiful Rocky Mountains. Follow her on Twitter @Gwen_Cooper10.

Jennifer Poff Cooper received a B.S. in Marketing from Virginia Tech and a M.A. in Liberal Studies from Hollins University. She is a wife and mother of two grown children. A freelance writer and public relations specialist residing in southwest Virginia, Jennifer is an avid reader who is active in her church and community.

Amanda Sue Creasey is married with dogs. She holds an undergraduate degree in German from Michigan State University and a graduate degree in creative writing from the University of Denver. She teaches high school English and loves hiking, running, reading, and writing, as well as her husband and dogs.

Teresa Crow, a freelance writer who lives on a small hobby farm, raises Miniature Australian Shepherds along with a small herd of goats that keep the farm weed-free. She has worked with children for twenty years and volunteers as a reader at the local school. She plans to write inspirational read-aloud books for children.

Alicia Curley is a recruiter by day and writer by night. She lives in the Midwest with her husband Brandon, dog (Moose) and cats (Daphnee, Guinness, Fredo). A graduate of Michigan State University, she is a member of SCBWI and blogs about her writing journey at www.aliciacurley.com.

Elizabeth Delisi received her B.A. in Creative Writing from St. Leo College. She's been married to her high school sweetheart for forty years and has three children and three grandchildren. She writes romance and mystery, and teaches online writing courses. She enjoys reading, knitting, playing piano and watching old movies.

Lindsay Detwiler is a high school English teacher and author. Her thirteen romance titles include *The Trail to You*, which features her Mastiff, Henry, as a main character. In addition, Lindsay's debut thriller, *The Widow Next Door*, released with Avon Books/HarperCollins UK in 2018.

Rebecca Edmisten is a twenty-one year teaching veteran of English and Theatre. She did not get her first dog until she was thirty years old, but says this *Chicken Soup for the Soul* book is the ideal place to showcase both her passion for writing and her love for all things canine!

Tracy Falenwolfe is a member of Sisters in Crime, Mystery Writers of America, and the Short Mystery Fiction Society. She's been published in several anthologies, and is currently writing a mystery series. She lives in Pennsylvania's Lehigh Valley with her husband and two sons. Learn more at www.tracyfalenwolfe.com.

Award-winning author **Ellen Fannon** is a veterinarian, former missionary and foster mom, and church musician. Her first novel, *Other People's Children*, the humorous account of life as a foster parent, is available online. She lives in Valparaiso, FL with her husband, son and assorted pets.

Linda Feist is proud to have her third story featured in the *Chicken Soup for the Soul* series. She enjoys writing, reading, and hanging out with her best friend, her husband. Published in newspapers and magazines this three-time Royal Palm Literary Award finalist continues her love affair with the written word.

Jenny Filush-Glaze is a licensed counselor who specializes in grief support and death and dying. She writes a weekly grief column for two newspapers, has published two books (available online) and writes a daily blog on her Facebook page: ZenJen's Mindful Living.

After two decades of working in fashion marketing in Europe, **Tara Flowers** returned home to Philly to raise her son. When not sitting in a carline or attempting to wrangle two very spirited black Labs, she operates her consulting business Le Papillon Marketing.

Valerie J. Frost lives in beautiful San Diego, CA with her husband Terry. She has three children, nine grandchildren, and one precious great-grandson. She loves God, her husband, her family and dogs. She is particularly enamored with the noble Doberman Pinscher and those mischievous little Jack Russell Terriers.

Lori Fuller teaches middle school and high school English at a small Christian school in Illinois. She has been a volunteer with animal rescue groups for more than seven years and has fostered many dogs, helping them find their forever homes. In her spare time, Lori works as a newborn baby photographer.

Leslie Garrett is an author and journalist whose work has appeared in *The Atlantic, O, The Oprah Magazine, The Washington Post* and more. Her books include bestselling children's biographies of Muhammad Ali and Helen Keller. She lives in London, Ontario, with her husband, three children, three cats and two dogs.

Tammy Collins Gibson grew up on a farm in rural East Tennessee. She is a nurse and recently received her Bachelor's in Nursing from Drexel University with high honors. She is married to her husband Jimmy and they have two adult sons, Joshua and Bradley. She has an adventurous spirit and loves spending time with her dogs.

Kathy Harris is an author by way of a three-decade detour into the Nashville entertainment industry. She writes romantic suspense and women's fiction and has contributed to several inspirational nonfiction books. Her debut novel, *The Road to Mercy*, was released in 2012.

Gwen Hart teaches writing at Buena Vista University in Storm Lake, IA. Her poems and stories have appeared in numerous journals and anthologies. Her second poetry collection, *The Empress of Kisses*, won the X.J. Kennedy Poetry Prize from *Texas Review Press*.

Kelly Hennigan has degrees in Human Service from Jefferson Community College, and Psychology from SUNY Oswego. Kelly had a fulfilling career in the field of human services. She is most proud of her roles as both a mom and wife. Kelly is a Crohn's warrior and loves to write. She enjoys country living and kind smiles.

Sharla Hintz is the author of the book *Love Again*. She had four children in four years time, but the kids are grown now so Sharla is finally able to have some hobbies. She loves to read, swim in the ocean, and travel as much as possible. Read her blog at www. whathappenedtomymarriage.app.

Zach Hively writes nonfiction, poetry, and "Fool's Gold: The Column." He dances and teaches Argentine tango, and he plays guitar and harmonica in the duo Oxygen on Embers. Dogs love him. He thrives in the desert, he wears fine hats, and he once changed his own tire.

Jan Hopkins-Campbell is a professional watercolor artist and children's author and illustrator. She has two children and one amazing grandson. She lives in Tennessee with her husband — as well as a dog and cat who do not realize that they are not the same species. E-mail her at wcartist1115@yahoo.com.

David Hull is a retired teacher whose life is now filled with cats instead of dogs. He enjoys reading, writing, gardening and spending time with family. E-mail him at Davidhull59@aol.com.

Nadia Ianakieva was born in Sofia, Bulgaria. In 2000 Nadia's family moved to America as immigrants. Her life has been filled with miracles and wonders since she became a believer in 1989. Nadia loves the *Chicken Soup for the Soul* series and has dreamt about getting her stories published. E-mail her at ianakieva@sbcglobal.net.

Susan A. Karas resides on Long Island with her adorable Teacup Maltese, Bentley. Susan won a coveted spot in a *Guideposts* national writing contest in 2004 and has been a regular contributor ever since. She has appeared in many *Chicken Soup for the Soul* books and other publications as well. E-mail her at SueZFoofer@aol.com.

Jeaninne Escallier Kato taught grades K-12 for thirty-six years in California. She has a B.S. degree and Master's in Educational Psychology, and three specialized teaching credentials. Jeaninne wrote the children's book *Manuel's Murals*. She has won and placed in several online literary magazines for her flash fiction pieces.

Yvonne Kays lives with her husband in the high desert of Central

Oregon with incredible views of the snow-capped Cascade Mountains. She loves being a grandmother, and is a member of Oregon Christian Writers. A four-time Cascade Writing Contest finalist in poetry and short story, she's working on a book about WWII.

Linda Kinnamon is the author of *Alchemy of the Afterlife*, an award-winning memoir about her life after death experiences as a hospice nurse. Jack, her rescue dog turned exercise coach, takes Linda for a long walk daily whether she wants to go or not. He also protects her from delivery people and squirrels while she writes.

Kelley Knott is a University of Alabama alumna, Florida native, and striving CEO of Intrepy Healthcare Marketing based out of Atlanta, GA. She married the love of her life Justin Knott in 2016 and the two of them enjoy building their company and spending time with their fur baby family. Kelley is a passionate animal lover.

Suzanne M. Kurth is a retired police officer with a doctorate in Sociology. She enjoys traveling, reading, hiking, music, weightlifting, and sharing life with her husband and dog. She writes fiction and nonfiction about issues and topics in policing and sociology.

Samantha LaBarbera lives in Pennsylvania with her husband, two children, and their sweet yellow Lab, Rosie. She works as an attorney in the pharmaceutical industry and received her B.A. from Franklin and Marshall College and J.D. from Villanova University School of Law.

Joyce Laird is a freelance writer living in Southern California with a menagerie of rescue "fur-babies." She is a regular contributor to *Woman's World* magazine and the *Chicken Soup for the Soul* series. Joyce is also a member of the Mystery Writers of America.

Natasha Lidberg spent her childhood days on the dirt roads of rural Michigan and is now a Southen California local. She's been married to her best friend, Adam, for ten years and together they serve at a local church in their community. Natasha loves her rescue dog Toby, traveling, cooking, rainy days, long walks, and musical theatre.

Vickie J. Litten lives in South Florida with her husband, two sons, three grandchildren, her deaf dog and a Savannah cat. She loves to write and also enjoys art, photography, cooking and gardening.

Patricia Lund tutors international students and is a Certified Funeral Celebrant. She began writing at a young age, creating comical poems to pass time on long road trips. She writes Celebration of Life services, song lyrics, and freelance articles, and is forever grateful for the ongoing support of her son and daughter.

Lisa Mackinder received her Bachelor of Arts degree at Western Michigan University. A freelance writer, she lives in Portage, MI with her husband and rescue animals. Besides writing, Lisa enjoys photography, traveling, reading, running, hiking, biking, climbing and fishing.

Irene Maran is a freelance writer and storyteller. Her stories revolve around family, animals and everyday topics humorously expressed in two bi-weekly newspaper columns, *The News-Record of Maplewood and South Orange* and *The Coaster in Asbury Park*.

David Martin's humor and political satire have appeared in many publications including *The New York Times*, the *Chicago Tribune* and *Smithsonian* magazine. He has published several collections of his humor, all of which are available online. David lives in Ottawa, Canada with his wife Cheryl and their daughter Sarah.

Richard Matturro has a Ph.D. in English with a specialization in Shakespeare and Greek Mythology. After sixteen years at the Albany *Times Union*, he taught literature at the University of Albany for fourteen years. He is the author of numerous newspaper articles, six published novels, and one audio book. Learn more at richardmatturro.com.

Debbi Mavity lives in West Virginia with her husband, Mark. She retired from the Federal Government and is a Lions Club and VFW Auxiliary member. She has rescued and fostered many dogs. She and her Golden Retriever, Rizzo, make monthly visits to the West Virginia Veterans Nursing Facility. E-mail her at mavsmutthouse@aim.com.

Louisa Godissart McQuillen has published stories and poetry since childhood, with writings in both national and international publications. She's written five booklets of poetry; her sixth booklet, *Stories to Help You Sleep,* is a compilation of short stories and sold via requests for $6.00. To order a copy, please contact her via e-mail at lzm4@psu.edu.

Hambone and Sadie, both orphans, were adopted by journalists Kevin Valine and **Linda Meilink**. Linda is the author of the book *What Your Doctor Doesn't Know About Fibromyalgia* and has been published in numerous national magazines. She writes poetry in her spare time.

Roberta Messner, RN, Ph.D., is a writer whose extensive work spans healthcare, inspirational, and home decor publications. She lives in a century-old log cabin in West Virginia where she pursues the creative, intentional life.

Taylor Reau Morris is an avid outdoorswoman and dedicated mother. She enjoys practicing archery, riding horses, and homesteading. She has both a daughter and a son, and loves spending time with them and her husband on their hobby farm. Taylor is an advocate for self-love and overall health, and mentors women from home.

Ann Morrow is a writer, humorist and frequent contributor to the *Chicken Soup for the Soul* series. She and her husband live in South Dakota and share their home with three dogs and two cats. Ann is currently writing her first middle-grade novel. Read more of her stories at annmorrow.net.

Sheryl-Ann Odell is a retired wife, mother of two and grandmother of six who has just begun her longtime dream of writing. She enjoys traveling, cooking/entertaining, reading and gardening. She and her husband hope to resume their side business, which includes recycling and up cycling old rusty metal and worn out wood.

Jenny Pavlovic, Ph.D. is the author of *8 State Hurricane Kate*, *The Not Without My Dog Resource & Record Book*, and many published stories. She lives in Wisconsin with her dogs Chase and Cayenne and her cat Junipurr. Bandit lives on in her heart. He and the eagles opened her eyes and her mind. Learn more at www.8statekate.net.

Andrea Peebles is retired after thirty-five years in the commercial insurance industry. She lives in Pendergrass, GA with her husband of forty-two years. She has had multiple stories published in the *Chicken Soup for the Soul* series over the past ten years. Along with writing, she enjoys travel, photography and time with her two spoiled dogs.

Award-winning nationally syndicated columnist, **Saralee Perel**, can be reached at sperel@saraleeperel.com or via her website at www.SaraleePerel.com.

Cassidy Porter is a small town girl with a big heart. She has a passion for rescuing animals and helping those in need, which she incorporates into ideas for her third passion — writing stories and song lyrics. Cassidy hopes to continue rescuing animals and writing, and to perform a few of her songs in the upcoming year.

Marsha Porter fell in love with writing when it was the punishment du jour at her grade school. She went on to write dozens of short stories, hundreds of articles and thousands of movie reviews. She also taught high school English for nearly thirty-five years.

The proud father of one daughter, **Ken Prehn** enjoys playing guitar, leading men's Bible Studies at church, part-time preaching, and ministering to widows and orphans.

Kay Presto's stories have been published in numerous *Chicken Soup for the Soul* books. She recently published a middle grade go-karting mystery adventure novel, *Chasing the Checkered Flag*, which won two national awards. Kay loves writing, and has written ten additional children's books. E-mail her at prestoprod6@yahoo.com.

Winter Desiree Prosapio is a humor columnist and novelist in the Texas Hill Country. She has written trivia books, mysteries, and a few truly hilarious e-mails. She is a mom, a rabble-rouser, and enthusiastic dog person. You can read more about her writing life at wdprosapio.com.

Evan Purcell is an English teacher from America. Right now, he's working with adult learners in Kazakhstan. He's also taught in Russia, Zanzibar, China, and Bhutan. Throughout his travels, he's made a lot of friends and was even featured on an official stamp in Bhutan.

Michele Bazan Reed spent forty years working in journalism and higher education before retiring to write travel articles and mystery fiction. She enjoys history, books, antiques, travel and, of course, dogs. Michele and her husband have two grown children and divide their time between upstate New York and France.

Sallie A. Rodman lives in Los Alamitos, CA with Mollie the Beagle. She received her Certificate in Professional Writing at CSULB where she now teaches Writing Creative Nonfiction at the Osher Lifelong Learning Center. Her stories have appeared in numerous *Chicken Soup for the Soul* books. E-mail her at writergal222@gmail.com.

Martha Roggli started writing stories after she retired from teaching for twenty-five years. She now belongs to two writing groups and is addicted to listening to their stories and sharing hers. She advises anyone interested in writing to start or join a group for feedback, support and encouragement.

Nikki Rottenberg has worked in social work helping women overcome trauma for a number of years. She began writing in 2009. Nikki lives in Canada with her family and enjoys hiking, photography and writing stories that inspire and give hope.

Rebecca Ruballos received her Bachelor's in Education from Nyack College (NY), and her Master's in Instruction and Curriculum from Kean University (NJ). She is a Learning Specialist at Berkeley College in New Jersey. Rebecca has two daughters, two grandchildren, and two pets. She enjoys writing and traveling.

Candace Sams was a Police Officer for the State of Texas, which included fourteen months on the Texas Department of Public Safety Narcotics Task Force. She was later a Reserve Police Officer for the city of San Diego, a Traffic Safety Instructor for the County of San Diego, and worked with an undisclosed agency in Alabama.

Mya R. Schwartz received her B.A. in Communication at CSU San Marcos. Her passions include long walks and hanging out with her buddy Rei, a beautiful yellow Labrador. Mya plans to continue writing great stories, and wants to remind you to please be kind to animals. E-mail her at WritingWithPassion2014@gmail.com.

Jennifer Sienes holds a Bachelor of Arts in Psychology and Master's in Education. After teaching middle school for several years, her husband encouraged her to quit to pursue her life-long dream of writing. She recently received her first book contract, and enjoys creating characters that inspire her readers.

Abigail Smith is a Registered Nurse in East Texas. Abigail loves to spend time with her husband, run, cook, travel, and play with her four rescue fur babies.

Diane Stark is a wife, mother of five, and freelance writer. She is a frequent contributor to the *Chicken Soup for the Soul* series. Diane writes about the important things in life: her family and her faith.

Sharon Struth writes books about life, love, and a little bit more. When she's not writing, she and her husband happily sip their way through the scenic towns on the Connecticut Wine Trail and pursue their travel passions. If you enjoy real life characters and a feel good story, visit her website at www.sharonstruth.com.

Mary Vigliante Szydlowski writes across several genres using this and other pseudonyms. She's the author of eleven adult novels and ten children's books. Her short stories, articles, essays, and poems have been published in anthologies, books, magazines, newspapers, and on the Internet.

Polly Hare Tafrate is an eclectic freelancer who has published numerous articles on a variety of topics — education, grand-motherhood, travel, health, volunteering, German Saturday Schools, cooking, Appalachian Trail Angels, and whatever else piques her interest. She welcomes assignments. E-mail her at pollytafrate@hotmail.com.

Lisa Taylor is a librarian with a master's degree from Texas Woman's University. In addition to being a librarian, she is a writer, wife, mother, and Phillies fan — not necessarily in that order, especially during base-ball season.

Jeana Tetzlaff loves to write both fiction and nonfiction stories. She works part-time at the Chamber of Commerce and enjoys reading, crocheting and working with kids. She is married with a grown daughter and a little dog named Daisy May.

Julie Theel lives in sunny Rancho Mirage, CA with her husband, two teenage daughters, three furry dogs and two fluffy cats. When not busy shuttling the girls to their many activities, Julie spends her time rescuing animals and running her business selling the Rippys, her patented rip-apart toys for dogs.

Lisa Timpf is a retired human resource and communications professional who lives in Simcoe, Ontario. Lisa enjoys organic gardening, bird watching, and spending outdoor time with her Border Collie, Emma. You can find out more about Lisa's writing projects at lisatimpf.blogspot.com.

Donna Collins Tinsley is a sister among you and a sometimes hormonally challenged wife, mother and grandmother (soon to be great-grandmother) who lives in sunny Port Orange, FL. She has been included in several magazines and many book compilations. Donna is a member of Word Weavers of Volusia County.

A E Troyer enjoys spending time with God, family, and friends. In her spare time she gardens and cares for her pets. Currently, she is pursuing counselor training to learn how to help others resolve issues in their lives and to help them bring those issues to Jesus.

Blossom Turner is a freelance writer/business woman with both articles and short stories published. A rich diversity of life experience is what she draws upon to write with inspiration and heartfelt authenticity. Watch for her first contemporary romance novel called *Anna's Secret* due summer 2019.

Cheryl E. Uhrig is a writer, illustrator, cartoonist and painter. Her work appears in children's books, magazines and local galleries. Cheryl lives in Newmarket, Ontario with her family.

Marilynn Zipes Wallace has a B.A. and M.A. in English. She worked in publishing in New York City and then in London, having fallen in love with England when she spent her junior year of college there. She is a great animal lover as well as a keen gardener. She loves writing creative nonfiction.

Jude Walsh is the mother of the best son in the whole wide world. She will always be grateful that Buddy barked. She writes self-help, memoir, and personal essays. Her writing is published in numerous literary magazines and anthologies. Learn more at www.judewalsh-writer.com.

Diana L. Walters works in an assisted living facility and is involved in a dementia ministry (www.touchinggrace.org). In her mid-sixties she began pursuing her life-long interest in writing. She's been published in the *Chicken Soup for the Soul* series, *Upper Room*, and other publications.

David Warren and his wife Angela live in Kettering, OH. They have a daughter Marissa. David survived cardiac arrest and jokes you only live twice. His stories blend humor with inspiration. David has appeared in six *Chicken Soup for the Soul* books, several magazines and had two children's books published. He's VP of Lutz Blades.

Roz Warren, the author of *Our Bodies, Our Shelves: Library Humor*, writes for everyone from the *Funny Times* to *The New York Times*, and has appeared on both *Morning Edition* and the *Today Show*. E-mail her at Roswarren@gmail.com or learn more at muckrack.com/roz-warren.

Aileen Weintraub is an award-winning children's book author living in New York. She also writes for *Glamour*, *Scary Mommy*, and *Kveller*, among other publications. She will stop you in the street to ask if she can pet your dog. Learn more at aileenweintraub.com or follow her on Twitter @aileenweintraub.

Born and raised among the West Virginia Hills, **S. J. Wells** loves God, her family, and books in that order. Married to a minister, she homeschools her daughters, often enlisting their help when creating new characters. In her spare time she loves to read, listen to music, bake and crochet.

Cheryl Wright resides in upstate New York and has produced a Contemporary Christian album. An animal lover from the start, she is currently writing a book that will include her personal experiences with the animals and pets that have touched her life.

Meet Amy Newmark

Amy Newmark is the bestselling author, editor-in-chief, and publisher of the *Chicken Soup for the Soul* book series. Since 2008, she has published more than 150 new books, most of them national bestsellers in the U.S. and Canada, more than doubling the number of Chicken Soup for the Soul titles in print today. She is also the author of *Simply Happy*, a crash course in Chicken Soup for the Soul advice and wisdom that is filled with easy-to-implement, practical tips for enjoying a better life.

Amy is credited with revitalizing the Chicken Soup for the Soul brand, which has been a publishing industry phenomenon since the first book came out in 1993. By compiling inspirational and aspirational true stories curated from ordinary people who have had extraordinary experiences, Amy has kept the twenty-six-year-old Chicken Soup for the Soul brand fresh and relevant.

Amy graduated *magna cum laude* from Harvard University where she majored in Portuguese and minored in French. She then embarked on a three-decade career as a Wall Street analyst, a hedge fund manager, and a corporate executive in the technology field. She is a Chartered Financial Analyst.

Her return to literary pursuits was inevitable, as her honors thesis in college involved traveling throughout Brazil's impoverished northeast region, collecting stories from regular people. She is delighted to have come full circle in her writing career — from collecting stories "from the people" in Brazil as a twenty-year-old to, three decades later, collecting stories "from the people" for Chicken Soup for the Soul.

When Amy and her husband Bill, the CEO of Chicken Soup for the Soul, are not working, they are visiting their four grown children and their first grandchild.

Follow Amy on Twitter @amynewmark. Listen to her free podcast — "Chicken Soup for the Soul with Amy Newmark" — on Apple Podcasts, Google Play, the Podcasts app on iPhone, or by using your favorite podcast app on other devices.

About
American Humane

American Humane is the country's first national humane organization, founded in 1877 and committed to ensuring the safety, welfare, and wellbeing of all animals. For more than 140 years, American Humane has been first to serve in promoting the welfare and safety of animals and strengthening the bond between animals and people. American Humane's initiatives are designed to help whenever and wherever animals are in need of rescue, shelter, protection, or security.

With remarkably effective programs and the highest efficiency ratio of any national humane group for the stewardship of donor dollars, the nonprofit has earned Charity Navigator's top "4-Star" rating, has been named a "Top-Rated Charity" by CharityWatch and a "Best Charity" by Consumer Reports, and achieved the prestigious "Gold Level" charity designation from GuideStar.

American Humane is first to serve animals around the world, striving to ensure their safety, welfare and humane treatment—from rescuing animals in disasters to ensuring that animals are humanely treated. One of its best-known programs is the "No Animals Were Harmed®" animals-in-entertainment certification, which appears during the end credits of films and TV shows, and today monitors some 1,000 productions yearly with an outstanding safety record.

American Humane's farm animal welfare program helps ensure the humane treatment of nearly a billion farm animals, the largest animal welfare program of its kind. And recently, the historic nonprofit launched the American Humane Conservation program, an innovative initiative helping ensure the humane treatment of animals around the globe in zoos and aquariums.

Continuing its longstanding efforts to strengthen the healing power of the human-animal bond, American Humane pairs veterans struggling to cope with the invisible wounds of war with highly-trained service dogs, and spearheaded a groundbreaking clinical trial that provided for the first time scientific substantiation for the effectiveness of animal-assisted therapy (AAT) for children with cancer and their families.

To learn more about American Humane, visit americanhumane. org and follow it on Facebook, Instagram, and Twitter.

AMERICAN★HUMANE
FIRST TO SERVE

Editor's Note: Chicken Soup for the Soul and American Humane have created *Humane Heroes*, a FREE new series of e-books and companion curricula for elementary, middle and high schoolers. Through 36 inspirational stories of animal rescue, rehabilitation, and humane conservation being performed at the world's leading zoological institutions, and 18 easy-to-follow lesson plans, *Humane Heroes* provides highly engaging free reading materials that also encourage young people to appreciate and protect Earth's disappearing species. To download the free e-books and learn about the program, please visit www.chickensoup.com/ah.

Thank You

We owe huge thanks to all of our contributors and fans. We were overwhelmed by the thousands of stories you submitted about your amazing dogs. Our Associate Publisher D'ette Corona, our Senior Editor Barbara LoMonaco, and our editors Elaine Kimbler, Laura Dean and Crescent LoMonaco made sure they read every single one.

Susan Heim did the first round of editing, D'ette Corona chose the perfect quotations to put at the beginning of each story, and editor-in-chief Amy Newmark edited the stories and shaped the final manuscript.

As we finished our work, D'ette Corona continued to be Amy's right-hand woman in creating the final manuscript and working with all our wonderful writers. Barbara LoMonaco and Kristiana Pastir, along with Elaine Kimbler, jumped in at the end to proof, proof, proof. And, yes, there will always be typos anyway, so feel free to let us know about them at webmaster@chickensoupforthesoul.com, and we will correct them in future printings.

The whole publishing team deserves a hand, including Executive Assistant Mary Fisher, Senior Director of Marketing Maureen Peltier, Senior Director of Production Victor Cataldo, and our graphic designer Daniel Zaccari, who turned our manuscript into this beautiful book.

Sharing Happiness, Inspiration, and Hope

Real people sharing real stories, every day, all over the world. In 2007, *USA Today* named *Chicken Soup for the Soul* one of the five most memorable books in the last quarter-century. With over 100 million books sold to date in the U.S. and Canada alone, more than 250 titles in print, and translations into nearly fifty languages, "chicken soup for the soul®" is one of the world's best-known phrases.

Today, twenty-six years after we first began sharing happiness, inspiration and hope through our books, we continue to delight our readers with new titles, but have also evolved beyond the bookstore with super premium pet food, television shows, a podcast, video journalism from aplus.com, movies and TV shows on the Popcornflix app, and licensed products, all revolving around true stories, as we continue "changing the world one story at a time®." Thanks for reading!

Changing the world one story at a time®
www.chickensoup.com